This is one of those rare  saga, part humor, and part reflection, Scott Abbott, who taught at BYU for more than a decade, chronicles his turbulent encounters with Mormon leaders and Mormon institutions. I found the chapters defending his BYU colleagues from overzealous bureaucrats both amusing and alarming. I also enjoyed his discussions on academic freedom, race, sexuality, and gender equality. Abbott's sense of justice, unflinching courage, and sheer humanity shine brilliantly throughout this book.

—Matthew L. Harris
author of *Watchman on the Tower: Ezra Taft Benson and the Making of the Mormon Right*

Scott Abbott must have questioned authority from his birth. He has spent much of his life speaking truth to power, often to power that didn't want to hear that truth. He has always defended open, rigorous debate and has always been as willing to consider criticism of his own ideas and actions as to offer criticism of others, particularly when their decisions were destructive to institutions and individuals Scott cared about, including Brigham Young University, intellectuals, feminists, and homosexuals. This compilation of Scott's essays, letters, and articles, spanning over thirty years, demonstrates many significant ideas: That reason and intellectual inquiry do not oppose faith but, rather, are necessary for authentic faith to flourish. That coercion kills growth and agency. That an eccentric individual is most likely not dangerous to an institution but rather the source of vital ideas that will help renew it. That individuals who are harmed by shortsighted policies matter as much as the empowered who make and carry out those policies. Reading this book will help administrators consider how to be more kind and farsighted. It also offers a model of how to speak out against the damaging and dishonest policies rampant in our contemporary culture, however they are disguised.

—Susan Elizabeth Howe
Emerita Professor of English, BYU,
and author of *Salt* and *Stone Spirits*

In these essays, Scott Abbott has sketched his personal odyssey. A boy from a Four-Corners oil town went away to college, became an ascendant academic, then pivoted, poignantly. A stirring in his deep parts pointed him toward the transcendent prospect of a consummate community, lustrous in its interweaving of humane quest with tokens of godliness. Eventually, contesting the interweave brought embroilment and sundering, an uneasy reality to which Professor Abbott has borne witness in ways heartrending and cautionary.

—Hal Miller, Jr.
Professor, Cognitive and
Behavioral Neuroscience, BYU

Dwelling in the Promised Land as a Stranger

SCOTT ABBOTT

By Common Consent Press is a non-profit publisher dedicated to producing affordable, high-quality books that help define and shape the Latter-day Saint experience. BCC Press publishes books that address all aspects of Mormon life. Our mission includes finding manuscripts that will contribute to the lives of thoughtful Latter-day Saints, mentoring authors and nurturing projects to completion, and distributing important books to the Mormon audience at the lowest possible cost.

Dwelling in the Promised Land as a Stranger

SCOTT ABBOTT

Dwelling in the Promised Land as a Stranger: Personal Encounters with Mormon Institutions
Copyright © 2022 by Scott Abbott

All rights reserved. Printed in the United States of America. No part of this book may be used or reproduced in any manner whatsoever without written permission except in the case of brief quotations embodied in critical articles or reviews.

For information contact
By Common Consent Press
4900 Penrose Dr.
Newburgh, IN 47630

Cover design: D Christian Harrison
Book design: Andrew Heiss

www.bccpress.org
ISBN-13: 978-1-948218-43-6

10 9 8 7 6 5 4 3 2 1

Dedicated to dear friends

Steven Epperson and Sam Rushforth

Your inspiration can be found on every page this book

Contents

Acknowledgments   xi

Preface by Cecilia Konchar Farr   xv

Foreword by William Evenson   xxi

Introduction   xxvii

1. "Mickelsson's Mormons"   1
   The Sunstone Review, September 1982

2. "House of the Temple, House of the Lord:
   A View from Philadelphia," with Steven Epperson   13
   Dialogue: A Journal of Mormon Thought, Fall 1987

3. "Will We Find Zion or Make Zion?
   An Essay on Postmodernity and Revelation"   37
   Sunstone conference on Zion, 1990;
   Sunstone, December 1994

4. "One Lord, One Faith, Two Universities:
   Tensions between 'Religion' and 'Thought' at BYU"   53
   Sunstone, September 1992

5. "The Provo Window" 89
   Annual of the Association for Mormon Letters, 1996

6. "Clipped and Controlled:
   A Contemporary Look at BYU" 99
   Sunstone, September 1996

7. "On Ecclesiastical Endorsement
   at Brigham Young University" 133
   Sunstone, April 1997

8. "Telling Stories"
   (review of Wayne Schow's *Remembering Brad:
   On the Loss of a Son to AIDS*) 151
   Sunstone, July 1997

9. "Sinister Virtue: The Effects of Cultural
   Despair on Academic Freedom at a
   Private Religious University" 161
   AAUP Conference on Religious Institutions and
   Academic Freedom, Chicago, 1997 (unpublished)

10. Debating the Possibility of a Mormon University:
    Documents from an Appeal 173
    1998 (unpublished)

11. "Lighting the Way with Autos da Fé" 203
    Boston Globe, 27 October 2002

12. Reviews of New Work by Brian Evenson:
    "Mormon Civilization and its Schizophrenic
    Discontents" and "Affliction Fiction" 213
    Open Letters Monthly, May 2012

13. "Hermeneutic Adventures in Home Teaching
    Mary and Richard Rorty"   229
    Dialogue: A Journal of Mormon Thought, Summer 2010

14. "New LDS Restrictions on Children of
    Gay Parents Make Perfect Sense"   237
    The Goalie's Anxiety, 6 November 2015

15. "UVU President Matthew Holland Continues
    His Battle against Marriage Equality"   241
    The UVU Review, 13 November 2017

    Final Thoughts   247

    List of Woodcuts   257

Bluff

Acknowledgments

Because a quarter-century has passed since many of these essays were written, this attempt to thank the people without whom they could not have been written will inevitably miss important contributors. If you are among them, please forgive me and know that the work we did together remains a highlight of my life.

The women and men who were officially part of the BYU Chapter of the AAUP buoyed my spirits and inspired my work: Sam Rushforth, George Schoemaker, Bill Evenson, Bert Wilson, Duane Jeffreys, Gary Bryner, Bonner Ritchie, Gene England, Susan Howe, Brandie Siegfried, Bill Davis, Cecilia Konchar Farr, and Rick Duerden. This group (I have surely forgotten several members) was once ridiculed by BYU President Merrill Bateman as consisting of a scant eight members—"there are only eight of them!" However many we were, it was an honor for me to associate with these fine people.

My colleagues in the Department of Germanic and Slavic Languages over the course of eleven years were wonderfully supportive, including the successive chairs of the department: Garold Davis, Alan Keele, and Gary Browning. Among the colleagues from other departments who were involved in our efforts, Nancy Rushforth, Tomi-Ann Roberts, Tim Heaton, Lynn England, Grant Boswell, and Reba Keele stand out in my memory.

There were many students over the years who fought for justice and academic freedom by publishing the independent

Student Review and through the women's organization VOICE. Some of the most resourceful of these included John Armstrong, Stirling Adams, Joanna Brooks, Kelli Potter, Bryan Waterman, Brian Kagel, and Kristin Rushforth.

Helpful administrators included Stan Albrecht (Academic Vice President), Don Jarvis (Director of the Faculty Center), and Hal Miller (Dean of Honors and General Education). One day Hal stopped me on campus and handed me John Ashbery's new book of poetry, *Flow Chart*. What for? I asked. I thought you would enjoy it, he said. Ashbery's explorations of truth and meaning beyond metaphysical certainty, as Hal surmised, came at an important time for me: "In time all excuses merge in an arch / whose keystone overlooks heaven, and / we must be patient if we are to live that far, at our own expense, this time, without that."

Colleagues George Schoemaker, Brian Evenson, David Knowlton, Cecilia Konchar Farr, Gail Houston, and Steven Epperson were forced to leave BYU during these years. The battles they fought in difficult circumstances were courageous, motivating the rest of us to work more thoughtfully and intently.

I have had the good fortune to write for several outstanding editors over the years: Peggy Fletcher of *The Sunstone Review*, Linda King Newell and L. Jackson Newell of *Dialogue*, Elbert Peck of *Sunstone*, Laraine Wilkins of *Irreantum*, Eric Robertson of *saltfront*, Kristine Haglund of *Dialogue*, and John Alley of The University of Utah Press.

Steve Evans generously reviewed my *Immortal for Quite Some Time* for the blog *By Common Consent* and then agreed to publish this book that will not, he wrote after reading the manuscript, be sold in the BYU Bookstore. That's not the problem it once would have been, I replied. BYU no longer has a bookstore. BCC's (unpaid) technically and visually talented staff members Andrew Heiss and Christian Harrison designed the book and its cover. Royden Card's woodcuts evoke the spirit of a strange and promising land. Without Andi Pitcher Davis's creative advocacy, Card's work would never have graced these pages.

Special thanks to Bill Evenson and Cecilia Konchar Farr for the preface and foreword to this book. They were both major players in the events these essays address.

Doug Moeller, BYU roommate and friend since our high-school years in Farmington, New Mexico, read and commented helpfully on the manuscript of the book, as did neighbors and friends Sterling Van Wagenen and Byron Adams.

My son Ben Abbott, an ecologist flourishing now as an assistant professor at BYU, thoughtfully critiqued an early draft of this book, giving me yet another reminder that I'm a fortunate man to be father to seven dear children. And speaking of our children—their mother never once suggested that I pursue another course than the one that felt right to me, although my activism at BYU had the potential for grave economic consequences for our family. I'll always be grateful for that generous and thoughtful support.

Day's Window

Preface

I recently attended a small family wedding in Minnesota, where I have lived for over 25 years. Afterwards, as we socialized (in masks, six feet apart) I found myself talking with the bride's brother, who told me that he had heard my name for years. "How lovely," I thought, "that his sister, my long-time book club buddy, had talked about me!" I was basking in the glow of our friendship when I realized, a few more sentences in, that he was referencing something completely different—not friendship, but notoriety. I stiffened. He had been at BYU during the challenging times that Scott writes about here, and he had worked for the *Daily Universe*. Now I had to be concerned about *what* exactly he associated with my name.

BYU was my first job out of graduate school. In 1990 with my new Ph.D., I was among the first cohort of scholars trained in feminist theory, so I had options for tenure-track positions across the country. I chose BYU because I knew I never would have been selecting an assistant professorship at all if I hadn't been raised Mormon, active in ward and stake activities that let me imagine myself outside of the working-class town north of Pittsburgh that formed the horizons of my school years. To put it simply, I knew I was "a child of God with unlimited potential." How huge is that? Quite huge, I promise you. It made all the difference in my life.

I had earned my M.A. at BYU, where I had been named Outstanding Graduate Student in the English Department (one of two that year), and left in 1987 to accept a Dean's Fellowship for my doctoral studies in literature and theory at Michigan State. I danced my way through that program, even when it was difficult, because I loved reading and talking, loved being a scholar and a writer. I also discovered that I loved my students and the learning communities I could construct with them in my classrooms, and I graduated from MSU with the Graduate Teacher/Scholar Award.

All this is to say, I was just learning how to be a professor when I arrived at BYU (at age 32, with a supportive spouse and my just-born first baby), but I was on my way. I knew I was a solid thinker and researcher, that my journalism background had honed my writing, and that I enjoyed teaching and was determined to be good at it. Now I was about to enter a new career that would call on all of these skills as I embraced the life of an intellectual. What a privilege! I could not have been more thrilled. I remember that time now as all potential—and joy.

But I don't think I was more than a few weeks into the job before I learned to steel myself for persistent encounters like the one at that Minnesota summer wedding. I was "That Feminist" that the English Department had hired, and lots of people had *opinions* about that. When, at a department meeting, I protested the persistent use of family metaphors that characterized women colleagues as daughter, sister or mother the tension was thick in the air. "What more does That Woman want?" they whispered to one another. I think now that I wanted only to be seen professionally, to be allowed to succeed or fail based on the work I did, not on some flawed preconception of a feminist or on an unreasonable standard of what motherhood required of me. I wanted what the young male assistant professors were granted without question—the aging professor's arm over the postmodernist's broad shoulders that said, "I was young once. I had some crazy ideas, too." Instead I was held at arm's length, treated as dangerous. I was a woman with a longtime habit of wanting it all—or at least to have the chance to earn it all.

Preface xvii

As I read through Scott's moving collection of essays, I was taken back to that time with a vivid awareness of how much those first four years as a professor taught me. BYU was clarifying. I learned to define my values as I embraced opportunities to stand up for them. I left knowing who I was, what it meant to "profess," and what I would sacrifice to do that with integrity. Like Scott, I also learned what it meant to be a stranger in our Promised Land.

And I realized as I read Scott's words how much I came to define academic life as he did. Together, in our community of strangers, we imagined a BYU that would never be—"an open space of democracy" to use Terry Tempest Williams's phrase, a university that cherished the free exchange of ideas, that treasured its fierce, and fiercely loyal, critics and embraced its feminists, gays and lesbians and "so-called scholars or intellectuals"; one that could see and nurture potential equally in its women students as in its men; a place where questioning was encouraged and curiosity ignited. We pictured a diverse and multicultural Zion, imagined ourselves into a beloved community, and, for a moment, there it was. And in that landscape, I learned how to be professor.

Moments in these essays felt absolutely revelatory to me. It was like re-encountering my dad's Serbian nose: "Oh, that's where I got that!" Sentences resonated as if they were my own origin story. Here, for example, I find myself in Scott's response to compulsion and oppressive authority:

> . . . do others respond to coercion the way I do? My nature is to do well the things I choose and to despise and evade what I am forced to do. Or, if I decide to knuckle under even while disagreeing with the requirement, I experience a diminished sense of dignity. Emphasizing the letter over the spirit shifts a people's sense of morality from heartfelt individual commitment to superficial observance of outward requirements. (139–139)

And there I am again in his failure to stay quiet about this coercion: "For reasons I don't fully understand, I cannot stand by and watch institutional power exerted unfairly" (249). This may, in fact, be the central theme of Scott's book—or so it was for me, as Scott fearlessly beards the lion in the den again and again in the name of his Mormon values, with his unwavering moral compass pointed toward the finest traditions of higher education. And when he drew my attention to our fledgling BYU chapter of the American Association of University Professors, I traced my academic roots, my activism and commitments since, to this pregnant moment. We were drawn to the AAUP's protection of "fairness and honesty and intellectual openness," because we/he first knew these principles "from the scriptures and practices of my faith" (249) and had committed to enacting them in our scholarly lives.

The passionate professor that Scott became has its own origin story in a young scholar at Princeton committing himself to the "holy work" of education, "to the responsibility of good thinking and good teaching and of being an active citizen of the academy." I hear his voice in the bold renewal of that pledge, even as he battled for promotion at BYU:

> There's no way in hell I could win this appeal. But as long as I am at BYU, as long as I am an educator, I'll continue to carry out the moral commitment I made in 1979 in Nassau Hall. Fairness matters. Academic freedom matters. Universities matter. Truth matters (188).

I want to avoid spoilers, but let's all agree that we can see where that was going. Scott left, as did my dear BYU colleagues from that time Tomi-Ann and Gail, Sam and Gene and Brian. And many of the young men and women we taught went on to graduate school and became the kind of stand-up scholars that these colleagues had modeled unfailingly in that moment when there was no easy place for them to stand. Our students became another generation of praiseworthy professors who had no place at BYU. Strangers in other lands.

Our beloved BYU community is scattered all over the world now: The chronic questioners in Chicago, Tulsa, Ann Arbor, New York and St. Paul whose gift to the faith is their constant doubt; the multi-generational-Mormons, intellectuals who take their heritage with them to Abu Dhabi, Boston, San Diego, New Haven, or Oxford, Mississippi; the believing women everywhere who struggle with a patriarchy that won't accept them whole; our wise elders who persist in Provo and Orem and the Salt Lake Valley, never giving up. For those few years, we invested in the future as we imagined a space where we could all thrive together, a promised land, as it were, a true university. And though that land was only imagined, it returns occasionally, magically like Brigadoon. Scott's book conjures it. I admire his vision and cherish how it became my own. In these pages, drawn together in faith and love, we professors and scholars, feminists and intellectuals are strangers no more.

—Cecilia Konchar Farr, Ph.D.

(Cecilia served as Professor of English and Women's Studies and a Carondelet Scholar in the Women's College at St. Catherine University in St. Paul, Minnesota and is now Dean of the College of Liberal and Creative Arts at West Liberty University.)

Peaks

Foreword

Institutions in general, when they grow large on a national or international scale, almost inevitably develop in ways that lose sight of individuals and serve institutional imperatives. Religious institutions seem to me to be especially susceptible to the problems of control and manipulation because they present themselves as representatives of the divine. Their relationship with their adherents is not a market relationship, although a great deal of money is involved. Rather, it is a social or community relationship where social norms prevail rather than market norms (as explored by Clark, Mills, and Fiske in a social psychology context). Where market norms might require transparency in the institution, religious institutions tend not to be transparent in their dealings. Think of the struggles of the Catholic Church in recent years with clerical sex abuse and corruption after decades (at least) of institutional cover up. Control and manipulation can be seen both in religious restrictions on particular behaviors and in promises of great benefits in the next life based upon sacrifices in mortality. Religious groups in America do not normally have coercive powers. Still, even mainstream religions in the U.S. often put great pressures upon their adherents to conform to particular views and behaviors. While religious institutions do much good, they are innately susceptible to exercising what Joseph Smith called "unrighteous dominion."

These characteristics of large institutions in general and of large religious institutions in particular are the central focus of Scott Abbott's essays in this collection. They bring general concerns powerfully to the particular. The fifteen deeply personal essays are full of insight, addressing religious beliefs, views, and principles from the perspective of one who grew up in Mormonism and continues to value the culture of Mormon communities even as his belief changes over time. This is especially interesting as Abbott grapples with authoritarian and controlling institutions and officials connected to the Mormon Church.

Abbott's truth-seeking is antithetical to the common inclination to defend institutions over principles. His writing is not comfortable; his questioning challenges readers to regard the foundations of their own beliefs and commitments.

The essays address a wide variety of topics, including issues of control, how to make a life in an imperfect world, what is truth, how we engage the search for meaning, and the importance of language in defining our place in this imperfect world. All grapple with complicated questions about meaning and uncertainty, especially with how attempts to grasp certainty by denying the legitimacy of questioning reveal an underlying insecurity in one's faith. These essays expose that underlying insecurity not just in individuals but in broader institutional cultures.

The first two essays in this collection pre-date Abbott's move to the BYU faculty. They nicely set the stage for exploration in the later essays of his commitment to Mormonism even while moving intellectually out of the mainstream of believers. Essays 3–7 and 9–11 address a BYU that loses its moorings in attempts to overtly and explicitly support the LDS Church, turning to apologetics and away from scholarship that would make LDS leaders or the general membership nervous. Essays 8, 11, 14, and 15 deal thoughtfully with the challenges faced by gay Mormons and their parents. Essay 12 reviews a range of writings by Brian Evenson as a meditation upon language and meaning, community and individualism, metaphor and fanaticism. Essay 13 is a delightful reminiscence of the possibility of being within Mormon culture while addressing some of the philosophical questions that may be uncomfortable in that culture. All the essays explore Abbott's struggles with faith and meaning and the difficulties associated with the institutional imperatives he faces.

I lived through some of the challenges Abbott addresses in his BYU essays. My reaction to these challenges was remarkably compatible with his. My own experience as a BYU academic administrator (associate academic vice president, dean of general education, dean of Physical and Mathematical Sciences) was filled with challenges of the kind explored in Essay 4, "One Lord, One Faith, Two Universities: Tensions between 'Religion' and 'Thought' at BYU." I enjoyed my time in those roles because I felt that we made more progress than lost ground. When the tide turned, the satisfaction of leadership at the university evaporated, and I temporarily left the university in 1994 and returned as a faculty member in 1995. During that period I was on the board of the BYU chapter of AAUP whose work is reviewed in Essay 9, "Sinister Virtue."

Essay 5, "The Provo Window: Late Night Thoughts on the Purposes of Art and the Decline of a University," deals with the case of my son, Brian, who had a reputation among students as one of the best teachers of fiction at BYU during the short time he was there. He has had a successful career elsewhere, but Abbott describes well the institutional costs of Brian's and other faculty members' cases. These cases and their related challenges are discussed further in Essay 6, "Clipped and Controlled: A Contemporary Look at BYU," and in Essays 9, "Sinister Virtue: The Effects of Cultural Despair on Academic Freedom at BYU," and 10, "Debating the Possibility of a Mormon University: Notes from an Appeal, 1998."

When the ecclesiastical endorsement policy for BYU employees was announced, I wrote an opinion piece that ran in the Provo *Daily Herald*. In that opinion I suggested that the new policy was likely to strain relationships between BYU employees and their ecclesiastical leaders, since it inserted local Church leaders into continuing employment considerations. I received calls from several BYU staff members who did not teach students but were responsible for repairing machines and supporting the teaching faculty. They expressed exactly the fears in their own relationships that I worried about in my public opinion article. They pointed out that they posed no risk to students and asked my advice on how to deal with the potential conflicts—advice that could only depend on the specific approach of their local bishop or stake president. Abbott's Essay 7 in this volume, "On Ecclesiastical Endorsement at BYU," reviews a particular case involving a faculty member of deep convictions to principle and a bishop who could see only one way to be faithful. The loss of that faculty member was in reality a major loss to the students and future students would never have the chance to be inspired by this unusually thoughtful and principled teacher.

Abbott is stunningly open and personal in this book of essays, engaging the reader and drawing her into thoughtful and eloquent examination of philosophical issues dealing with our relationships to others, to religion, and to the making of meaning, all in the context of his relationship with Mormonism.

—William Evenson,
Emeritus Professor of Physics, BYU
Corvallis, Oregon

Salt Valley

Sky Stone

Introduction

I began writing seriously about Mormonism after an epiphany. Walking home after a long day in Princeton's Firestone Library, my daemon spoke to me: you don't believe in God. Okay, there was no daemon, but I did have that sudden, unexpected thought, and it unnerved me. I looked around to see if anyone had noticed. I wondered, in that moment, if my moral world would crumble. Fortunately, at least it felt fortunate to me, it didn't alter my fundamental sense for right and wrong. The patterns of life that had proven productive for me had been chosen pragmatically. The reasons for my choices still made sense. I could go on.

That's the concise version of the event. In an early draft I wrote that "my choices had been practical and not based on superstition." My son Ben pointed out that superstition was a loaded word in this context, disrespectful even. I changed the sentence to say my life choices hadn't been based on metaphysical beliefs. But that's not quite right either. There were many choices based on belief, or at least situated in belief. For a quarter of a century I believed in and prayed to a Heavenly Father, a belief that shifted slightly with each new experience—shifted, took new form, faded, strengthened, adjusted.

On my German mission, for instance, a grey-haired man opened a door we had knocked on, heard our description of ourselves as missionaries with a message that could change his life, and invited us in on condition that we listen to his message after delivering ours. We agreed, of course, and after we spoke about Joseph Smith's first vision it was his turn. I'm a Freemason, he said, and the story I'll tell you is from an eighteenth-century play written by a Freemason and leading figure in the Enlightenment: Gotthold Ephraim Lessing. *Nathan the Wise* features representatives of three religions: a rich Jew named Nathan, Saladin—the Muslim ruler of Jerusalem at the time, and a young Christian crusader. Saladin needs money and in an attempt to compromise Nathan asks him which of those three religions is the true one. Nathan answers with what he calls a *Märchen* or fairy tale. Ages and ages ago, he says, there was a man who possessed a ring whose opal stone made whomever wore it beloved. He passed on the ring to his most beloved son, who passed it on to his most beloved son and so on until the ring came to a man with three sons, all of whom he loved equally. As he approached death, he had a jeweler make two rings indistinguishable from the original. On his deathbed, he called in his sons one by one and gave each a ring. When his sons discovered there were three rings, they argued and asked a judge to decide which was the true ring. You say the ring has the mysterious power to make its wearer beloved, the judge said. Come back in a thousand thousand years and we will see whom the ring has so affected. Deeply moved, Saladin asks Nathan for his friendship. I left the Freemason's apartment with a story that still rings true to me half a century later.

Peering through a seerstone used by Joseph Smith (part of the Western Americana Collection of Princeton's Firestone Library) and thinking "this is just a geode" was important to me, as was the thrill I felt listening to President Hinckley's 1992 speech to faculty and staff at BYU ("May God bless you my beloved associates, both young and old, in this great undertaking of teaching and learning"). I am inspired when I read the Psalms and I have been filled with peace while praying. I interpret some of these events differently now, and I no longer pray, but for almost two decades after my epiphany I continued to practice my religion because I found it deeply rewarding.

Discussing Mormonism with people who truly believe in a Heavenly Father and Mother, I sometimes think I don't belong in these conversations, that I have no real standing in their community. Several reviewers of *Immortal for Quite Some Time* wished I had revealed my atheist epiphany earlier in the book; the experience colored everything that followed, they felt. But as I review the essays I wrote after that singular event, I don't think that my unbelief distorted my commitment to Mormonism any more than the sudden insight into my disbelief affected my moral commitment in general. And isn't it possible, I ask now, that my unorthodox perspective enabled contributions that others could not have made?

In a peculiar 1973 commencement speech at Utah State University, Elder Boyd Packer excoriated people who leave the Church but continue to attack it. "Have you ever wondered," he asked, "what it means when [your professor] can leave [the Church], but . . . cannot leave it alone? Normal behavior would have him cancel his affiliation in the church and let that be that. Not so with this individual. He can leave it, but he cannot leave it alone" (*That All May be Edified*, SLC: Bookcraft, 1982, p. 165). There are, to be sure, critics of the Church who spend their lives revealing troubling historical facts to undermine people's faith in the restored gospel and the supposed infallibility of Church leaders. My fundamental disbelief, however, meant that my belief couldn't be challenged by historical discrepancies and infallibility had never made sense to me. So what did I believe? Why didn't I leave Mormonism alone? The essays collected here are products of my belief in principles and possibilities I found and still hope for in the religion that profoundly influenced and continues to color who I am.

When I left a newly tenured position at Vanderbilt University, I explained to the curious dean that I was leaving because I missed the scent of sage and wanted to contribute to the education of my fellow Mormons. I didn't believe in God, but I did believe in the ability of Mormonism to foster goodness and to inspire and challenge. My criticisms of structures and policies—and there are plenty of criticisms in these essays—were meant to improve rather than to tear down. I couldn't let my religion go because I believed in it, even in my disbelief.

Freud argued in *Civilization and Its Discontents* that humans are instinctually aggressive toward one another and that the structures of civilization are meant to restrict aggression. Prohibitions that are too strong, however, lead to unhappiness and neurosis. One theme running through these essays is that over the course of several decades people governing the Church's institutions increasingly exerted control that vitiated Joseph Smith's counsel: "Teach them correct principles and let them govern themselves." Only decades after the fact, after reading Greg Prince's descriptions of the power struggles Leonard Arrington had to negotiate as Church Historian, did I realize that not only were my arguments for less restrictive institutional practices beside the point, but that they were totally irrelevant in the hierarchical system in which BYU's policies were determined. Still . . . time passes, things change, and in some naïve corner of my soul I remain hopeful for the future of my religion.

Highway 24

Castle Valley

ONE

Mickelsson's Mormons

Review of John Gardner's novel *Mickelsson's Ghosts*

***The Sunstone Review*, September 1982**

Rereading this review of John Gardner's last novel (he died in a motorcycle crash in September 1982, months after the novel was published and just before my essay appeared), I am struck by the frequent references to "we Mormons." I was writing for a Mormon audience, to be sure, but the references were personally meaningful as well. The essay feels a bit prudish, but the only thing I really regret is my dismissive reference to Fawn Brodie's *No Man Knows My History*. My stake-president grandfather had a copy of Brodie's book with Hugh Nibley's booklet *No, Ma'am, That's Not History* tucked inside the front cover; but by the time I wrote the review I was well aware that Brodie was a better historian than Nibley. My question near the end—why "doesn't Mickelsson think of spirituality, intellect, wisdom, pacifism, success in the arts and education, and social consciousness when the Mormons come to mind?"—still feels like a good question.

That the *Sunstone Review* existed and that its editors thought my ideas worth printing gave me an early sense that even from Vanderbilt University in Nashville, Tennessee, I might be part of engaging conversations about Mormonism.

John Gardner, the late novelist and literary critic, is as controversial as he is prolific. His several volumes of criticism on medieval subjects, most notably *The Life and Times of Chaucer* (Knopf, 1977), have received both praise and condemnation, the latter primarily for a novelist's habit of recycling ideas without appropriate acknowledgement. But it was Gardner's *On Moral Fiction* (Basic Books, 1978) that really ruffled feathers in the literary aviary. Using Tolstoy as his shibboleth, Gardner divided contemporary authors into those who write "moral fiction" (fiction that "affirms life") and those whose fiction tends toward destruction. Bernard Malamud and John Fowles belong to the former, with perhaps the addition of John Cheever, Guy Davenport, Eudora Welty, and Joyce Carol Oates. The latter list includes John Updike, John Barth, Thomas Pynchon, Norman Mailer, Joseph Heller, and Kurt Vonnegut Jr.

Gardner's dogmatic judgments evoked swift and stormy protests (and, in fact, continue to arouse hostilities). Robert Harris's June review of *Mickelsson's Ghosts* in the *Saturday Review*, "What's So Moral About John Gardner's Fiction?" begins with the statement "It is a good bet that John Gardner enjoys writing his novels far more than the public enjoys reading" and ends with "Late in the novel, Gardner defines religious fundamentalism as 'permission not to think.' Some of his own fundamentalist ideas about how to write fiction seem to invite the same definition.'"

But among Mormons, Gardner's "fundamentalist" call for moral fiction was generally well received. We agree for the most part with assertions like the following:

> Art's incomparable ability to instruct, to make alternatives intellectually and emotionally clear . . . ought to be a force bringing people together, breaking down barriers of prejudice and ignorance, and holding up ideals worth pursuing. . . . But what we generally get in our books and films is bad instruction: escapist models or else moral evasiveness, or, worse, cynical attacks on traditional values such as honesty, love of country, marital fidelity, work, and moral courage.

. . .

Mickelsson's Ghosts, Gardner's newest novel, illustrated with photographs by his son Joel, could be expected to join other works of "moral fiction" on the preferred reading lists at BYU. But two serpents lurking in the new novel may provoke Gardner's expulsion from paradise. The first: explicit sexual description, arguably necessary in the context of this novel, may cost him some of his more "moral" readers. And the second? Let us allow that serpent to lurk a while longer while we turn to the novel.

Peter Mickelsson, a professor of philosophy at SUNY Binghamton, "once the most orderly of men," now lives a life of magnificent disarray. Vast stacks of unopened mail dominate his desks, creditors hound him, his estranged wife receives nearly all of his salary, rubber check follows robber check, and the I.R.S. stalks him for tax evasion. Mickelsson suffers from loneliness and chronic drunkenness, his students drain his energy and his liquor cabinet, he finds it impossible to write, and the summer heat of the city is more than he can stand. The solution, he decides, is a house in the country. After a long search Mickelsson finally chooses an old house near economically depressed Susquehanna, Pennsylvania. The lies he tells the bank's loan officer about his finances surprise him (he is a professional ethicist), but the house gives him a sense of purpose and new beginning.

Mickelsson's story now has two centers—small, superstitious Susquehanna and the university in Binghamton. Bouts of drinking and all-night binges of full scale house renovation alternate with classroom discussions about Plato, Aristotle, and fascism. Arguments in class about the ethics of abortion on demand (Mickelsson is opposed) are followed by nights with Donnie, Susquehanna's seventeen-year-old prostitute. When Donnie announces that she is pregnant by Mickelsson and demands money for an abortion, Mickelsson won't allow it—on ethical grounds.

Mormon readers will find it fascinating that Mickelsson has moved into a house once inhabited by Joseph Smith Jr. And that is only the beginning. One morning, a little before noon, hung over and sore from having lifted weights the night before, Mickelsson answers his door:

> On his front porch stood two young men, wearing ties and long black coats. Their plain black, carefully polished shoes looked like government-issue, and both young men had their hair cut short, like marines. He clung to his first thought, that they were I.R.S. men, or maybe F.B.I. men. . . . There was something drab, even pitiful about them.
>
> The blond one said, "Mr. Mickelsson, we're representing the Church of Jesus Christ Latter-Day Saints [sic]. We understand you recently paid a visit to Salt Lake City—". . . .
>
> He realized that almost unconsciously he'd said "Yes," nodding, admitting that he had once visited Salt Lake City, yes. Perhaps, the blond one said, he would like to know more about the Mormons. Again Mickelsson failed to react. He could have told them he knew a good deal about the Mormons. He'd had a student, some time ago, who'd broken away from the Mormon Church and had been hounded for months by their soft-spoken, black-suited squads. He'd had

a colleague in California who'd been hounded in the same way for fifteen years. Mickelsson thought of the underwear he'd been told their women wore, marked with holy gibberish and never taken off, not even in the shower—a sin against life, if it was true, he would have told them—and once, in a motel somewhere, he'd read a ways into their incredibly dull bible, the adventures of the archangel Moron. He knew the good that could be claimed for their company—their music, mainly (according to Ellen, it was vastly overrated); also the fact that they were family people, unusually successful in business and agriculture, non-drinkers, non-smokers, statistically more healthy and longer-lived than any other group in America. He would even grant that sometimes, as individuals, they were apparently good people, no real fault but dullness.

Shortly thereafter, speaking with his neighbor about the townspeople's reluctance to sell historical sites to the Mormons, Mickelsson hears the following explanation:

"They're clubby," Pearson said, and squinted. "There's somethin unnatural abowt people all hangin together like that. The Baptists, now, they may be mean sons of bitches, but there's no way they're ever gonna take over the world. . . . But the Mormons, now. . . ." He stared at the dowsing rod, lips compressed, trying to come up with exactly what he thought, and at last brought out, "Clubby."

"Well, they're healthy, you've got to admit that," Mickelsson said, and grinned. "They live practically forever."

"Yup." Pearson nodded.

One of the most interesting conversations about Mormonism takes place between Mickelsson and his young friend Donnie. She can't understand how people can believe in Joseph Smith as a prophet. Her great-great-grandfather actually knew him, she says, and claimed he was "tricky as a snake." Donnie is full of vague ideas about how Mormons torture people while pretending to be stupid and sweet, and her thoughts lead Mickelsson to contemplate the Mormons even further:

> "They're a strange people," he said. "We all work from premises we can't fully defend, but the Mormons are true, deep-down absurdists. They're people that know that nothing makes sense, the whole universe is crazy, or so they claim, but they go right on acting as if things make sense. . . . The Mormons start with this insane, made-up history—Jesus Christ coming to someplace like Peru, where he meets not only Indians but also white people who look exactly like Charlton Heston playing Moses—and out of this craziness they make a huge, rich church, complete with army and police, or anyway so people will tell you out in Utah; they make a whole new style of architecture, new theory of the universe, new system of family relationships. . . . It's an amazing accomplishment, when you think about it. They've stepped out of normal time and space, and so far as you can tell, most of 'em aren't even aware of the fact."
>
> "All religions are like that," she said.
>
> "I don't know. The Mormons seem pretty special. Anyhow, they take care of each other. There's something to be said for that."

In another conversation, Pearson and Mickelsson talk about Mickelsson's house, the ghosts there, and Joseph Smith, who is reputed to be a previous owner. Mickelsson claims not to have known the house belonged to Smith, and Pearson answers:

> "Must not've looked over the title search when you bought it, then—unless the stories ain't true. I 'magine they are, though. Anyway, most people think they are. He was a strange man, that Smith. Hahrd to say if he was crazy or the cleverest man of his time—or both."

Pearson goes on at length about the disreputable, dirty young Joseph—crystal gazing, treasure hunting, blessing and cursing fields. Then he launches into "the Joseph Smith story" with phrasing sure to tickle the ear of the ex-missionary:

> "I don't remember the *de*tails, but it was time time of—what do they say—religious foment. The established churches was falling apart . . . and around Palmyra, New York, where the Smiths lived, all kinds of new religions was shooting up. . . . It was a good time for a man like Joseph Smith Jr. I don't remember the whole story—Joseph Smith hisself would get confused about it, time to time."

Pearson describes the writing of the Book of Mormon as a mixing together of *The Manuscript Found* and some Masonic foolishness—"you have to admire the *labor* of it all. . . ." Joseph is further depicted as handsome and as an excellent rhetorician. But as sincere as "that man Jones with the People's Temple" Smith was not, Pearson concludes. "He was a thief, con-man, libertine, murderer—organized a band of assassins called the Sons of Dan. . . ."

Later in the novel, thinking about his son Mark and his battle against the nuclear establishment, Mickelsson again thinks of the Mormons:

> "Society," "the Establishment"—those fat, hollow words became a sea of drab faces, dutiful bent-backed Mormons like stalks of wheat, hurrying obediently, meekly across an endless murky plain toward increasingly thick, dark smoke. There were thousands of them, millions—timidly smiling beasts, imaginationless, good-hearted, truly what they claimed to be, the saints of the world's latter days. . . . "Here now," one might say to one's students, "is the real. Who could dream, having seen this grisly vision, of any possible ideal?" And the colorless accepters of what their betters decreed—Mickelsson's Mormons—were the least of it.

As Mickelsson's apocalyptic vision continues, he sees other vast armies, as terrible as the Mormons, advancing from the east and the north—lawyers, businessmen, congressmen, public ministers, terrorists, militant women and children. An old crooked man explains who these people are: "My son, those are the People Who Believe."

And finally, an "Avenging Angel," a "Son of Dan," forces Mickelsson at gunpoint to dismantle his newly restored house in search of documents that, in the wrong hands, would prove Mormon scriptures fraudulent. While Mickelsson works, the Danite expounds on an esoteric version of Mormon kingdom-building. What the membership of the church does not know, he says, is that the leaders have built up a hierarchy of knowledge and control similar to that of the Freemasons. With the help of their Avenging Angels, the leaders are freeing people from their humanity, allowing them to be comfortable, healthy beasts. There is a universal hunger, he says, for security, easy answers, magic, somebody to blame. The Danite concludes that he believes

> "with all my heart and mind in the vision of Joseph Smith Jr., as modified by Young and Pratt and, most important, modern circumstances. A vision, essentially, of man as he is: a small group of brilliant, imaginative thinkers supported in their work by a vast army of obedient, superstitious fools who give us half of all they earn—that's their tithe—which we 'invest' for them."

We are left, then, to ask: Is Gardner simply one more in the long line of novelists to exploit past and present Mormons, to joke about polygamy, to use the Danites for a gothic subplot, to fall for the hackneyed pun on Mormon and moron? Can't we dismiss him with a sneer after the dropped preposition in our formal name or deride his mistakes about tithing, underwear, and the length of missionary service? Shouldn't we point to his acknowledged sources, Brodie's *No Man Knows My History* and William Wise's *Massacre at Mountain Meadows*, and wonder scornfully how he can impugn *our* sense of history? Don't we have a right to be offended by the suggestions that Joseph Smith was less sincere than Jim Jones or that the Nazi SS could have taken lessons from Mormon dedication to a cause? Perhaps. But might we also learn from the novel?

We can benefit, I think, from the descriptions of the two missionaries and the "network" that allows them to know of Mickelsson's visit to Salt Lake, the missionary system that provides them with rote answers, and the assumption that the end justifies the means as they search for converts. (I remember weeks spent on my own German mission with a devious questionnaire designed solely to get us past the door and into a discussion.) We can be flattered by the descriptions of ourselves as musical, family oriented, successful in business and agriculture, healthy people who take care of each other and are good with computers. But such flattery has an ironic bite. Why doesn't Mickelsson think of spirituality, intellect, wisdom, pacifism, success in the arts and education, and social consciousness when Mormons come to mind? Is the image we are spreading in fact one of dullness, thoughtlessness, organizational greyness? Is the image a true reflection? Do we indeed "know who we are, what we are here for, in other words know nothing, question nothing, learn nothing"? ...

Mickelsson's Ghosts is a novel about epistemological and ethical uncertainty, and as such questions the reality of ghosts, focuses on shifting ethical foundations, and relativizes our understanding of sanity and insanity. Those who "know" are drab, dull, and destined to rule the world. Those who don't "know" are more human, but tortured and powerless. The individual has no communal source for ethical decisions, but those in the community tend to be "colorless accepters of what their betters decree." The view of Mormonism presented in the novel is a double one, combining the original, highly individual creation of order out of chaos, the stepping out of "normal time and space," with the unsuspecting, locked-together minds of a mass movement. The living order and meaning Mickelsson seeks may have existed in the time of and through the efforts of Joseph Smith, but the worn keys Mickelsson finds in the old house no longer reveal the treasures of the past. And his attempt to rebuild the house that Joseph built ends in failure when an insane Danite attempts to defend his religion.

Sage V

Line Pole II

TWO

House of the Temple, House of the Lord: A View From Philadelphia

Scott Abbott and Steven Epperson

Dialogue: A Journal of Mormon Thought,
Volume 20, Number 3, Fall 1987

I met Steven Epperson, co-author of this essay, in the Princeton, New Jersey Ward. After graduating in 1979 with a dissertation on Freemasonry and the German novel, I was in my second year as a full-time lecturer in the Princeton German Department. Steven had graduated from Brown University and then from the Divinity School of the University of Chicago. He had a free year before starting a Ph.D. program at Temple University (where he would write the prize-winning dissertation eventually published as *Mormons and Jews*), and he and his wife Diana Girsdansky decided to spend the year in Princeton. We became fast friends.

The Princeton Ward, like many wards that stretch over a large geographical landscape, comprised a wide variety of human beings. Bob Clark, for instance, who somehow convinced the Church Building Committee to let us build a beautiful non-standard chapel, was professor of art history at the university. The wife of an abusive alcoholic brought her children to church every Sunday. The bishop, town manager for a neighboring township, hired me one summer to take a questionnaire about septic systems door-to-door. Mary Rorty, a Ph.D. in Greek philosophy, was married to one of the world's outstanding philosophers. A counselor in the bishopric, a veterinarian, hired me another summer to paint his barn and sheds and house. Alfred Bush was curator of the Western Americana Collection of Princeton's Firestone Library. One member confirmed the New Jersey state motto (The Garden State) by growing delicious tomatoes in tall cages that required a step ladder to harvest. Another was an electrician who took on the electrical system for the chapel under construction and had us pulling wire through conduits on many a late night. One member was a landscaper who bought a used sod cutter with which we ran a small sod-laying business to raise money for the new building. We also sponsored a successful funnel-cake booth at various county fairs, at one of which I watched Bill Bradley, former Princeton and New York Knick basketball player and candidate for the U. S. Senate, work the long line waiting for our funnel cakes. And there were several Princeton students.

Once a week I met with LDS students in my campus office. I was the nominal Institute teacher, but we met together as a discussion group rather than a formal class. Once each semester a congenial Church Education System employee joined us from his base in New York City. On Sundays, I taught what was called the Gospel Essentials class, designed for people investigating the Church, missionary work that led to my ordination as a Seventy. A diminutive truck driver and his diminutive wife attended the class before they were baptized and we began a friendship that lasted for years. One Sunday the Bishop invited me into his office and said the missionaries had complained that I was telling investigators that we believed we had a Mother in Heaven as well as a Father in Heaven. That is one of the best parts of our theology, I said. He concurred.

Sacrament meeting was at five p.m. and during the summer the late sun came slanting in through a long west window to play against the front wall of the chapel. "Now the day is over," we sang, "Night is drawing nigh; / Shadows of the evening / Steal across the sky." A gentle tune, a prayer for "calm and sweet repose." And that evening light—Nature's visible spirit.

In 1981, I took a job at Vanderbilt University. By then Steven was engaged in graduate work at Temple University in Philadelphia. We exchanged letters, I visited him and his family in their sketchy neighborhood wedged between a freeway and a rail line, and we decided to weave his experiences in Philadelphia and my experiences doing research in the archive of a Washington D.C. Freemasonic temple into a single text. By the time we published our essay, Steven had become a curator at the Church Museum of Art and History in Salt Lake.

Steven's letters—long, handwritten, and haphazardly folded missives filling whatever pages and scraps of paper he had at hand—are, I realize as I peruse them again after nearly forty years, works of passionate and generous genius. Confessional, searching, scholarly, mundane, poetic, challenging, and fraternal, Steven's intense rambling thoughts inspired me when they appeared in my mailboxes in Tennessee, in Tübingen, Germany, and in Orem, Utah. They inspire me still.

> The lord whose oracle is at Delphi neither speaks nor conceals, but gives signs.
>
> —Heraclitus

Three steps. A terrace. Five steps. A terrace. Seven steps. A terrace. Nine steps. A final broad terrace. Stone sphinxes (one for wisdom, one for power) flanked me on either side. Above me, like an ancient Egyptian mountain carved by holy men, towered the massive House of the Temple, deliberately intimidating any "profane" seeking admittance.

I pressed a tiny button as a small sign directed (really wishing I could knock with the big brass ring hanging from the mouth of a flaming lion's head) and waited.

The pyramidal, columned edifice, headquarters of the Mother Supreme Council of the Thirty-Third and Last Degree, Ancient and Accepted Scottish Rite of Freemasonry, Southern Jurisdiction, U.S.A., stands at the corner of Sixteenth and S streets in Washington, D.C., not far south from the fine old Mormon chapel whose stained glass representations of the Restoration now shed their muted light on committed followers of the Reverend Moon. Taking their cue from the Great Architect of the Universe, Freemasons have always meticulously ordered their physical environments. Space is organized to facilitate mental change. Initiates pass along a symbolic route meant to transform them. Put most simply: the building makes the man.

I looked around at the ritually measured steps, the sphinxes, the thirty-three columns surrounding the building, the heavy, locked doors, and contemplated the wealth, power, and exclusivity the building represented. Would passage through this building change me? A second time, I rang the bell. The day before, I had come by train from Philadelphia to Washington to gather information for a paper on "Aspects of Freemasonry in the Mormon Temple." Waiting at the station for my cousin, I bought a copy of the *Washington Post* and in the book review section read the story of Robert Fitzroy, captain of the *Beagle*, that doggy ship we remember because the young Charles Darwin was among its passengers. Like Darwin, Fitzroy was a young upper-class Englishman. But unlike his soon-to-be famous passenger, he was a passionately fundamentalist Christian (and a strong advocate of slavery). Fitzroy visited the same exotic places as Darwin and witnessed the same phenomena, but his own lens of understanding (literalistic Biblical) led him to experience a radically different world from Darwin's. When Darwin began publishing his findings soon after his return to England, Fitzroy felt implicated in the rise of an idea that threatened his traditional Christian view of the cosmos. He was tortured by the thought of his own complicity, tormented—until one day he burst into a room where scientists had gathered to discuss evolution. Theatrically, desperately, touched by a spirit inimical to the new science, Fitzroy waved an open Bible over his head and shouted to the flabbergasted scientists: "The Book! The Book! the B-o-o-o-o-o-o-o-o-o-k!"

My cousin and I are not as different as were Darwin and Fitzroy, although what he told me on the way to his apartment about his work on Ronald Reagan's re-election campaign gave me the feeling that our politics would not lead to a sudden and perfect rapport. Nor would our economic situations, I thought, as we neared his home in the condominiumed splendor of Pentagon City. We did agree, however, that we would both like to attend sacrament meeting that afternoon at his ward.

The Potomac Ward parking lot looked like a well-stocked BMW dealership. The chapel breathed pastel elegance. The congregation listened intently as a speaker bore mellifluous witness to "the most correct book on the face of the earth."

Immersed in the pervasive well-being of the suburban Washington chapel, electronically amplified words washing around me, I perversely rebelled against the prevailing spirit of ease and resolution. Unavoidably I began making perilous and ludicrous contrasts between the well-heeled, cultured piety of this environment and the deprivation, ruin, and violence of north Philadelphia (where my wife and I were eking out a student-family's existence). Synapses opened and closed, adrenaline shot into my blood, very recent memories hurtled through my consciousness.

Last week, while standing in the Broad Street bus, I stupidly ignored the process of my own victimization by a skillful pickpocket: the unnecessary jostling by a commuter at my back, the conspiratorial looks of confederates on either side, young men disarmingly lost to the driving rap beat in their head-phones. Robbed for the second time in a month. (The first had been a useless break-in—what did we have that they would want anyway? It's a wonder they didn't trash our place out of spite.) But the pickpockets expertly fleeced me of the money for my research trip to Washington—and the precious means for Elizabeth's art lessons. Now when someone brushes up against me on a subway or crowded sidewalk, my hand goes to my wallet and lurid scenes of imagined violence pass through my mind's eye.

Fortunately, a grant from our bishop (he says a generous couple once supported his education) foiled the pickpocket and got me to a pastel chapel in Washington, where I now heard an undersecretary for something-or-other report on how hospitably the saints in Paris accepted her during a recent visit. "The Church is the same wherever you go."

That night my cousin and I had a long talk. I was thankful for his hospitality; but in spite of that and the fact that the Church is the same wherever you go, we were repeatedly at odds. He expressed concern over the topic of my paper, suggesting that the Mason-Mormon connection might be better left untouched. Instead of derivation and congruence, why not talk about this Church's uniqueness? Why write speculative history anyway? All history is analogical and speculative, I pointed out. Was he suggesting that history be forgotten? I tried to see things his way but had difficulties getting past my own prejudices. So did he. His faith seemed based on answers whose questions undergird my own. Although we disagreed on almost everything, we still conversed for hours. Perhaps that itself was a small victory for us both.

The next morning, on my way to the House of the Temple, my cousin kindly initiated me into urban masonry, the first order of which comprehends the computerized efficiency and antiseptic cleanliness of the new subway system. He led me down a swift and silent escalator into a vast, vaulted chamber. In exchange for a green bill bearing Masonic symbols (a pyramid capped by an all-seeing eye), we entered the subway. Conversing quietly, we rode a swift car through dark passageways: from Pentagon City to Arlington National Cemetery, on to Foggy Bottom, and into the heart of the city. There we ascended from the secret bowels of the earth to sidewalks where the world's largest contingent of lawyers and secretaries rushed to work. My cousin joined the phalanx of lawyers, and I made my way up Sixteenth Street to the House of the Temple.

A third time I pressed the bell, nervous about what awaited me.

The longer its doors remained closed, the more intimidating the building grew. Part of the Masons' attraction is that they don't try to attract. Proselytizing is forbidden, and frightful oaths protect the secrecy of their rituals.

I peered through the glass door. Through semidarkness a little man approached and opened the door. I showed him my letter of invitation, then followed him through a large atrium, prodigiously appointed with white marble, polished green granite, and heavy oak beams. Doric columns competed with black Egyptian figures, Greek vase paintings with Egyptian hieroglyphics.

The stone, wood, and gold paint were impressive; but the library, reached after progressing through a series of halls and rooms, struck my literarily educated senses as the ultimate in enclosed space. Books of every size, age, language, and shape rose in varicolored ranks to a vaulted, skylit ceiling.

The librarian, a kindly, middle-aged German-American woman, greeted me warmly. At her request, I gave her a list of books I wanted to see first. As she bustled away with energy I came to admire over the next days, I again contemplated the room. It reminded me of similar places, other sancta dedicated to the word, other protected inner rooms housing written visions and revisions, harboring texts both public and intimate, exoteric and esoteric: library rooms in New York, Provo, Tübingen—and Princeton.

It was at Princeton that I met Alfred Bush, head of the university library's Western Americana collection. Over several months (I drove up daily from Philadelphia), he introduced me to his collection of texts and artifacts, both Mormon and Masonic. One day he showed me a first edition of the *Book of Commandments* he had just purchased for the library. Another day it was a letter from Brigham Young to a wayward wife, offering to come pick her up himself if she would come back. I read about Joseph Smith sounding the Masonic distress cry—"Is there no help for the widow's son?"—in the moments before his death. Most fascinating of all was the seerstone, once used by Joseph, now encased in a velvet-lined box. Through the geode's hollow center, guided by a triangle of crystals, I could pretend, could long to see the world as Joseph Smith saw it. This stone acted for a time as his Delphi. I wondered about the signs it gave.

The librarian brought me a large stack of books—eighteenth- and nineteenth-century volumes for which there had been no great demand over the last century or so. I blew very fine, black dust from each book before I opened it, making liberal use of the disposable hand towels the librarian provided and wondering about documented cases of black lung in library workers.

Lunchtime came and the librarian directed me to a McDonalds a few blocks away (she had sized up my pocketbook rather handily). Outside, blinking in the harsh light of midday, I ritually left the House of the Temple behind—nine steps, seven, five, and three—and walked through a neighborhood of once fine townhouses. My coat and tie had fit in well enough in the subway among lawyers and in the library, but walking among the new tenants of the decaying buildings (the people whose threatening presence may have contributed to the sale of the old Mormon chapel), my clothing set me apart. Under the golden arches, however, all are equal, and I ate my lunch in a plastic environment among people with culinary tastes as indiscriminating as my own.

Back in the library, under the soporific influence of McDonalds' grease and sugar, drowsily trying to read a deadly sociological study of Freemasonry, my mind wandered to the vivid image of the bearded, sallow, shivering, overcoated man I had seen propped against the outside of the House of the Temple (oblivious to the ninety-degree heat). Strands of memory grew taut and resonant, and I relived a winter journey through Philadelphia, a trek necessitated by a sudden need for funds. Personal history. Existential history. The figured history of my life as opposed to the abstract history I was tracing on paper.

I hiked and hitchhiked through the city, through the litter-strewn woods in Fern Rock, through North Philadelphia bombed back into the Stone Age by age, neglect, and malevolence. Men stared at me as I passed their fires lit in drums, the ascending flames stoked with the ripped-out ribbing of building carcasses great and humble. I stumbled over rusting tracks running in once-purposeful grids through the gaunt ruins of commerce. I passed Dropsie University, festooned with graffiti and blackened by exhaust fumes and arson, and came to the Interstate Blood Bank. Four weeks earlier I'd bled for thrombosis research. Good money on a one-pint basis. The interval between then and now was too short, but mine was an immediate, non-trifling need: a birthday dress for Elizabeth, a denial of the marginality of our poverty.

I joined the early morning lineup of regulars, the several dozen other residents of that forlorn territory, hoping to get in on the plasma donors program. Men warmed chilled bodies by sitting on open heating grates in the sidewalk; others gathered, arms extended, fingers spread out toward the intense heat cast out from great, perforated barrels. I tried not to stare too hard at these or at others: the men with the DTs in front of me in the line, the one moaning, sweating, and stinking behind me. Peering in, I read the familiar, worn sign near the door: "Would you like to earn $87 a month? Ask about the Plasma Program. Donors with poor hygiene and body odor will not be processed." Most of us were turned away that morning. I didn't have enough identification, the man behind me was rejected when the medical technicians found the tracks between his thighs and toes.

Finally that night I stood at the end of the platform at the old Reading terminal off North Broad, under an implacable sky, a tender, star-dappled sky, imploring, like a child, for simple answers to numbing complexities and for the easing of that city's pain.

Back from dream memories of Philadelphia, refreshed by a furtive nap, I worked through the afternoon. Periodically the man who had let me in the front door led small groups of people through. I could hear his tour-guide intonations (boyish pride laced with bored familiarity) in adjoining rooms:

"This Bible, 150 years old, has each letter printed in gold."

"The silver ball here opens up to reveal a complete set of Masonic jewels or symbols. Notice the trowel, compass, square, and plumb line."

"This is the universal room. Each bookcase houses Masonic books from a particular country. We used to have each country's flag displayed above the cabinets, but today so many countries are communistic, and we won't allow communistic flags here, so we just took them all down."

"In this room is our Robert Burns collection, the most complete set of published material outside of Scotland written by and about our illustrious brother. The hammering and drilling you hear down the hall is from our Dynamic Freedoms Room. We are installing a new display there: torture instruments of the Catholic Inquisition, recently donated by an Italian brother."

While I worked and the tours went on, the librarian answered her telephone: "Lib'ry! . . . No sur, we do not have the Knights of Columbus ritul . . . That is what I said, ritul. You should call the Lib'ry of Congress . . . Thank you, sur."

"Lib'ry! . . . The Bolivian delegation is bringing how many extra pursons? . . . But I only ordered two cars for them. Are they small people?"

In the meantime, I read a novel (published in Germany in 1870) in which one of the characters writes eccentric letters from Salt Lake City describing the Mormons. He explains "Mormon Masonry" by referring to W. W. Phelps's supposed years of study at Göttingen under the philosopher/Masonic reformer Krause. (That was new to me and may have surprised W. W. Phelps as well.)

I emerged from the dim coolness of the House of the Temple at four o'clock with a satisfying stack of notes in hand.

Tuesday and Wednesday were much like Monday: riding the subway in with my cousin (we continued to agree on little, but we were still talking), reading old books from eight to four, and discovering the city in the late afternoons and evenings.

B'nai Brith and the National Rifle Association have headquarters on the same block. The Australian Embassy was tearing up great expanses of reinforced concrete to install heating wires under the entrance to an underground garage (the ambassador must have had a difficult winter). The Russian Embassy really does have a forest of antennae on its roof. The National Gallery closes at five, so if you walk through a rain storm for forty-five minutes after working until four and then hope to spend the rest of the evening there, you should forget it, go home, and dry your shoes.

Twice I fled from the prevailing heat and light into theaters. I saw *The Brother from Another Planet* and *The Gods Must Be Crazy*, two films about men thrust into alien cultures. The stories of those two black men dealing with their absurd, liminal conditions in shockingly new habitats evoked images of the winter we spent at the literal edge of Philadelphia.

Finally, after weeks of apartment hunting (while grossly overstaying the hospitality of our home teacher whose large family already made his house small), we found a place. Not elegant, and in a tough, ragged neighborhood, but with two bedrooms and a rent we decided we could afford. With two-thirds of our savings we paid the security deposit and the first month's rent. Two days later we arrived with our first load of belongings.

A disheveled woman with crying children behind her skirts and in her arms confronted us as we opened the door.

"What you doin' in my apartment?"

Over the next hour we established that the manager who had taken our money was no manager, but rather an enterprising former tenant still in possession of a key.

Too bad.

We decided that with our remaining money we could outfit ourselves with a tent, sleeping bags, and cooking equipment. It was mid-February, and spring was no more than a month away. We would be our own landlords in a state park just outside the city. Three times a week I could drive in to Temple University to teach the class for which I received a slim stipend; my own studies would simply have to wait.

Through the flattening patina of memory, the deprivations are obscured, most details washed out. But some resist the benign mendacity of passing time and are still served up piping hot like the fish and barley soup upon which we largely subsisted during our sojourn in the woods. Spring that year did not arrive until mid-April; the winter was bitter and protracted. What returns to mind are our acts of survival, shorn of ambiguity, so unlike the academic, urbane assertions to which I was habituated and which routinely die a death of a thousand qualifications. Here wood had to be gathered and protected from impending storms and food eaten carefully, with thought for our limited stores. Had the tent been re-staked? Was there enough fuel for the lantern? Would the socks dry overnight? I remember melting chunks of snow and ice over a wood-stoked flame, then boiling the water to heat milk bottles for two young boys; cracking open black walnuts with stained fingers and savoring their crushed meat; noting deer tracks in the snow and the depressions left by their bodies near our pitched tent and glowing coals; and seeing Elizabeth, stripped to the waist, bathing her supple frame, washing golden hair under the spout of frigid water from a rustic pump.

Once we began a rather bucolic walk to feed scraps to the ducks who inhabited a tiny portion of the lake kept liquid by a warm spring or a current or a glitch in the universe. Our two-year-old, Avi, and our four-year-old, Michael, layered in snowsuit over snowsuit, looked like ambulatory balls of clothing. Neither boy sensed the precariousness of our existence, and they jabbered happily while we fed the ducks. Elizabeth and I were picking up sticks of fallen wood for our fire when we heard a soft, liquid plop behind us. Michael began to call his brother's name: frightened, envious, admonishing—maybe all three. We turned and found Avi floating on his back in the freezing water, not yet frightened, only accepting, like a gentle Zen bundle. He began to sink, and I splashed to his rescue. Elizabeth ripped off layers of his already freezing clothing and thrust his little body inside her own clothing. We raced to the car and careened down slippery roads to Birdsboro, some miles distant. There in a laundromat we dried the only clothes he had, layer after layer, like the street people we nearly were. At night, in the scarcely tempered cold of our tent, I lay awake gnawing on the bitter bone of the effects of my choices on our children and on Elizabeth. At what point had the "nobility" (I've been so self-righteous about this!) of *Torah L'shmah*, or learning for its own sake, taken on such a sobering, mortal, threatening aspect? I dreamed that night of handing over my children to the dean of students and receiving a slim folder in return: "Aspects of Freemasonry in the Mormon Temple."

On Thursday I read a nineteenth-century exposé of Masonic rites, a book that came out of the William Morgan affair in upstate New York. (Morgan, a renegade Mason, disappeared after publishing what he had sworn to keep secret. Joseph Smith later married his widow.) The book was despicable, an expose of the worst sort (the author gave participants in the ritual names like "Woodenhead"), but I needed the information. I mollified my conscience by considering how Freemasons themselves would profit from my work.

As I read, I was struck by the fact that Joseph Smith drew symbols, tokens, and even whole phrases from the Masonic rite. I could see why Masons were upset by the unauthorized and creative use Joseph and Brigham made of rituals they had learned in Freemasonic lodges. But Mormons have assiduously maintained the secrecy of the rites Masons themselves regard as most sacred. In fact, I thought, Masons might be somewhat gratified to know that many Mormons believe, more strongly than most contemporary Masonic historians, that parts of the Masonic rituals descend directly from Solomon's temple.

That evening, after reading Masonic rituals all day in the House of the Temple, I joined my cousin and members of his ward in the House of the Lord—the Washington, D.C., Temple. Although it was a real pleasure to see all those fashion plates in standard issue white, fat, polyester ties, unnerving critical feelings disturbed the more profound pleasures I had hoped to find in the temple. I began to fear that I had lost the spirit of this place, which I valued above all other places. The entire building seemed to me a sacrifice on the altar of efficiency: the inner architecture featuring locker rooms (where ritual goods are exchanged for money), the plastic theater seats, the intrusive binary-minded computers. Like other temples, this building is intended to affect those who pass through it; but less scrupulously crafted, it lacks the symbolic density of our older temples. Remembered visits to the Manti Temple, a fine building illuminated by hand-wrought beauty and intended symbolic details, made the new, machine-tooled efficiency feel shallow.

Dominated by the critical feelings and cares I so wished to be free of in the Lord's house, I wondered about my own unworthiness, my own lack of charity. Were they blocking the light I had come to find, or was this modern temple, partially uprooted from its historical and symbolic context, "making the man"?

While I tried to sort truth from self-deception, the lights dimmed and the film began. My critical mood continued as a plethora of celluloid images specifically interpreted and limited a text much richer as a sparse, live, intense drama. Finally, however, as the great story of creation unfolded before me and the drama of the fall was enacted one more time, I found myself responding to the ritual with alertness and a gratefully open mind and heart.

Having just read the Masonic rite, I was immediately struck by the contrast. While our ceremony shares some wonderful phrases and symbols with the Masons, it has a substantial body and broad context of its own. The Masons focus on different matters: on the building of Solomon's temple, for instance, on allegories drawn from the craft of masonry, on predominately moral concerns. They have a decidedly different sense of who we are and of our relationship with God. I was impressed by how much of the ritual was exclusively our own, and I was thrilled by the message I was getting.

Our theology is largely narrative, and what we find in the temple is no exception. As a result, our learning in the Lord's house depends upon our personal interpretation. The insights I had that Thursday night changed my view of the world. But my reading of the temple ceremony is just that, my reading. Without the keys of authority (or even with them), attempting to specify *the* meaning of the ritual text automatically limits it, as does the overly specific film. *Caveat lector!*

As the Bible tells us (and I choose the account in Genesis so as to unencumber my telling of the ritually protected story), God created man (male and female) in his own image. He gave them two commandments: (1) to multiply and (2) not to eat of the fruit of the tree of knowledge of good and evil. Eve, however, realized that the fruit would make her like God. Although Adam at first refused to partake of the fruit, choosing instead what he took to be obedience (there was no curse mentioned for not multiplying), Eve recognized the value of the fruit, desired it, and partook. In Greek myth, Prometheus stole fire from the gods and suffered eternally for his assault on Olympus. As Mormons interpret Genesis, however, God *wanted* Eve to become like him. The second half of becoming like him, however (the half the devil, in his blindness, did not understand), involved the obedience Adam chose in the beginning. Adam and Eve, together, did the Lord's will and were collectively like him. Individually, both were flawed. Eve (dis)obediently reached for the fire; Adam chose obedience. The two experiences or attitudes were *both* necessary, although obviously contradictory. After single-mindedly taking the fire/fruit, Eve proved herself more fully worthy by bowing to the commandment that required not only her obedience to God but also, symbolically, to Adam.

As the story continued in the temple, the same lesson was repeated again and again in different forms. Through various symbolic structures, we (women and men) were offered the fire and then required to be obedient. We moved in the often-repeated dialectic from binding to unleashing, from obedience to (dis)obedience, from the strictures of sociality to the freedom of independence. For every law given there were extraordinary promises of freedom; for every spark of fire there were strict conditions.

In my interpretation of the ceremony, God desires at once our faithful disobedience and our fidelity. He wants us to leap and strive and grasp for his fire, while at the same time submitting ourselves to his will. He justifies neither the rebellious nor the obedient exclusively, but only rebellion *and* obedience. He bade Moses approach the burning bush and yet commanded him to remove his sandals. A Mormon reading of the Fall honors Eve for the fruit of her transgression and Adam for his fidelity to the law and to his mate—which bring us an interesting point, which I might label "and not for Eve's transgression." In 1984 the Southern Baptist Convention overwhelmingly endorsed a resolution stating that as Eve brought sin into the world, women should not be ordained to the ministry. I suppose that any Jewish or Christian practice that subordinates women to men justifies itself through Genesis 3:16: "Your desire shall be to your husband, and he shall rule over you." Have we not acquiesced, in our own practices, to this traditional reading, although our theology states specifically that "men [and women] will be punished for their own sins, and not for Adam's [or Eve's] transgression." Both sexes are created in the image of God and must learn similar lessons in order to fulfill that measure of their creation.

I know that what seemed so clear to me leaves out selected parts of the story (as do all interpretations)—the rib, the millennia of patriarchy, polygamy, and the near invisibility of our Mother in Heaven. But for a brief shining moment I felt I had cut through a knotty problem with a laser beam of insight.

In the celestial room after the ceremonies, I sat with my cousin and discussed the symbolic experience we had just had. His face lit up as he agreed and disagreed with my reading of the ceremony, and my understanding of what had transpired was enriched by the particularity of his experience. Gone were the tentativeness and distrust that had clouded our first discussions. The terms and spirit of our conversation were transfigured by a shared desire for faithful inquiry, a desire nourished by the spirit of the place, and perhaps even by our previous, seemingly unfruitful discussions. Whatever our final conclusions, we had momentarily, gracefully, entered together into the spirit of a blessed house of shared priesthood, a "house of faith, a house of learning, a house of glory, a house of order, a house of God" (D&C 88:119).

That night in a dream I found myself in the small New Mexican town where I grew up. With two friends I approached the high school (scene of many youthful awakenings). In place of the old buildings was a temple, drawing us towards it with great power. We scrambled up the hill, worried that we might miss something, for we knew we were late. Once inside, however, all sense of tardiness vanished. I felt warmly accepted, comfortingly, timelessly enclosed.

Waiting to enter the main room I saw Žarko Radaković and Zorca Papadopoulos, anarchically creative Yugoslavs I met one summer in Germany. Žarko held a huge bottle of wine in his hand and a long loaf of bread under his arm. I was surprised and then filled with delight to see them in a Mormon temple, Žarko drank deeply from the bottle and smiled broadly at me.

Inside a huge, lofty room (I never did see the ceiling), we joined a larger group of people. To one side a drama was being performed. One actor was a man who had insulted me several years before. Now he reached over and gave me a peculiar and warm handshake. Waves of cleansing forgiveness washed through my soul.

Children in the room were singing a happy song and clapping in unison. I could hear a quiet, cerebral jazz improvisation played on a piano in an adjoining room.

I felt no sense of time or of hurry. We were all in the place we most wanted to be and were settled in for a long stay.

In one corner I found a smooth, white wall, cans of paint at its base. With brilliant hues and lavish strokes I painted enormous poppies on the wall. Around the corner a friend decorated another wall with mythical Eastern figures.

All around me people were engaged in animated conversations. I walked among them until I found my family in the center of the room. Thomas was tired, but when I carried him around and showed him the paints, the drama, and all the happy people, his spirits lifted.

As the dream drew to an end, I heard two women discussing how they were created in the image of their Heavenly Mother. "I'll see you in the celestial room," one of them said, and the dream ended.

Friday was my last day at the House of the Temple. Amid the rush of making last-minute notes, I happened on a 1917 *History of the Ancient and Honorable Fraternity of Free and Accepted Masons*. In a section on Masonry among nineteenth-century Mormons, after a short, angry description of irregularities in the Nauvoo lodge, the author gives his impression of the pioneers:

> In 1846 the Mormon hegira took place, when Nauvoo and other places in Illinois and Camp Far West, and other towns in Missouri were evacuated, and that strange community took its departure from the borders of a land of civilization and enlightenment, to seek

an asylum in the Great Basin by the Great Salt Sea of the Deseret.

For a period of nearly twenty years, by alliances with hostile tribes of Indians, and their own armed bands of murderers and marauders, the Danites, they plundered and murdered the emigrants on their way to the Pacific Coast and massacred whole trains of both men and women, and, in successful armed defiance, fortified the national highways to prevent the passage of United States troops over the rightful territory of the government.

Refreshing to see yourself from another point of view.

Late that afternoon I said good-by to my cousin and boarded a train to Philadelphia. In one hand I carried a briefcase full of scholarly notes; within me I carried the seeds of a more personal essay. Could I, perhaps, in the intimate environment of home, write something about the places I had just visited? About how they relate to my understandings, doubts, loves, and fears? About the spirits I felt in those places?

The sky is quite blue today, not hung so heavily with humid, silver-blue veils. The week since I returned home has been awful. I have lived under the fan. I sleep poorly, and then, too tired to read, I watch movies until I am bored to tears and try sleeping again. I wander through the house, stepping on creaking floor boards, listening to the scuttling dances of cockroaches, to the children softly snoring, and to Elizabeth talking in her sleep.

Though our backyard is minuscule, still we have room for a rose bush, some pole beans, marigolds, a small wading pool for the boys, and a few square feet of grass. Around eight, fireflies rise and fall, entwined in a glowing rhythm. A neighbor two doors up sits in Bermudas and a pork pie hat and smokes a slow cigar. Pie tins, cut in sections and strung over tomato and pepper plants, wave and jostle in slightest breezes. This sliver of an old Polish working-class island in blighted north Philadelphia has its own pleasures.

Two nights ago I dreamed that all the stars disappeared and the old heavens rolled up like a scroll. Elizabeth and I set out to find a terrestrial place where celestial evidences of new heavens would be manifest.

Today I wash clothes in our broken machine. I beat and stir with a old cane, then hang up garments intercalated with socks, little boys' briefs, and sheets, to dry and flap, whipping in the breeze. I peg them with wooden pins, step back, and see accent marks at scored intervals strung along the taut, bowing line, the line bearing our wraps and linen and sacred wear, bearing marks, notes—music? If I could only hear it more clearly. It moves against currents so strongly, and its voice is drowned out in quotidian din.

Cities. I think how hard it is for me to find God here. As a child I grew amid archaic, wild landscapes and touched them, raw, vivid with divinity. In the city, layers and layers of peeling veneer seem to have totally obscured the grain of the earth and the succession of rings around the core of divine years and seasons. So much blight. So much toughness. We abandon the cities again and again to the paradigms of Babylon, Sodom, Gomorrah. Abandon them to the Catholic Church and the AME churches, the Bethel Baptist churches, the Holy Spirit Alliance Tabernacle of Prayer. But now the times of the gentiles in the suburbs is passing and the Church seeks new fields for its husbandry. Will we find God in these cities? What Latter-day Saint will find the interpretive ministrational key and gift to liberate these captives for God's kingdom? What new paradigm, what vision-alternative do we have?

The temple is a paradox, an earthly home for a transcendent God. It cannot house his glory, yet he bids his children raise its walls, adorn its chambers, weave its veil. For he chooses just this place and not celestial spheres to disclose and veil his presence among the children of Israel. Signs of fellowship and wisdom, signs of sovereignty and orientation hewn upon the temple's sheer face betoken the knowledge and endowment bestowed within. Mortal hands and eyes are led by ones immortal to frame the fearful symmetry of his form, his house, his kingdom here on earth. We cannot place the crown upon his kingdom—cannot bind all wounds, sate all hunger, pacify all violence, wipe away all tears. Yet he bids, he demands a realm of equity and justice, now, from our flawed hearts and feeble hands.

The House of the Lord is the matrix for the kingdom of God on earth. The temple transmutes city and wilderness: it pursues neither Eden, nor the heavenly Jerusalem. It sanctions neither a naive return to a romanticized past, nor the negation of the sensuous present, the real, for an abstract future. Rather, by a mysterious alchemy conjured through the conjunction of words from an improbable rite, it would bridge the rift between parents and children, the whole estranged family of Adam and Eve, and it would establish Enoch's city here, in this world, through unnumbered acts of charity and justice.

It has been months since my visit to two of Washington's temples. I still have not completed my essay on "Aspects of Freemasonry in the Mormon Temple." It seems such an abstraction: the philosophical and historical winnowing out, the surveying and staking of positions. Missing is the living of life, the liturgical power of the temples, the spirit moving through gathered sisters and brothers, the bidden power coursing through a servant of God, and even the groping around in doubts and weariness.

Works Cited

Heraclitus. "Fragment 93" as cited in Charles H. Kahn, *The Art and Thought of Heraclitus.* Cambridge: Cambridge University Press, 1979, p. 43.

Stillson, Henry L., ed. *History of the Ancient and Honorable Fraternity of Free and Accepted Masons.* Boston: The Fraternity Publishing Company, 1917.

Steven's letters contained those wonderful paragraphs about the temple as the matrix for the Kingdom of God on Earth and that riveting account of his family's frigid camping in a wintery Philadelphia park. I wrote about the Freemasonic temple and about attending the Washington, D. C. temple with my cousin Brent Israelson. The thoughts about Adam and Eve and the dream about friends and family in an expansive and inclusive temple are mine. Structured as a ritual drama, the dramatic temple ceremony invited interpretation, inspired new ideas, suggested new possibilities for living a good life.

But how did I, an atheist, get into the temple?

While I worked with Steven on the essay, I was active in the Nashville 3rd Ward. For several years I was the Scoutmaster, despite my aversion to uniforms. Inspired by my parent's generosity and my own experience over the years, I continued to pay a generous tithing. I obeyed the Word of Wisdom. I was a dutiful Home Teacher. I was true to my spouse. We held regular family home evenings. When Norman Tolk, a Vanderbilt physicist and one of the original founders of *Dialogue*, asked me to be a counsellor in the Stake Mission Presidency, I agreed. That calling required an interview with the Stake President, Todd Christofferson, for which I drove from the university into downtown Nashville for an interview in the office he inhabited as Senior Vice President and General Counsel for the Commerce Union Bank of Tennessee. A couple of years later, when Vanderbilt announced my forthcoming book *Fictions of Freemasonry*, I responded to an invitation from another bank vice president and again ascended that tall building for lunch with three 33° Freemasons. And while I'm digressing from the main question of my worthiness to enter the temple, I'll note that Norman's colleague in the Vanderbilt physics department, Richard Haglund, was busy raising a future editor of *Dialogue*.

But that begs the question of the temple-recommend questions about belief in God and in Church leaders as prophets, seers, and revelators. My affirmative answers to those questions over the years were based on my experiences with the powerful *idea* of God, with the life-enhancing stories told in the scriptures, and with the inspiring writings of Joseph Smith, Brigham Young, Spencer

Kimball, and many others. Those men were, for me, revelators like the poets and mystics who also inspired me—Goethe, Walt Whitman, Thomas Merton, Hildegard von Bingen, and so many others. Did it matter that my belief was metaphorical rather than literal? It didn't to me. And I did love the temple.

Wasatch

THREE

Will We Find Zion or Make Zion? An Essay on Postmodernity and Revelation

First presented at the *Sunstone* conference on "Plotting Zion" in 1990; a fuller version published in the *Student Review*, June 1990; and a final one published in *Sunstone*, December 1994

A month after achieving tenure at Vanderbilt, I accepted an offer from BYU. I had interviewed at BYU with two academic vice presidents, both scientists who were curious about whether I read outside my discipline. I did, and, assuming they did as well, anticipated stimulating exchanges with them and others at BYU. Colleagues in the Department of Germanic and Slavic Languages welcomed me warmly. My students gave me hope for the future. Wondering what that future might look like and how we at BYU might help shape it, I responded to a call from Elbert Peck for papers for a *Sunstone* sponsored conference on "Plotting Zion."

> The resulting essay is an attempt to think about the idea of Zion from the pragmatic perspective I first encountered in the work of Richard Rorty, ideas that continue to be a major influence on how I view and live in the world.

———

Early in Umberto Eco's novel *Foucault's Pendulum*, the narrator describes the effect on him of that famous pendulum that first demonstrated the earth's rotation:

> I knew the earth was rotating, and I with it, and . . . all Paris with me, and that together we were rotating beneath the Pendulum, whose own plane never changed direction, because up there, along the infinite extrapolation of its wire beyond the choir ceiling, up toward the most distant galaxies, lay the Only Fixed Point in the universe, eternally unmoving.
>
> . . . The Pendulum told me that, as everything moved—earth, solar system, nebulae and black holes, all the children of the great cosmic expansion—one single point stood still: a pivot, bolt, or hook around which the universe could move. And I was now taking part in that supreme experience. I, too, moved with the all, but I could see the One, the Rock, the Guarantee, the luminous mist that is no body, that has no shape, weight, quantity, or quality, that does not see or hear, that cannot be sensed, that is in no place, in no time, and is not soul, intelligence, imagination, opinion, number, order, or measure. Neither darkness nor light, neither error nor truth.[1]

---

1. My thanks to Steven Epperson, whose ideas and even words are evident throughout this essay. Umberto Eco, *Foucault's Pendulum* (San Diego: Harcourt Brace Jovanovich, 1989) 5. Note that these attributes of the fixed point are drawn from theological descriptions of the nature of God intended to describe God as absolute and unlimited in every sense. Compare that to LDS descriptions of a more definite and thus philosophically limited God, a God of body, parts, and passions.

In the course of Eco's novel, the narrator and two colleagues, disbelieving in "the One, the Rock, the Guarantee," playfully construct a grand conspiracy theory to *act* as the fixed point, the guarantor of meaning and truth in history. Knights Templar, Rosicrucians, and Freemasons become the movers of history, possessors of occult keys to absolute truth. As the novel ends, however, the three conspirators have been captured by their own exquisite philosophical construction. Devotees of the occult have taken the construction as truth; and to force the final truth from one of the constructors, they wrap the wire of the pendulum around his neck and finally, when he refuses to divulge the supposed secret, hang him:

> Then . . . Belbo's body, through a grisly addition and cancellation of vectors, a migration of energies, suddenly became immobile, and the wire and the sphere moved, but only from his body down; the rest—which connected Belbo with the vault—now remained perpendicular. Thus Belbo had escaped the error of the world and its movements, had now become, himself, the point of suspension, the Fixed Pin, the Place from which the vault of the world is hung, while beneath his feet the wire and the sphere went on swinging from pole to pole, without peace, the earth slipping away under them, showing always a new continent. The sphere could not point out, nor would it ever know, the location of the World's Navel.[2]

Eco's novel provides images for the abstractions of postmodern or postmetaphysical thought. First, confronting the age-old desire for metaphysical certainty. Second, the argument that truth is made, not found, that supposed grounded, certified, natural truths are in fact arbitrary, contingent, constructed. Third, the image of Belbo hanging from the wire of the pendulum, his head now a new, mediating, fixed point changing the motion of the pendulum and thus deflecting access to the World's Navel, is a strong

---

2. Eco, 597.

metaphor for the argument that even were metaphysical truth to exist, it would always be mediated through human language.

This language that is our primary means of knowing is, to quote Nietzsche, "a mobile army of metaphors." One metaphor points to another in an endless chain. We live in what Nietzsche calls a prison house of language, in a world made by language and thus dependent on or contingent on language.

Richard Rorty argues in *Contingency, Irony, Solidarity* that our languages, our selves, and our communities are contingent, although there is no reason to lament with Yeats that "the center cannot hold."[3] We ought, rather, to celebrate the concomitant gain in freedom and responsibility:

> If we could ever become reconciled to the idea that most of reality is indifferent to our descriptions of it, and that *the human self is created by the* use *of a vocabulary rather than being adequately or inadequately* expressed in *a vocabulary*, then we should at last have assimilated what was true in the Romantic idea that truth is made rather than found. What is true about this claim is just that *languages* are made rather than found, and that truth is a property of linguistic entities, of sentences....
>
> What the Romantics expressed as the claim that imagination, rather than reason, is the central human faculty was the realization that a talent for speaking differently, rather than for arguing well, is the chief instrument of cultural change. What political utopians since the French Revolution have sensed is not that an enduring, substratal human nature has been suppressed or repressed by "unnatural" or "irrational" social institutions but rather that changing languages and other social practices may produce human beings of a sort that had never before existed.[4]

---

3. William Butler Yeats, 'The Second Coming," in *Selected Poems and Two Plays of William Butler Yeats*, ed. M. L. Rosenthall (New York: Collier Books, 1962) 91.
4. Richard Rorty, *Contingency, Irony, Solidarity* (Cambridge, England: Cambridge University Press, 1989) 7.

Rorty is often attacked as a relativist, as one who has jettisoned access to the basic truths that must inform ethical decisions. He might answer that in one sense an awareness of contingency in fact enables ethics, delivering us from the dominating, dehumanizing insistence on exclusive views of absolute truth. The history of such dominations is sobering. Historical claims of access to the fixed points of truth have themselves produced conflicting, unsettling, and sometimes destructive sets of ethical standards.

Theologian John Dillenberger addressed this problem of truth and violence, of paradoxically attempting good but achieving a greater evil:

> How to believe in a single eschatological coherence without acting as if it existed is humanity's lot and task.... The translation of vision into particular actualities demands the recognition that such achievement is beyond reach and that the direct effort to do so frustrates and distorts what might be achievable. That Pascal knew so well when he said, "Man is neither brute nor angel; and he who would act the angel will end by acting the brute." The direct translation of vision into action is exactly the boundary that cannot be crossed, the essence of the rent in creation which we cannot attempt to expunge, except at greater peril.[5]

Although contingency seems to fly in the face of the truth claims of religion, Paul Ricoeur suggests that religions owe a debt to Nietzsche and Freud and others who have cleared the ground for a new faith:

> We must acknowledge that the critique of ethics and religion by the "school of suspicion" has been an asset. From it we have learned to question the authority of a weak superego too easily identified with the will of God and to recognize that the commandment which

---

5. "The Diversity of Disciplines as a Theological Question: The Visual Arts as Paradigm," *Journal of the American Academy of Religion*, 48:2, 235.

gives death but not life is merely a projection of our own weakness.[6]

Ricoeur and Dillenberger investigate the interface between religion and postmetaphysical thought extensively and insightfully, but I would like to move on to ask their basic question once again, this time in a specifically LDS context: What can our revealed religion gain from a philosophy that denies every sort of transcendence?

First, I should mention some obvious and powerful differences between LDS theology and postmodern thought. Our scriptures, we believe, are divinely inspired. We speak of an Adamic language and the gift of tongues. And we call our beginning "the Word" (John 1:1). Doesn't this negate a supposed contingency of language?

We believe we are coeternal with God: intelligences, spirits, corporeal human beings, and finally gods. How could we then speak of a contingency of self?

Central to our thought is the concept of Zion, of a people consecrated and led by prophetic political/religious leaders. It is a community in which there are no poor, a community in which each receives according to needs, in which individual growth and community growth are mutually advantageous. Doesn't Zion repudiate a contingency of community?

Further, our scriptures are replete with assertions concerning truth:

> And truth is knowledge of things as they are, and as they were, and as they are to come; And whatsoever is more or less than this is the spirit of that wicked one who was a liar from the beginning. The Spirit of truth is of God. I am the Spirit of truth, and John bore record of me, saying: He received a fulness of truth, yea, even of all truth; And no man receiveth a fulness unless he keepeth his commandments. He that keepeth his commandments receiveth truth and light, until

---

6. Paul Ricoeur and Alsadair MacIntyre, *The Religious Significance of Atheism* (New York: Columbia University Press, 1969) 68.

>he is glorified in truth and knoweth all things. (D&C
>93:24–28)

I could go on and on with examples from our theology that demonstrate that truth is indeed out there in the presence and person of our creator. So why bother with the concept that truth is made by humans, not found?

My point will be that even if truth is "out there," it is largely inaccessible in our present condition. That is an advantage to us, as is our mortality.

A few quick examples:

There is a veil between us and the pre-mortal life, between us and God's presence. Is it perhaps the purpose of that veil to let us experience the exigencies of contingency? Are our attempts at masking that contingency through various methods of reduction, possession, mastery, or totalization attempts to bypass that important experience? (*Reduction* of the majesty and mystery of God to something we can fit our minds around. *Possession* of a dogmatic God for the purpose of dominating others. *Mastery* instead of humility. The pretense of *totalization* to gain control and power.)

Don't we believe in a creative God who makes truths? And don't we believe, Christian heretics that we are, that at some time God had to learn to be a maker of truths? As we learn to be like our Heavenly Parents, we learn to make truth as they do. Would that be possible without a veil? Would we not otherwise simply mirror the existence we saw clearly in God's presence? Isn't it possible that we live this life not to discover transcendent truths through revelation, but rather to learn by creating contingent truths, having to live with them, exploring what serves us well and what doesn't, developing ideas and customs and languages that make us interesting human beings—in fact, working out what it is to be human? Why would God leave us so alone if we were best served by divine presence, by truth, by totality?

There is, of course, a second side to this story. We may sense, in blessed moments, that we are not left entirely alone. While

God created the veil, God may also part it to offer us a divine hand of fellowship. The Spirit speaks heat and light to our souls. Still, we are left to respond contingently to even the most glorious revelations of a transcendent deity. Our understanding of such experiences is obviously both facilitated and limited by our languages, our traditions, our prejudices. In the very short history of the latter-day Church, we have hundreds of examples of change, of progress and regress as we describe and re-describe our visions of God and ourselves by means of language reeking of history and culture.

Take, for example, our most sacred latter-day story—Joseph Smith's First Vision, that marvelous, direct encounter with God. Joseph recounted this event in at least four different ways, obviously struggling to translate his encounter into language. It is inspiring to observe just how assiduously Joseph worked to understand the nature of God in the years after his vision, how the traditional Trinitarian God that had dominated his mind at the time of the vision gradually gave way to a sense of Father and Son as distinct beings. One version of the First Vision was eventually canonized. Still, Joseph Smith's search itself is instructive, as is our wonderfully open canon.

But don't we already know who God is? Roger Keller, whom I first met in Nashville where he was an administrator of Scarritt College, a Methodist graduate school, and who is now a professor of Religion at BYU, has as good an answer as I have heard anywhere. He suggests that he converted to Mormonism because here, in contrast to the perhaps 5 percent of truth taught by other great religions, he found 6 percent of the truth. A sense for what we don't know, like the knowledge of ignorance Plato's Socrates must inculcate in his interlocutors before he can teach them, is indispensable if we are to continue to learn about our Lord.

The Jewish tradition is replete with examples of how new metaphors aid in approaching God. Consider, for instance, Arthur A. Cohen's description of a rather startling metaphor:

> I prefer the gentle and exceedingly simple formulation of Saint Silvester: "God is like an onion. He is very simple and he makes one cry."
>
> The onion is all of a piece, it is generally recognized. There is nothing different at its core than what appears at its surface. Nothing new is revealed if we begin to remove its layers. Nothing at all. We weep, however, as we pare away each layer.[7]

Another metaphor, this time a burning bush, reminds us of God's wish for us to approach and simultaneously to keep our distance: "Moses . . . do not come near; put off your shoes from your feet, for the place on which you are standing is holy ground . . . and Moses hid his face, for he was afraid to look at God" (Ex. 3:5–6).

Two examples show Joseph Smith's own humility before the face of God:

> 28 April 1842 (Thursday Afternoon).
> Upper Room, Red Brick Store.
> Nauvoo Relief Society Minutes
>
> [Joseph] said the reason of these remarks being made was, that some little things was circulating in the Society, that some persons were not going right in laying hands on the sick, &C. . . . these signs such as healing the sick, casting out devils &C. should follow all that believe whether male or female. . . . if the sisters should have faith to heal the sick, let all hold their tongues, and let every thing roll on. . . . Who knows the mind of God? Does he not reveal things differently from what we expect?
>
> Respecting the females laying on hands, he further remark'd, there could be no devil in it if God gave his sanction by healing—that there could be no more sin in any female laying hands on the sick than in wetting the face with water[.] It is no sin for any body to do it

---

7. Arthur A. Cohen, "Myths and Riddles: Some Observations about Literature and Theology," *Prooftexts* 7 (1987) 107–22.

that has faith, or if the sick has faith to be heal'd by the administration.[8]

This wonderfully pragmatic statement demonstrates Joseph's own desire not to reduce, possess, or master the mind of God: "who knows the mind of God?" He is also perfectly willing to change what others saw as truth in the service of what works. He here creates a new ritual practice—or supports a practice already created by faithful women—of women healing by the laying on of hands. In subsequent history, that practice has been disavowed.

There is also the remarkable passage in Joseph Smith's letter of 27 November 1832 to W. W. Phelps that shows Joseph sharing his intense longing to escape the strictures of language *and* his pragmatic desire to publish the *Star*:

> Oh Lord when will the time come when Brothe[r] William thy Servent and myself behold the day that we may stand together and gase upon Eternal wisdom engraven upon the hevens while the magesty of our god holdeth up the dark curtain we may read the round of Eternity to the fullness and satisfaction of our immortal souls Oh Lord God deliver us in thy due time from the little narrow prison almost as it were totel darkness of paper pen and ink and a crooked broken scattered and imperfect language I would inform you that I have obtained ten subscribers for the Star. . . .[9]

Most, if not all of our revelation, if we investigate it closely, involves very human attempts to work through problems in a condition of contingency. Even if, as we believe, revelation does occur through the intervention of the Holy Ghost, even if the Church is indeed led by Jesus Christ, such revelation and guidance are always in the context Joseph Smith described as studying it out in our minds. Elder Bruce McConkie's description of

---

8. Lyndon Cook and Andrew Ehat, eds., *The Words of Joseph Smith* (Provo, Utah: Religious Studies Center, BYU , 1980) 115–16.

9. Dean C. Jessee, comp. and ed., *The Personal Writings of Joseph Smith* (Salt Lake City: Deseret Book. 1984) 261–262.

the revelation allowing blacks to hold the priesthood is a case in point. He writes that the revelation only came when President Kimball asked the right questions. It was made possible by open debate among the general authorities. And it led to the understanding that earlier revelation—the Book of Mormon scripture proclaiming all alike before God, black and white, male and female (2 Ne. 26:33)—had not been understood.[10] Such studying out has an element of finding truth, but does it not also involve a courageous making of truth?

What are the advantages of emphasizing made truth over found truth? Circumspection, humility, openness, tolerance, and, surprisingly—where many might suspect loss of will or commitment—a new responsibility. We will pay closer attention to the metaphors we have created and by which we live. We will recognize some of them as potentially troublesome. Taking responsibility for those metaphors, we will forge better ones. Elder B. H. Roberts wrote that Mormonism

> calls for thoughtful disciples who will not be content with merely repeating some of the truth, but will develop its truths; and enlarge it by that development. . . . The disciples of 'Mormonism,' growing discontented with the necessarily primitive methods which have hitherto prevailed in sustaining the doctrine, will yet take profounder and broader views of the great doctrines committed to the church; and, departing from mere repetition, will cart them in new formulas; cooperating in the works of the Spirit, until they help to give to the truths received a more forceful expression and carry it beyond the earlier and cruder states of its development.[11]

Consider what we lose, for example, by limiting our understanding of morality to chastity, or by glorifying faith over

---

10. Mark L. McConkie, ed. *Doctrines of the Restoration: Sermons and Writings of Bruce R. McConkie* (Salt Lake City: Bookcraft, 1989) 159–171.
11. B. H. Roberts. "Book of Mormon Translation," *Improvement Era* 9:712–13.

knowledge, or by defining all differences of opinion as contention, or by being satisfied with the negative assurance that "they will never lead us astray," or by propagating military and sexist metaphors. What do we lose or gain by creating metaphors like "iron-rod and liahona Mormons," or like the metaphors that are the titles of *Dialogue* and *Sunstone* and of this symposium: "Plotting Zion"? Haven't we been enriched at this conference by new and renewed visions of Zion: geometrical order, work or labor as opposed to capital, iniquity as inequity, a handful of rice, Jesus among the poor, feet-on-the-ground theology? We have decided that rather than waiting for God to establish Zion, we will own up to our stewardship as creators and not just conservators. We will be active instead of passive. We will have a sense of mission that includes but isn't exhausted by proselytizing. We will experience a renewal of wonder, awe, humility, curiosity, creativity.

In *Ruin the Sacred Truths*, Harold Bloom says that "The sage must rise to the agon, as Abraham and Jacob did, and so behave pragmatically as if he were everything in himself, while knowing always that, in relation to the Lord, he is nothing in himself."[12] Of course we long for absolute truth and divine presence. History shows that that has always been the case; but the same history shows that, with the exception of the city of Enoch, which we know only through the briefest narratives, the moments when perfection is achieved are moments of totalitarianism, and not in fact the utopias we had in mind. We are religious in part because of a longing for oneness with God and for the promises of transcendent unity. The thrill of religious ecstasy, of possession by the Holy Ghost, is one of our most powerful experiences, compared often and with reason to sexual ecstasy; but these moments, however wonderful, are fleeting.

Transcendent experiences give direction but not form to our lives. And even directions from God must be interpreted by

---

12. Harold Bloom, *Ruin the Sacred Truths* (Cambridge: Harvard University Press. 1989) 22.

humans, leaving us, in a sense, awash in contingency. But that state of ambiguity, in my opinion, is better than being awash in dogmatism. In humility we refer to most of our personal revelations as promptings.

Elder Stephen L. Richards, in an essay reprinted in *Line upon Line*, a collection of essays on developments in Mormon theology, expressed strong feelings about supposed knowledge of truth:

> I fear dogmatism. It is a tyrant guilty of more havoc to humankind than the despot ruling over many kingdoms....
>
> In matters of church government and discipline, the judgment of presiding officers is mandatory and controlling. In matters of individual guidance to members, their counsel is directory and persuasive only. In the interpretation of scripture and doctrine, they are dependent on their knowledge and experience and inspiration....
>
> The very elasticity of prayers, ceremonies, and procedure is additional evidence to me of the adaptability of our religion to human needs and therefore of its divinity...
>
> Dogmatism and bigotry have been the deadliest enemies of true religion in the long past.... They have garbed it in black and then in white, when in truth it is neither black nor white any more than life is black or white, for religion is life abundant, glowing life, with all its shades, colors, and hues, as the children of men reflect in the patterns of their lives the radiance of the Holy Spirit in varying degrees.[13]

When I returned from my mission I was sure what truth was. In a fireside talk I gave to adults in my home ward, I used passages from the *Doctrine and Covenants* to argue that truth could and should be found and that the Lord would establish Zion in

---

13. Stephen L. Richards. "Epilogue: Continuing Revelation and Mormon Doctrine," in Gary James Bergera, ed., *Line upon Line* (Salt Lake City: Signature Books, 1989) 183–85.

His own good time. In retrospect, the fervent and committed talk was abstract and bare. I was committed to a concept. Today I find myself skeptical of found truth, committed to making truth in the context provided and limited by my understanding of the scriptures and the rich religious heritage we share.

Zion is an abstraction until someone creates metaphors for it. What are the metaphors we will live by: wide streets with sparkling water running down the gutters, a specifically ordered commonality of property, a community characterized by productive diversity, a homogenous mass of people who have a consolidated meeting schedule and correlated instruction? Zion will not will simply come—it must be created. Zion, at least the only Zion we will know is the Zion we create through the metaphors we use.

I am suggesting finally, that we wed those strangest of bedfellows—postmetaphysical contingency and latter-day revelation—that, like Abraham, "[by] faith [we] sojourn in the land of promise, as in a foreign land" (Heb. 11:9).

Hidden Valley I

Canyons

FOUR

One Lord, One Faith, Two Universities: Tensions between "Religion" and "Thought" at BYU

Sunstone, Issue 89, September 1992

Two weeks after the annual *Sunstone* symposium in the summer of 1991, LDS leaders released a statement warning members of the Church not to participate in symposia "that result in ridiculing sacred things or injuring the Church . . . detracting from its mission, or jeopardizing the well-being of its members." As Bryan Waterman and Brian Kagel point out in *The Lord's University: Freedom and Authority at BYU*, this followed several years of intensified entreaties by Church leaders not to criticize authorities.

About this same time, BYU Religion professor Stephen Robison reviewed a book edited by Dan Vogel: *The Word of God: Essays on Mormon Scripture* (Salt Lake City: Signature Books, 1990). Published in the 1991 *FARMS Review of Books on the*

Book of Mormon 3/1, Robison's review begins with a provocation: "Korihor's back, and this time he's got a printing press." The new book, Robison argued, "proposes the ultimate oxymoron—empirical religion, a faith-less faith. Come all ye who no longer believe, but who still want religion, and enter ye in!" I, of course, was one who no longer believed, at least in God, but who very much wanted religion. Robison's assessment galled me.

In February, 1992, a letter to BYU president Rex Lee signed by members of the sociology faculty was made public. The sociologists argued that restrictions on participation in symposia like *Sunstone*'s would have a chilling effect on the study of Mormonism and that they were a clear abridgement of academic freedom. An editorial in BYU's student newspaper, *The Daily Universe*, argued that the *Sunstone* symposium was not an academic conference and that professors should obey their leaders' prohibition on presenting the results of their research there (26 February 1992).

Provoked by this debate, I decided it was time for me to speak, for the first time, at the annual symposium. I proposed a talk about the idea of Mormon scholarship and its role in a Mormon university. The proposal was accepted. I wrote the paper and delivered it in a session devoted to recent events at BYU. Omar Kader spoke in that session as well, recommending that the Church simply divest itself of the university, given the impossibility of accommodating its current distrust of academics with the work of a real university. I was critical of current practices, but more hopeful than Kader. Surely changes could be made.

At another session of the symposium, Lavina Fielding Anderson delivered a paper titled "A Chronology of the Intellectual Community and Church Leadership," laying out cases of what she called "ecclesiastical abuse." When she was done, Eugene England leapt to the podium and, echoing Zola's letter in defense of Alfred Dreyfus, said "J'accuse!" He had just learned, he said, that there was an official committee of the Church called "The Strengthening Church Members Committee." The Committee was gathering statements by Church members that could conceivably do harm to the Church and passing them on to ecclesiastical leaders for possible discipline. Gene found that outrageous. He later apologized for his "outburst," but I thought his initial impulse was a good one. We began to refer to the committee as "The Lengthening Church Members Committee."

At the age of eighteen I left the oil-boom town of Farmington, New Mexico and headed north for my first year at BYU. The lush campus at the foot of the mountains seemed like paradise and at the center of that paradise was the honors program, its challenges and stimulations assuring that paradise was more than a country club. Informing the entire experience was a complex web of religious theory and practice. A philosophy professor taught my Book of Mormon class and was my ward bishop; a psychology professor was my stake president. The education I got from these and other religiously committed professors, trained in good programs around the country, qualified me for eventual graduate work at Princeton; it also prepared me to teach an LDS institute class for Princeton undergraduates. After graduating from Princeton I taught for seven years at Vanderbilt University in Nashville, Tennessee. Those were good years: I wrote articles and published my first book; I taught good students and associated with good colleagues and again taught an institute class. I was granted tenure in March of 1988; by April I had decided to move to BYU. Answering questions of an incredulous dean and various colleagues, I explained my desires to work at the university that had shaped me and that would shape my fellow Mormons in years to come. Some of them understood. Others did not. To further explain myself in my subsequent correspondence with Vanderbilt friends, I have recounted the following positive experiences at BYU.

At BYU I moved into a warm, supportive, and competent department. My teaching load is the same as it was at Vanderbilt.

I have received generous research grants every summer and have had a semester of paid research leave. I have traveled to numerous conferences at my department's expense. BYU's library is good and, at a time when state universities are cutting library budgets, we have an aggressive acquisitions policy. The academic climate at BYU is even more stimulating than when I was a student. Faculty colleagues across the university are dedicated, morally committed scholars with diverse opinions. I have participated in faculty seminars on feminist thought and on the French philosopher Emmanuel Levinas. Richard Rorty, Terry Eagleton, Alan Bloom, and Martha Nussbaum have led lively seminars. BYU has more women faculty members and more black students than when I was a student. Our Women's Research Institute and an active group of women students have gained national attention with their innovative and forceful work on women's issues. Women students now receive half of the university's most exclusive scholarships—offered, in my day, only to males. Sexist language is officially discouraged at BYU and university policy on hiring women requires affirmative action. This year when my department wanted to hire a bright non-Mormon woman who also had an offer from UCLA, the university administration and the board of trustees decisively waived normal deadlines and hired her. After four years I am grateful to be at BYU and am sure I made a good choice.

Though the university is a better place than the paradise I experienced in my student years, it is not yet what it could be. Let me give a few examples. I bring them up here because I am immensely proud of the university fellow Mormons have built up over the last century and I want to be part of the continuing development.

Ironically the most pressing issue on the BYU campus is Mormon scholarship. With few exceptions, Mormon and non-Mormon faculty are free to pursue their research wherever it takes them. I can write freely about Freemasonry and the German novel, and a friend writes uninhibitedly about Dante and the Latin sexual vocabulary. As long as the work is unrelated to Mormonism, and as long as it is real scholarship, BYU will permit it and it may be well funded. But when professors write about sexuality among Mormon adolescents, or query working Mormon women about their opinion of President Ezra Taft Benson's advice that they stay at home, or speak about Mormon women from a feminist perspective, or ask why Mormon chapels are bombed in South America (these are four recent, actual cases), immediate pressure is applied. The pattern is that a single general authority will contact a university administrator, who then contacts the faculty member's dean and department chair to request action. BYU administrators are forced to defend faculty at meetings with the Board of Trustees, especially after sensationalized reports in the press. More often than we know, university officials shield faculty members from pressure from "above." And there are surely many instances when board members bite their tongues when thoroughly provoked. But when board members don't, and when our administration doesn't act as a buffer, a pattern of arbitrary micromanagement arises that inhibits research on Mormon topics. We scorn efforts at the University of Utah to declare Mormonism an uninteresting and unfruitful research topic, but we produce our own climate in which faculty know they are safer pursuing topics unrelated to what may be most dear to them. And Mormon research at a Mormon university becomes controversial.

Although the new "Statement On Academic Freedom at BYU" argues that academic freedom must include the individual's freedom "to ask hard questions," it also requires that faculty behavior or expression must not "seriously and adversely affect the University mission or the Church." What behavior or expression might "seriously and adversely affect BYU's mission or the Church"? Who knows? We have enough examples of arbitrary judgments during the Wilkinson years to cause unease. Historically, efforts to prevent deviations from supposed political and doctrinal purity have adversely affected BYU and the

Church. Spy scandals and secret committees that keep files on members "contradict fundamental Church doctrines" more radically than does, for example, a private belief that the Book of Mormon is the word of God but perhaps not an archeological record, or than do suggestions that we talk more openly about our Mother in Heaven. Enforced "goodness" is infinitely more destructive than unorthodoxy; it is personally destructive.

Like the problem of doing research on Mormon topics, the gulf opening between teachers of religion and the rest of the faculty is crucial to our idea of a Mormon university. I'll focus on one example. The pattern of hiring in Religious Education indicates an increasing preference for candidates with BYU Ph.D.'s and Ed.D.'s and Church Education System (CES) faculty.[1] In the department of ancient scriptures, only three full professors have their final degree from BYU, while nine have degrees from other universities. Of the associate professors, three are BYU graduates and five are from other programs. Of the most recently hired faculty, the assistant professors, five are from BYU and only two from elsewhere. The percentage of faculty with BYU credentials thus progresses from 25 percent to 37.5 percent to 71 percent in the department of Ancient Scriptures. In the department of Church History and Doctrine the numbers are even more skewed toward BYU and the trend is similar. Of full professors, seven are from BYU and four have degrees from other schools. Among associate professors nine have degrees from BYU and only one from elsewhere. And all six assistant professors have their degrees from BYU. The percentage of home-grown faculty here progresses from 64 percent to 90 percent to 100 percent. Another way to put this is that only six of twenty-three faculty hired from 1984 through 1991 have degrees from schools other than BYU. Faculty hired for 1992 change this picture only slightly.[2]

---

1. Information from the *BYU General Catalogue*, 1992–1993.
2. No other department on campus even approaches these percentages of hiring faculty with BYU degrees.

This kind of analysis doesn't tell you which of the BYU graduates in education or history have been excellent scholars and teachers and which of the graduates of Duke and USC have not been assets to the program. What it does tell you is that Religious Education has experienced the kind of inbreeding that weakens any academic department—they have hired teachers rather than teacher-scholars, and they have chosen, to use their phrase, the "tried and true" former seminary and institute teachers rather than the products of good graduate schools. While other departments attract increasingly good faculty, and while BYU students become increasingly brighter, this kind of religious inbreeding will lead inevitably to second-rate status.

Members of the Religious Education faculty argue that it is nearly impossible to find candidates with degrees from other schools who teach well and who fit their standards of orthodoxy. Perhaps their standards are too timid. I know of one faithful LDS candidate with extraordinary credentials in both teaching and scholarship whom they chose not to hire because he did not fit the unctuous seminary-teacher mold. The normal procedure for any academic department, designed to make creative risk-taking possible, is to bring a young scholar/teacher to campus for two three-year trial periods on tenure track. On the basis of that trial they are then given tenure or asked to leave. Religious Education faculty tell me that they could not bear to let someone with a family go and so they must be absolutely certain when the person is first hired. Those are difficult decisions for any department, of course, and the better the initial hire, the less pain later; but good departments are built only with hard decisions. CES employees are a comfortable fit in one way, for already they have their proven loyalty to the Church. They have not, however, shown that they are scholars or that they are suited to a university academic department.

One solution to the pressure exerted on a relatively small religion faculty by the thousands of students required to take religion classes is to borrow faculty from other departments to teach religion classes. This arrangement has been used fruitfully for as long as I can remember; but it has been recently curtailed somewhat by Religious Education policy. Hal Miller, dean of Honors and General Education, recommends reversal of this policy in a recent memo, reasoning as follows:

> By involving those outside Religious Education, students can be alerted to the fact that the Gospel is what is most important here, that we are (nearly) all about the business of pursuing it, of plumbing its depths, of savoring its inexhaustible richness, of encountering its matchless spirituality. Most important is the message that we are in this together, so we teach and learn the Gospel with one another. There is no corner of purchase on that effort. Moreover, it may alert students to the diversity of methods by which the gospel may be effectually apprehended and the Spirit invited.

For BYU to be a healthy Mormon university, Religious Education faculty and other faculty must be united in hiring and retaining only teachers and scholars of the academic, spiritual, and moral first rank (for those three are intimately related). As a friend of mine is fond of saying: "First-rate faculty hire first-rate faculty. Second-rate faculty hire third-rate faculty."

It has been almost a year since the First Presidency's statement suggesting that Church members not take part in symposia like *Sunstone*'s. Many of us on campus saw this as an order to mind our own academic business in chemistry and law and humanities and to quit thinking and talking about Mormon topics. Faculty in the sociology department drafted a letter to Rex Lee protesting the statement and asking for clarification.[3] At about the same time an assistant professor who had read a paper at the last symposium was called in by his ecclesiastic leaders in what seemed an attempt to intimidate him. Several departments

---

3. "Church Issues Statement on 'Symposia,'" SUNSTONE 15 (September 1991): 58–5; BYU Memo Highlights Academic Freedom Issue," SUNSTONE 16 (February 1992) 62–66.

sent letters or delegations to Rex Lee in support of the sociology department's positions and argued against arbitrary limitations of academic freedom. A persistent rumor was heard and often denied that the administration had been given a hit list of six faculty members whose employment was to be terminated. A faculty member named as co-editor of *Dialogue: A Journal of Mormon Thought* received abusive anonymous phone calls and was attacked in the press. When BYU's academic vice president resigned rumors flew. Members of the Board of Trustees told faculty members privately that tension between the board and BYU faculty had never been as high.

In its absurdity, one specific example shows just how bad things are. Recently, a member of the Board of Trustees mistakenly and in private expressed contempt for a faculty whose elected advisory committee had recommended that we no longer call one another brother and sister at BYU. There was no such recommendation; the faculty committee wrote a draft, subsequently tabled, that recommended that we should not refer to male faculty as professor and women faculty as sister, that we should instead refer to them as brother and sister or professor and professor, and that we be careful with distinctions between LDS and non-LDS faculty. But some excitable faculty member with access to this general authority board member reported that we were all going to hell in a handbasket and the board member, already disposed to believe the worst, all-too-easily fit this into his picture of a university spinning out of control.

BYU administrators' biggest headache, one administrator says, are ill-informed, biased end runs to members of the Board of Trustees. I suspect that the Board of Trustees sees itself as enormously patient. But when complaints by members of the John Birch Society to a trustee about botanist Sam Rushforth's lecture on the need for a new ecological world order can produce a request by a board member for a faculty member to be reprimanded, as recently happened, something is amiss.

Apparent distrust among some trustees has led to attempts to further control Church employees. The statement on symposia is one such action. And this spring, when BYU faculty received their 1992–93 contracts, they contained a new paragraph:

> Brigham Young University is a private university. It has unique goals and aspirations that arise from the mission of its sponsoring institution, The Church of Jesus Christ of Latter-day Saints. By accepting a contract of employment here, faculty members choose to accept, support and participate in the University's religiously oriented educational mission, to observe and support the behavior standards of the University, including the Honor Code and Dress and Grooming Standards, and to further the University's objectives by being role models for a life that combines the quest for intellectual rigor with the quest for spiritual values and personal character. Faculty who are members of BYU's sponsoring Church also accept the spiritual and temporal expectations of wholehearted Church membership.

There is nothing particularly obnoxious in the paragraph (except, perhaps, for the morally misleading dress and grooming standards), for most of us came to BYU precisely to "further the University's objectives." But the sudden, unannounced, and unexplained change in our contracts indicates that someone doesn't trust us and finds it necessary to remind us of the letter of the law. In the context of such newly exerted control, the new document on academic freedom and competency reads like a legal document making it easier to fire unruly faculty. In all fairness, it may simply be that the current tensions and paranoia on campus cause it to be read this way, for there is much language in the document defending faculty rights to free expression.

So much for my litany of complaint. Every university has its problems. I'm grateful ours don't include racially segregated and alcoholic fraternities or a provost whose vision of a university doesn't include a library—two of Vanderbilt's most pressing problems when I left there. But BYU's problems concern me deeply. I am also aware that I can't see all sides of any of these issues. *Caveat lector.*

Many unsavory things at BYU (sexist hiring practices, attempts to disallow certain non-traditional viewpoints, harassment and backstabbing in the name of orthodoxy) involve individuals and departments within the university who inflict wounds on themselves and others despite concerted actions and policies of the administration and Board of Trustees. I say despite, and I have mentioned just how good Church support of BYU is, but I also want to say because of. Our collective stupidities aren't happening in a vacuum. While supporting education with economic gusto, some of our leaders say and do things that make education difficult. There is a virulent strain of anti-intellectualism in the Church. This is nothing new. Joseph Fielding Smith, for example, wrote in his journal in late December 1938: "The more I see of educated men, I mean those who are trained in the doctrines and philosophies of men now taught in the world, the less regard I have for them. Modern theories which are so popular today just do not harmonize with the gospel as revealed to the prophets."[4]

In my view, the basic and most destructive mode of this anti-intellectualism is to distinguish between faith and reason, setting one against the other and one above the other. And its purveyors are, among others, members of BYU's Board of Trustees. I don't think they mean to be anti-intellectual. In their writings and talks they indicate they not only support thought and education, but they link them integrally to faith. These are, in fact, our spiritual leaders; and as an academic vulnerable to the pride they warn against I am thankful for their reminders that, in the end, I am not as smart as I think I am. The anti-intellectualism I am talking about, however, is the message heard and used by people

---

4. Joseph Fielding Smith, quoted in Gary James Bergera and Ronald Priddis, *Brigham Young University* (Salt Lake City: Signature Books, 1985) 62.

at BYU and elsewhere who disdain the intellect and suppose they can live by what they think is faith.

I will give examples of this anti-intellectualism from several recent statements by current members of our Board of Trustees. These are men I admire immensely, each of whom has moved me spiritually sometime in my life; I would not now be at BYU or in the Church if I had not felt the spirit of their words. What follows will be seen by some as "contradicting or opposing, rather than analyzing or discussing, fundamental Church doctrine or policy" or "deliberately attacking or deriding the Church or its general leaders"—to quote the document on academic freedom. I wish that the readers who see it that way would recognize the damage to our leaders, damage to the Church, and damage to our own souls caused by assumptions of infallibility and by quashing attempts at discussion.

Elder Dallin Oaks quotes President Harold B. Lee at the beginning of his discussion of religion and academia in his book *The Lord's Way*: "The educational system of the Church has been established to the end that all pure knowledge must be gained by our people, handed down to our posterity, and given to all men. We charge our teachers to give constant stimulation to budding young scientists and scholars in all fields and to urge them to push further and further into the realms of the unknown."[5]

This was the experience I had as a student at BYU. I felt I was "urged to push further and further" into science and philosophy of every kind, fearlessly, certain that I would never face an unbridgeable dilemma. That happened because my mentors were simultaneously scholars and faithful Mormons. Today's students have similar experiences, I think, with a new generation of faithful scholars.

But after quoting Harold B. Lee, Elder Oaks continues: "Unfortunately, some of the practitioners of study and reason

---

5. Dallin Oaks, *The Lord's Way* (Salt Lake City: Deseret Book, 1991) 45–46.

are contemptuous of or hostile toward religion and revelation."[6] Although the chapter returns several times to the argument that "the view of religion . . . includes the methods of reason and the truths determined by them"[7] and although there is a section on how revelation needs reason, the chapter emphasizes the negative. It warns that while there may be "nothing wrong" with reasoning about the principles of the gospel in journals and symposia, there is nothing especially right about that either. It argues that while religion does not reject reason, "spiritual verities can be proven only by spiritual means . . . we comprehend secular truths predominantly by study and reason and spiritual truths finally only by revelation."[8] Elder Oaks' text is an attempt to produce a balanced discussion of reason and revelation; but splitting the two so drastically, and asserting the primacy of one over the other while spending almost half the chapter warning against reason and professors and universities, his net effect is to foster anti-intellectualism.

Along with the people in my ward who pick up on this kind of negative portrayal and justify their own lack of intellectual curiosity, some professors at BYU find it comforting to assert "us (spiritual giants) vs. them (academic pygmies)." Neil Flinders, for example, uses Elder Neal Maxwell's division between the "tongue" of secular language and the "mother tongue of faith" to lament that "academic practice at BYU is clearly dominated by contemporary academic norms"[9] and to ask why we don't "see the secular domain as foreign to the spiritual domain."[10] BYU Provost Bruce Hafen's distinction between the passports Mormon academics have earned to Athens and their citizenship

---

6. Oaks, 46.
7. Oaks, 49.
8. Oaks, 64.
9. Neil Flinders, "Our Celestial Agenda," in *Laying the Foundations: A Symposium Initiated by the Moral Character and Agency Education Research Group and Sponsored by the College of Education* (Provo, UT: Brigham Young University) 5.
10. Flinders, 8.

that must remain in Jerusalem[11] unwittingly feeds the same unproductive fires.[12] And when Elder Maxwell asserted at the 1992 BYU Education Week that a few modern individuals seem to favor a life of the mind over a life of devotion, that "exciting exploration is preferred by them to plodding implementation," anti-intellectual dogmatists nodded knowingly.[13]

Two influential talks in the last decade by Elder Boyd Packer, another board member, have likewise served to divide the spirit and the mind and to denigrate reason while praising it. One talk mentions blending, wedding, and mixing the spirit and mind: "The fusion of reason and revelation will produce men and woman of imperishable worth. . . . The combining of reason and revelation is the test of mortal life."[14] Elder Packer describes here some of my most meaningful experiences. But the speech leaves these thoughts behind and identifies the following as its crux: "Now listen carefully! It is crucial that you understand what I tell you now. There is danger! Church-sponsored universities are an endangered species—nearly extinct now." The talk quotes a passage from the recent debate on the secularization of church-sponsored colleges that asserts that "the schools that lost, or are losing, their sense of religious purpose, sincerely sought nothing more than a greater measure of 'excellence.' . . . The language of academic excellence is powerfully seductive."[15] The talk further asserts that BYU can only be kept "in faith with the founders" if the prerogatives of this unique board of trustees are neither diluted nor ignored. . . . Theirs, and theirs alone, is the right to establish

---

11. Bruce Hafen, talk given at BYU, reported in *Y News*, 13 September 1991.
12. Bruce Hafen, "The Dream is Ours to Fulfill" (Provo, UT: Brigham Young University, 1992) 15–22. Hafen's talk to faculty at the beginning of the 1992 school year deftly and meaningfully wed reason and faith, and yet still insisted on a hierarchy.
13. Neal A. Maxwell. (Not in print that I know of.) This statement was repeated in Elder Maxwell's 1992 October general conference talk.
14. Boyd K. Packer, "I Say Unto You, Be One," 1990–1991 Devotional and Fireside Speeches (Provo, UT: Brigham Young University, 1992) 90.
15. Packer, "Be One," 88.

policies and set standards under which administrators, faculties, and students are to function—standards of both conduct and of excellence.... History confirms that the university environment always favors reason, and the workings of the spirit are made to feel uncomfortable. I know of no examples to the contrary."[16]

Why the defensiveness? Why the distrust? Why the need to assert exclusive control? Why the absolute division between the faithful Board of Trustees and the unfaithful university—the very university that is and can be an "example to the contrary"?

I find a clue in attitudes expressed in an earlier talk by Elder Packer. "It is an easy thing," he states, "for a man with extensive academic training to measure the Church using the principles he has been taught in his professional training as his standard. In my mind it ought to be the other way around. A member of the Church ought always, particularly if he is pursuing extensive academic studies, to judge the professions of man against the revealed word of the Lord."[17] And why shouldn't academics "measure the Church using academic principles"? Because, the talk asserts, academics will vitiate religion and true religious scholarship whenever possible. Elder Packer gives as an example a friend, a CES employee who went East to do a doctorate in counseling and guidance. He chose as his dissertation topic, "The Ward Bishop as Counselor." He was forced by his professors to delete references to power of discernment and revelation. If he would do so, he was promised, he would become "an authority in the field, his dissertation would be published and his reputation established." In the end he both compromised and didn't compromise, and the dissertation became neither the inspired document it might have nor the academic success promised by his professors. The writer, the talk reports, returned to the modest income and to the relative obscurity of the CE System. Elder

---

16. Packer, "Be One," 88–89.
17. Boyd K. Packer, "The Mantle is Far, Far Greater Than the Intellect," Address to the Fifth Annual CES Religious Educators' Symposium, 1981, also in *Let Not Your Heart Be Troubled* (Salt Lake City: Bookcraft, 1991) 101–22.

Packer reports that "He summed up his experience this way: 'The mantle is far, far greater than the intellect.'"

The audience was to conclude from this that professors don't understand things of the spirit, that academics are forced to produce spiritually sterile work, and that truly wise men and women will retreat from academia. The example was so foreign to my experience that I went looking for the dissertation mentioned in the talk. It turned out to be typical of so many dissertations written for weak departments. "The purpose of this study," the author wrote, "is to measure the counseling attitudes of bishops and seminary instructors of The Church of Jesus Christ of Latter-day Saints, and to compare their counseling attitudes with various measures of activity in their wards and class rooms." The startling conclusions were that "There is a relationship between counseling attitudes of bishops and their effectiveness as bishops. . . . Also the amount of training received in counseling is positively related to counseling attitudes."[18]

This example is bogus. The dissertation is clearly a weak piece of work. To use it as the key example in a talk pitting academia against spirituality is unfair. Contrast the anti-intellectual spirit of that example with this passage from Joseph Smith's letter to Isaac Galland, 22 March 1839: "the first and fundamental principle of our holy religion is, that we believe that we have a right to embrace all, and every item of truth, without limitation or without being circumscribed or prohibited by the creeds or superstitious notions of men, or by the dominations of one another, when that truth is clearly demonstrated to our minds, and we have the highest degree of evidence of the same."[19]

Academia, at its worst, is indeed sterile, mind-numbing, and spiritually destructive. So is religion at its worst. We don't

---

18. "Counseling Attitudes of Bishops and Seminary Instructors of the Church of Jesus Christ of Latter-day Saints," (Boston: Boston University School of Education, 1961).
19. Joseph Smith. *The Personal Writings of Joseph Smith*, ed. Dean C Jessee (Salt Lake City: Deseret Book, 1984) 415.

choose to be academics or practitioners of a faith because of how bad they can be, but rather because of the power they give us to live good and productive lives.

My recurring question is why, with our extraordinary theological background in which all truth is meant to be circumscribed into one great whole, we insist on fearfully dividing instead of fearlessly circumscribing? Why the weak anecdotes about academic misfits instead of the academic and spiritual triumphs like Steven Epperson's Mormon History Association prize-winning book on Mormons and Jews in the nineteenth century?[20] Epperson wrote his dissertation at Temple University in Philadelphia. His non-Mormon dissertation committee was thrilled by the project and supported him while learning from his religious commitment. Or why not the example of Susan Taber's oral history of her Delaware ward, a study academic readers of the University of Illinois Press found stimulating and academically challenging?[21] Why not choose, as an example of scholarship growing out of faith, Richard Bushman's fine history of Joseph Smith's early years that helped him move into a distinguished chair at Columbia University?[22] Or Hugh Nibley's massive set of writings on Church-related subjects?[23] Or Paul Cox's brilliant work in Pacific rain forests?[24] Or Lamond Tullis's Latin-America studies?[25] Or Royal Skousen's work on Book of Mormon

---

20. Steven C. Epperson, *Mormons and Jews* (Salt Lake City: Signature Books, 1993).
21. Susan Taber, *Mormon Lives: A Year in the Elkton Ward* (Urbana: University of Illinois Press, 1993).
22. Richard L. Bushman, *Joseph Smith and the Beginnings of Mormonism* (Urbana and Chicago, IL: University Press, 1984).
23. Hugh Nibley, *The Collected Works of Hugh Nibley* (Salt Lake City: Deseret Book, 1986).
24. Paul Cox, *Islands, Plants, and Polynesians: An Introduction to Polynesian Ethnobotany* (Portland, OR: Dioscorides Press, 1991).
25. Lamond Tullis, *Handbook of Research on the Illicit Drug Traffic: Socioeconomic and Political Consequences* (New York: Greenwood, 1991).

manuscripts?[26] Or Fred Gedicks's book on religion and law?[27] Or Alan Bergin's psychology?[28] Or Wilford Griggs's Egyptian archeology?[29] Or Laurel Thatcher Ulrich's Pulitzer Prize work in women's history?[30] In these "Mormon scholars" work and lives there is no whining supposition that it's us vs. them, that if the so-called secular academic world were just spiritually minded they would award us all Guggenheim fellowships and Nobel prizes. (Note that although Ulrich's women, Cox's rain forests, and some of the other subjects are not Mormon, the work and conclusions fit squarely into Joseph Smith's anti-sectarian vision of the truths we seek.)

But the trustees whose texts I have described give primarily negative examples and warn mainly of the seductive power of reason over faith. Again I ask, why do they and so many others defend faith over reason in what our theology teaches is a false dichotomy? Let me give several examples to argue that there should be no split between the two.

Hugh Nibley, in his now classic "Zeal Without Knowledge," quotes Joseph Smith: "'The things of God are of deep import and time and experience, and careful and ponderous and solemn thoughts can only find them out. Thy mind, O man! if thou wilt lead a soul unto salvation, must stretch as high as the utmost heavens.'" Nibley's interpretation: "No shortcuts or easy lessons here! Note well that the Prophet makes no distinction between things of the spirit and things of the intellect."[31]

---

26. Royal Skousen, a professor of English at BYU is working on a critical edition of the *Book of Mormon*.
27. Frederick Mark Gedicks and Roger Hendrix, *Choosing the Dream: The Future of Religion in American Public Life* (New York: Greenwood Press, 1991).
28. Alan Bergin, *Handbook of Psychotherapy and Behavior Change* (New York: Wiley, 1986).
29. Wilford C. Griggs, *Early Egyptian Christianity* (Leiden: New York: E. J. Brill. 1990).
30. Laurel Thatcher Ulrich, *A Midwife's Tale: The Life of Martha Ballard, Based on Her Diary, 1785–1812* (New York Vintage Books, 1990).
31. Hugh Nibley, "Zeal Without Knowledge," *Nibley on the Timely and the Timeless* (Provo, UT: Religious Studies Center, Brigham Young University, 1978) 261–78.

Many "Mormon scholars" will tell you that the process of study and inspiration is the same whether the subject is physics, art history, a talk for ward conference, psychology, or choosing counselors for a Relief Society presidency. A. LeGrand Richards, for instance, writes that "In my own life, I can't draw a specific line between those experiences which have been 'religious' and those which have been 'secular.'"[32]

When we distinguish between religious experience and intellectual experience (or religious experience and secular experience, for that matter), we disregard the verses in the Doctrine and Covenants that describe the light of Christ:

> And the light which shineth, which giveth you light, is through him who enlighteneth your eyes, which is the same light that quickeneth your understandings; Which light proceedeth forth from the presence of God to fill the immensity of space. The light which is in all things, which giveth life to all things, which is the law by which all things are governed, even the power of God who sitteth upon his throne, who is in the bosom of eternity, who is in the midst of all things. (D&C 88:11–13)

All experience of life and light, as I interpret this, is experience of God.

The following episodes from *The Personal Writings of Joseph Smith*, made accessible by Dean Jessee's meticulous scholarly work, have had a profound effect on how I view faith and reason. Just one month before receiving the revelation about light, Joseph bought a book in which to record his thoughts. On the flyleaf he wrote his name and then the phrase: "Record Book Baught for to note all the minute circumstances that comes under my observation."[33] These are the misspelled and intensely meant words of a man of great capacity hungry for knowledge. The

---

32. A. LeGrand Richards," God or Mammon: Not Both/And, But Either/Or" in *Laying the Foundations*, 95.
33. *The Personal Writings of Joseph Smith*, ed. Dean Jesse (Deseret Book, 1984) 15.

following years, between 1832 and 1836, were a time of intense "getting wisdom" of the broadest kind. Attending class daily in the "Elders School" with its lectures on medicine, grammar, Egyptian artifacts, and finally Hebrew, Joseph filled his diary with entries like the one on 3 November 1835 in which he links study and the temple endowment: "I then went to assist in organizing the Elders School called to order and I made some remarks upon the object of this School, and the great necessity there is of our rightly improving our time and reigning up our minds to a sense of the great object that lies before us, viz, that glorious endowment that God has in store for the faithful."[34] A few months later Joseph made the following entry:

> Wednesday the 17th [February 1836] attend[ed] the school and read and translated with my class as usual, and my soul delights in reading the word of the Lord in the original, and I am determined to pursue the study of languages until I shall become master of them, if I am permitted to live long enough, at any rate so long as I do live I am determined to make this my object, and with the blessing of God I shall succeed to my satisfaction,—this evening Elder Coe called to make some arrangements about the Egyptian records and the mummies.[35]

One month later (27 March) Joseph dedicated the Kirtland Temple. His dedicatory prayer is full of his enthusiasm for learning, and he quotes from the aforementioned revelation that will become section 88 of *The Doctrine & Covenants*. The temple will be a place where "the Son of Man might have a place to manifest himself to his people." And what will allow that to happen?—"Seek learning; even by study, and also by faith. Organize yourselves; prepare every needful thing, and establish a house, even a house of prayer, a house [of] fasting, a house of faith, a house of learning, a house of glory, a house of order, a house of

---

34. Smith, *Personal Writings*, 72.
35. Smith, *Personal Writings*, 161.

God."[36] The extraordinary outpourings of knowledge through the endowment are only possible in minds prepared through intense study and prayer.

The temple, as we use it today, is no longer a place where we can receive instruction in Hebrew grammar or the latest medical discoveries—although it has often been the locus where a scholar's mind is set free to make discoveries, like John Widtsoe's in organic chemistry or my bishop's in civil engineering. But the temple's shift in function need not lessen the marriage of religion and thought. Church universities are, in the best and broadest sense, houses of learning. The fact that meetings of student wards are held in science lecture halls and English classrooms connects religion and thought physically and symbolically in ways our students cannot misunderstand.

Finally, President Joseph F. Smith says it as well as anyone has: "With God all things are spiritual. There is nothing temporal with him at all, and there ought to be no distinction with us in regard to these matters. Our earthly or temporal existence is merely a continuance of that which is spiritual."[37]

My reuniting of reason and faith in this essay is not simply a theological game. Separating the two has grave consequences. In the pages of the journal *First Things* there has been a recent flurry of articles about the secularization of American universities. Our university administration, the authors of the new document on academic freedom, and members of our Board of Trustees have quoted from these at some length. One supposition of several of the articles is that "the real danger comes from a much larger group of persons who believe that [church universities] can strive for ever-higher standards of academic excellence—and use the same criteria of excellence by which the best secular universities in the land are judged to be excellent."[38] This makes no sense to me. What is wrong with secular standards of academic

---

36. Smith, *Personal Writings*, 176.
37. Joseph F. Smith, *Gospel Doctrine* (Salt Lake City, Utah: Deseret Book, 1966) 70.
38. David W. Lutz, "Can Notre Dame Be Saved?" *First Things* (January 1992) 35.

excellence? Where are the conflicts between academic excellence and the Mormon theology I have just outlined? The author of the article supposes that there is a fundamental difference. Imagine Joseph Smith saying that "If there is anything virtuous, lovely, or of good report or praiseworthy (as long as academics don't think it is excellent) we seek after these things."

Many American colleges founded by religious groups have become secular, and our board and administration are worried that we might follow a similar path. Alan Keele, former associate dean of General Education and Honors, argues that the analogy is wrong-headed:

> Joseph Smith and Brigham Young would, I fear, roll over in their respective graves at the very suggestion that the founding of a school in Zion might be comparable in any way to the founding of what they would have called 'sectarian' colleges. The LDS theological imperative for learning . . . with its grand vision of the compatibility of all truth, is so unlike the typical 'sectarian' view that it has in fact become a focal point of anti-Mormon rhetoric down to our own time.[39]

Fears that BYU will become secular should be balanced by fears that it will become sectarian after the model of Liberty Baptist or Bob Jones University. The document on academic freedom should include this fear in its language.

One *First Things* article on the subject is especially helpful to us in our situation. In "The Decline and Fall of the Christian College," James Burtchael first reviews the history of Vanderbilt University.[40] Vanderbilt was founded in 1875 by the Methodist church, financed initially by Cornelius Vanderbilt. A Methodist bishop, Holland McTyeire, led the university until 1889. During the next twenty-five years Vanderbilt moved away from the Methodist church, becoming fully independent in 1914. Burtchael

---

39. Alan Keele, personal memo.
40. James Burtchael, "The Decline and Fall of the Christian College," *First Things* (April 1991) 16–38.

identifies several related causes for the break. Here are the ones that strike me as most relevant to our situation:

> There was a period of great intellectual turbulence, when fresh findings and methods and disciplines raised fearful philosophical challenges to theology. Spokesmen for the church's concerns, by a compound of incapacity and animosity, exacerbated the apparent hostility between the church and rigorous scholarship. (I have described moments in our own recent BYU history when these conditions were met precisely.)

> There was a transfer of primary loyalty from the church to the 'academic guild,' especially on the part of the faculty" Why? Burtchael asks. Because the "angry General Conference . . . had narrowed its view of what it meant to be Methodist to things like a religious test for all faculty and disciplinary control over students. Absent any larger vision of Christian education, this program was unrelievedly negative, and assured the educational reformers that the church had no stomach for ambitious scholarship. (I have been trying to show that while not unrelievedly so, much of our current vision of what it means to be Mormon at a Mormon university is negative and that we fear ambitious scholarship.)

> There was a progressive devolution of church-identifiers: first from Methodist to generically Christian, then to generically religious, then to flatly secular. Why? Burtchael's answer is because "an effective bond to the Methodist Church instinctively evoked references to bigotry, exclusion, narrowness, sectarianism, and selfishness." There is no acknowledgment of "any intrinsic benefit for the mind in Methodism . . . and no exploration of the [more general Christian] faith which would suggest that it was illuminative of the mind."

We are similarly at risk here—the word "Mormon" can and does evoke bigotry, exclusion, narrowness, and sectarianism. In John Gardner's 1982 novel *Mickelsson's Ghosts*, for example,

Mormons are described as a "sea of drab faces, dutiful, bent-backed, hurrying obediently, meekly across an endless murky plain ... timidly smiling beasts, imaginationless ... family people, unusually successful in business and agriculture, non-drinkers, non-smokers ... no real fault but dullness."[41] Or in Tony Kushner's 1992 play, *Angels in America*, a Mormon woman describes Salt Lake City as a hard place, "baked dry. Abundant energy; not much intelligence. That's a combination that can wear a body out."[42] Edward Abbey sees us similarly in *Desert Solitaire*,[43] as does John Le Carré in *The Russia House*.[44] Burtchael's point is that when a church begins to harp on the faith/reason distinction, denigrating its supposed academic enemy, those who know the value of reason will abandon ship. Although our theology radically affirms intelligence as the glory of God, our actual practice makes us imaginationless and intellectually dull. Non-Mormon writers see this, and so do increasing numbers of faithful Church members.

Most of Vanderbilt's second-generation faculty were loyal to the church as well as being academics, Burtchael writes, yet this was the group that laid the groundwork for the later, complete secularization of the university. This is, I think, the present situation at BYU. Most of the faculty are loyal to the Church as well as being academics. There are some, of course, who aren't loyal to the Church and there are some who aren't academics. But if we and our Board of Trustees continue to proceed from a foundation of fear, we too will create either a sectarian or a secular university.

If we aggressively asserted the connections between reason and faith on Joseph Smith's (and Brigham Young's and John Taylor's and Joseph F. Smith's) model, both sectarianism and secularization would be rendered impotent. In 1972 as president of BYU, Dallin Oaks argued similarly in a discussion of BYU's

---

41. John Gardner, *Mickelsson's Ghosts* (New York: Knopf, 1982) 225 ff.
42. Tony Kushner, *Angels in America* (New York: Theatre Communication Group, 1993) 82.
43. Edward Abbey, *Desert Solitaire* (New York: Simon & Schuster, 1990) 235 ff.
44. John le Carré, *The Russia House* (New York: Knopf, 1989) 176.

connection with Jim Jensen's work with dinosaurs: "Jensen points out . . . that the bones are there and cannot really be ignored by a major university that is almost literally sitting on top of them." Oaks suggested that the board "give controlled but expanding support to research in Rocky Mountain paleontology and pursue the private funding of a museum to exhibit findings. [In so doing] . . . we demonstrate that the church has nothing to fear from any legitimate research; in fact, the church university fosters it."[45]

What keeps us from fulfilling this vision? Distrust, I think, and fear. Again I quote then President Oaks:

> While church authorities know we have testimonies, they question our judgment and sensitivity. . . . We must not have anything done at BYU or said publicly by BYU teachers and administrators that can be misinterpreted. . . . It doesn't matter that it couldn't reasonably be so used, or that it was distorted. We must not give occasion for retaliation or give ammunition to our enemies.[46]

Bruce Hafen reiterated this advice to walk carefully in his most recent address to BYU faculty and staff: "If a few among us create enough reason for doubt about the rest of us, that can erode our support among Church members and Church leaders enough to mortally wound our ability to pursue freely the dream of a great university in Zion." Both of these university leaders imply that some powerful members of our Board of Trustees do not understand how generally faithful the BYU faculty is, nor do they share our "dream of a great university in Zion."[47]

This is not a climate in which faithful scholarship will flourish. Realistically, pragmatically, President Oaks and Provost Hafen are surely right. But divinely inspired leaders should not let a few differences between them and BYU faculty get in the way

---

45. Gary James Bergera, Ronald Priddis, *Brigham Young University* (Signature Books, 1985) 163.
46. Bergera and Priddis, 223.
47. Hafen, "The Dream Is Ours to Fulfill," *BYU Studies Quarterly* (Vol. 32, 3, 1992) 22.

of a century-long effort to build a Mormon university. We have in our recent history many examples of the kind of vision that will make us whole. Hugh B. Brown's 1969 talk at BYU, for example, featured a kind of aggressive pro-intellectualism:

> Preserve, then, the freedom of your mind in education and in religion, and be unafraid to express your thoughts and to insist upon your right to examine every proposition. We are not so much concerned with whether your thoughts are orthodox or heterodox as we are that you shall have thoughts."[48]

Elder Marlin Jensen has quoted the following inspiring passage from a letter by J. Golden Kimball, a statement that sums up my view of BYU:

> Elder Maeser visited Bear Lake Stake in the interest of the Brigham Young Academy, and filled an appointment at Meadowville, Rich County, Utah, in 1881. The meeting was held in a log school house. Language cannot explain the impression made. The spirit and personality of the man burned into my soul and awakened me to a realizing sense of what life and religion mean—I drank in his words, as I was an hungered. I repented in sack cloth and ashes—no power could prevent me from attending Brigham Young Academy. My brother, Elias, and I together with our mother went to Provo at great cost and sacrifice, and all who know us can look back to 1881 and ascertain just "what Dr. Maeser did for me"[49]

In addition to the testimony of the powerful effects of an educator and an education, two things stand out in this passage: the fact that Karl Maeser is referred to both as Elder and Dr., and Kimball's phrase combining life and religion—"he awakened me to a realizing sense of what life and religion mean." Life and

---

48. Bergera and Priddis, 71.
49. J. Golden Kimball, quoted by Elder Marlin Jensen in an unpublished talk as honored alumnus of the College of Humanities, October 1991.

religion are one and the same. We don't need two universities at BYU.

Addendum

In what may prove to be a landmark BYU devotional address, President Gordon B. Hinckley spoke to faculty and students on 13 October 1992 about his expansive vision of the university. Statements like the following take the edge off some of the tensions described above:

> I am confident that never in the history of this institution has there been a faculty better qualified professionally nor one more loyal and dedicated to the standards of its sponsoring institution.
>
> This institution . . . is a continuing experiment on a great premise, that a large and complex university can be first-class academically while nurturing an environment of faith in God.
>
> "Trust is what makes an army work, and trust comes from the top down." (Gene Smith, published in condensed form by Reader's Digest Condensed Books, Vol. IV, page 299.)
>
> May God bless you my beloved associates, both young and old, in this great undertaking of teaching and learning, of trust and accountability.

I am honored and grateful to be called President Hinckley's associate: he inspires me to help build this university for the greater glory of God.

"One Lord, One Faith, Two Universities" was published in the September issue of *Sunstone*. Discipline followed swiftly. My stake president was a member of the Religion Department I criticized for hiring seminary teachers rather than scholar/teachers. He had famously told the men in a stake priesthood meeting that the problem with women in the stake was that they were not "priesthood broke." For the next couple of years he set out to break me.

His first requirement was that I write an apology to the three apostles (Boyd Packer, Neal Maxwell, and Dalin Oaks) I had quoted in the paper as setting faith against thought. I did so readily. When I sent the three letters I thought the apostles might read my essay, recognize that my purpose was to improve the quality of the university, and understand that my stake president was exerting unrighteous dominion. From the distance time affords, I'm surprised by the naiveté of that assumption. And a little proud of it.

24 May 1993

Dear Elder Packer [Maxwell, Oaks],

Ten days ago, Keith Perkins, a member of the Religious Education faculty here and president of the Orem Stake in which I reside, asked me to talk with him, my bishop, and the rest of the stake presidency about my recent *Sunstone* article, "One Lord, One Faith, Two Universities: Tensions Between 'Religion' and 'Thought' at BYU." President Perkins expressed his belief that I had "spoken evil of the Lord's anointed" and that I had offended you. He asked me for my temple recommend and said there would be further disciplinary action if I did not write to you to apologize and also publish a public statement of retraction.

My immediate response was that I could not, in good conscience, retract what I believed to be true, but if I had offended you I would welcome the chance to apologize and to explain that that was not my intent. I had hoped, as part of my duties as a BYU faculty member, to raise productive questions about the university. As I look over my article I do find several words and sentences whose tone is counter-productive, and for this I am sorry. Perhaps further maturity will polish some of my rough edges.

As I wrote my essay I wanted very much to express my lifelong gratitude and support for you and others who have influence and inspired me. I hoped the result would be a balanced, faithful, truth-seeking document. To the extent that I failed to achieve this, I beg your forgiveness.

Sincerely,

Scott Abbott

The replies arrived in envelopes stamped CONFIDENTIAL.

10 June 1993

Dear Brother Abbott:

You wrote extending something of an apology for statements you made in your recent *Sunstone* article entitled, "One Lord, One Faith, Two Universities: Tensions Between 'Religion' and 'Thought' at BYU."

I readily accept your apology for those things which you have said or published concerning me personally. In your letter you also stated that there were "several words and sentences" in your article which might have been misinterpreted. Any of us may, in our speaking or writing, say things which can be misunderstood or misinterpreted. That, I think, is not a serious matter.

However, it is not individual words or sentences, but rather the entire spirit of your article which causes us very serious concern. You acknowledge that you are familiar with the statement made by the First Presidency and the Quorum of the Twelve Apostles counseling members concerning certain symposiums and organizations. Particular concern is expressed therein for "the participation of our own members, especially those who hold Church or other positions that give them stature among Latter-day Saints and who have allowed their stature to be used to promote such presentations." You then proceed to misinterpret the statement and continue in a tone which projects a spirit of bitterness, even defiance.

For one to do so who has made sacred covenants and, in addition, is under contract represents a fundamental breach of integrity; particularly when one's livelihood is drawn from the tithes and offerings of the Latter-day Saints.

May I suggest that you counsel, very seriously counsel, with your wife as to the direction you intend to pursue in life and thereafter counsel with your stake president, whose responsibility it is to resolve this matter.

May you give prayerful consideration to these serious matters and receive the blessings of the Lord.

Sincerely yours,

Boyd K. Packer

jm
cc: President Keith Perkins

The apostles with less seniority replied more briefly, generally agreeing with Elder Packer's assessment and noting that the tone of my essay troubled them as well. The essay is certainly brash (I do say, for instance, that Elder Packer's example is "bogus). But my account is also hopeful. It is quite possible that there are good counterarguments to my assessment. Rather than make them, however, the responses addressed only the tone.

My essay warns that if we aren't careful, we'll become as Kushner sees us: "Abundant energy; not much intelligence" and as Gardner portrayed us in *Mickelsson's Ghosts*: "a sea of drab faces, dutiful bent-backed Mormons like stalks of wheat, hurrying obediently, meekly across an endless murky plain toward increasingly thick, dark smoke." After publication, *Sunstone* editor Elbert Peck sent me a letter he received from a reader of the piece. "I don't give a rat's ass," the man from Heber, Utah wrote, "what Kushner and the others think about Mormons."

A few weeks after he received copies of the apostles' letters, my stake president sent me a long letter praising me for having done what he, inspired by the Lord, had required. He gave me extensive counsel about humbly submitting to Church authority. And he enclosed the purloined temple recommend with the suggestion that I use it often.

I never used that recommend again.

Soon after the essay was published, the BYU Faculty Center announced a series of discussions on "Revelation and Reason at BYU: Crossing the Cultural Divides":

> Most of us at BYU have strong loyalties both to our spiritual heritage and to academia. We continually mull a number of questions arising from this dual allegiance:
>
> What is the appropriate integration of my belief system into my teaching and my scholarship? Is my freedom to seek and proclaim truth adequate at BYU? How can we cross the cultural divides that seem to separate different disciplines and intellectual/theological persuasions?
>
> As a result of extraordinary faculty interest, the Faculty Center has scheduled four discussions on the above subjects:
>
> Thursdays at 11 a.m., October 15, October 29, November 12, December 3. Varsity Theater
>
> The first session will begin with Scott Abbott (Germanic and Slavic). We hope you will come, share your insights, and learn with us. If you would like to nominate someone to lead one of these discussions or if you have written something yourself on the topic, please share that with us by calling the Faculty Center at 8-7419 or by getting us a paper at 167 HGB. We only have these four sessions scheduled, but we want to have as many good alternatives as possible.

My presentation was taken in large part from the published essay, but there were some new thoughts as well. A few of them here:

> Where there is much desire to learn, there of necessity will be much arguing, much writing, many opinions; for opinion in good men [and women] is but knowledge in the making.
> —John Milton, *Aeropagitica*

(Don Jarvis, Director of the Faculty Center and my colleague in Germanic and Slavic Languages shared this with me)

Riding home on my bike the night before last, I glanced up at the mountain in front of me and was overcome by the beauty of the evening light on its slopes. I stared at what felt like a vision, wanting to draw it out, but the light soon faded. I extrapolated, thinking that all love must be love at first sight and that we need repeated moments of first sight to keep relationships alive. Over the last year there have been several experiences that have clouded relationships we share as members of the BYU faculty and administration. But this Tuesday, as President Hinckley spoke, I and perhaps many of you had caught a new vision....

I, and maybe you as well, have been feeling powerless in regard to directions BYU is taking. Something, whatever it is, is being done to us. The university is being defined out from under us. By whom? By members of our Board of Trustees. Consider Elder Packer's recently assertion that BYU can only be kept "in faith with the founders" if the "prerogatives of this unique board of trustees are neither diluted nor ignored.... Theirs, and theirs alone, is the right to establish policies and set standards under which administrators, faculties, and students are to function -- standards of both conduct and of excellence."

Our university (and it is ours as well as theirs) is an ongoing experiment. Risks are necessary if we hope to be productive. The administration is risking something as they encourage or at least allow this series of discussions. Our religious leaders risk much as they encourage real scholarship here. And yet, if you truly believe, as President Hinckley reminded us, that "the glory of God is intelligence," you are risking nothing. The true risk would be to quit seeking, to close down shop, to fearfully conserve rather than to forge ahead.

Tuesday morning, in a meeting of the subcommittee of the Faculty Advisory Council on Academic Affairs, we were talking about a new policy. I argued against codification of the letter of the law when the law's spirit would be more effective. Duane Jeffrey, also on the committee, argued against me, citing long experience in which the lack of codification worked to his disadvantage and allowed arbitrary decisions by past administrations. In a note to me after the meeting Duane wrote: "Keep up the good work, brother. Your insights are valuable to the well-being of both Church and university." I was thrilled to be called brother.

Update

6 March 2021

This morning Peggy Fletcher Stack published a piece in *The Salt Lake Tribune* titled "BYU shifts its hiring for religious studies, puts faith-building before scholarship." She begins by noting that "through the decades, Brigham Young University's college of religious education has swung back and forth between emphasizing its faculty's academic credentials (think famed ancient scripture scholar Hugh Nibley) and its devotional bona fides (cue apostle Boyd K. Packer)." The latter era, of course, was the context for my *Sunstone* essay. BYU President Kevin Worthen, Stack reports, recently spoke to "the religious education faculty to reiterate that the school would give hiring preference to candidates who had taught in the faith's Church Education System, which includes high school 'seminary' classes and college 'institute' courses."

Responses to the new policy came from Michael Austin, BYU alumnus and executive vice president for academic affairs at the University of Evansville and Samuel Brunson, professor of law at Loyola University. Both men, Stack writes, see the policy in terms related to the ones I outlined in "One Lord, One Faith, Two Universities." Austin emphasizes that a curriculum and faculty with a one-sided devotional approach "create graduates who are very sure of their own perspective and less likely to see the world through anybody else's eyes." Brunson argues that college courses taught by professors without the requisite academic training do "pastoral disservice" to students. "When we tell them that our religion isn't worthy of in-depth study... we tell them that their religious beliefs aren't intellectually defensible."

Besides reminding me that I'm an aging man who took classes from Hugh Nibley, argued with Boyd Packer over the nature of BYU, and now face another swing of the religious studies pendulum, Peggy Stack's piece gives me an odd sense of hope. Fears that drive the devotional retrenchment may well be the result of internal forces demanding more thoughtful and inclusive policies related to racial and gender issues. Last Thursday night, for instance, LGBTQ students and allies lit the "Y" with rainbow colors. BYU responded that "BYU did not authorize the lighting of the Y tonight"; maybe someday they will. And on February 26 of this year, BYU released a faculty-committee report on racism that recommends important changes. Maybe those changes will be made. I hope so.

Update

Tonight, the 29th of January 2022, I'm not so hopeful. Over the past two weeks BYU administrators have announced two new policies. The first governs protests, explicitly forbidding protests on "Y Mountain" like the rainbow one that elicited hope for a better future. The second, announced two days ago, will require all new LDS employees of BYU to be temple recommend holders. My blog post today was titled "Cycles of Coercion at BYU."

North of Goblin

Hidden Valley II

FIVE

The Provo Window

Late Night Thoughts on the Purposes of Art and the Decline of a University

Annual of the Association for Mormon Letters, **1996**

1996 was an especially troubling year at BYU. English professor Gail Houston left BYU after being denied tenure and Brian Evenson left the university when he was told he couldn't continue writing fiction like his previous work. At the Annual Meeting of the Association for Mormon Letters, I spoke about Evenson and what his loss would mean to BYU. The panel was chaired by Marni Asplund-Campbell and contributors included Susan Elizabeth Howe, Bruce Jorgensen, and Brian Evenson.

If Brian Evenson were a painter (and maybe he is, for all I know), and if he were to paint something related to the violent themes of some of his stories, he might depict the following scene, which I imagine, for whatever reasons, in the fleshy forms and colors of the school of Rubens:

> Dominating the front center of the painting, a strong and beautiful woman stands before a long banquet table on which are a loaf of bread and a whole lobster. One guest grips a large glass of red wine. A servant holds aloft a platter with a cooked pheasant. The woman wears a flowing red dress, a dangerously provocative dress, cut impossibly low over taut breasts. Her hair is pulled back and done up in jewels. Her right hand holds a platter whose cover her coy left hand lifts to reveal the soggy head of a bearded, long-haired man. On her face is a smile both mischievous and erotic, and her bright eyes offer a necrophilic challenge to a king who sits convulsed at the head of the table. Although the phallic sword hanging from his belt signifies his power, the king's eyes bug out of his reddened face as he sees what the woman has brought him. Next to the king, wearing a dainty black hat, pearls, and a brown satin dress with décolletage, sits a young woman with a curiously satisfied expression. Her left hand reaches for the plate the woman in red proffers, and her right hand, bent daintily, holds a little three-pronged fork to the head's black lips. A dwarf stares out of the painting at the viewer, confronting us with questions about our own involvement: our complicity, our pity, our deviant desires, our outrage, our religious sensibilities—our reasons, in short, for studying the painting so intently. If we take up his invitation, becoming self-conscious guests at the feast, we put ourselves in positions of risk. We can never be quite the persons we were before the artistic confrontation.

It's an old story, of course: Salome offering the head of John the Baptist to Herod. As you may have already surmised, the painting I have described is not my own invention but is from the school of Rubens and hangs on the fifth floor of the BYU Library across from the humanities reference desk. It is mostly ignored, with the exception of an occasional child who looks at the painting and says "gross."

That, I think, is a fair description of what has happened at BYU with Brian Evenson's book *Altmann's Tongue*. On the basis of passages cited out of context in an anonymous letter, several authorities have said "gross." (In fact, in a statement quoted in the *Daily Universe* [11 July 1995] BYU President Rex Lee used that very word: "If [Evenson's] future work follows the same pattern of extreme sadism, brutality and gross degradation of women characteristic of *Altmann's Tongue*, such a publication would, in our view, not further his cause as a candidate for continuing faculty status.") Possessing power the child does not, members of our administration have forced Brian to leave BYU. I don't use the word "force" loosely.

On January 16 of this year, the chair of the English Department wrote to Academic Vice President Todd Britsch that he "met with Brian just a few days following the meeting with Elder Eyring [Commissioner of Education] Nov. 9. . . . The bottom line is that he knows that this book is unacceptable coming from a BYU faculty member and that further publications like it will bring repercussions." Brian appealed this summary judgment in a meeting with BYU President Rex Lee and Provost Bruce Hafen; he reports that they failed to listen to his arguments.

Subsequently, members of the executive committee of BYU's newly formed chapter of the American Association of University Professors met with President Lee to express concerns about Brian's case and academic freedom in general. We asked what there was about the stories in *Altmann's Tongue* that the administration found objectionable. President Lee referred to the title story and said it was about a man who killed another man after he suggested he cut out the tongue of Altmann, whom he has just killed. I had just published a short piece in the *Student Review* on the story and walked President Lee through my argument.

The narrator states at the beginning that after he killed Altmann someone named Horst told him that if he were to eat Altmann's tongue he would be wise; he would speak the language of the birds. The narrator says that he then knocked Horst down and killed him. He had been right to kill Altmann, he thought, the choice had been a good one. Killing Horst wasn't quite as clearly justified, he says, but still, he feels remarkably calm. All people are either like Horst or Altmann, the narrator thinks, except for himself. He is either the sole exception or the unique exception, he can't quite decide. Then he flew about, a foul bird: "I stuttered, spattered a path through the branches of trees, sprung fluttering into blank sky."

The story comes alive when you recognize that Klaus Barbie, the infamous Nazi "Butcher of Lyon," went by the name Altmann while hiding in South America. That explains, for example, the narrator's justification for killing Altmann: "There are people, Altmann among them, who when you have sent a bullet through their skull, you know you have done the right thing."

And what about Horst's devilish promise of wisdom, of the ability to speak the language of the birds if the narrator would eat Altmann's tongue? It happens: the narrator kills Altmann, kills Horst, and then begins thinking and talking in the language of the mass murderer. He is the "sole exception, so different from the rest of humanity that his violence is justified. And he flies off, in the end, smelling his "foul feathers and flesh." Through his acts of violence and subsequent justifications he becomes what he has killed.

It feels like an important story for students and faculty in my department (Germanic and Slavic Languages), I said. And, in fact, most of the faculty in the department had met the previous Tuesday for a productive discussion of the first three stories of the book. The weight of the Holocaust must be borne. The lessons of history must be recalculated constantly. We must remember where language can take us. Our rhetoric must not justify violence. We must not kill.

Are all the stories about the Holocaust? asked a visibly surprised President Lee. Many are, I answered, including "Killing Cats," "The Munich Window," "The Abbreviated and Tragical History of the Auschwitz Barber," and "A Conversation with

Brenner." What about the story where the serial killer carves stars in the backs of his victims? There's nothing moral in that. Bruce Jorgensen has just read a paper, I said, that interprets that story as a depiction of

> a restless, frustrated, destructive male will. . . . [R]unning on No-Doz, he drives a truck, a tangible, even trite, symbol of male will, through Utah, Wyoming, Colorado, New Mexico, and into Texas, killing as he goes, and loading "her other bodies" into the dark and otherwise empty cargo compartment behind the cab. The truck has to be a U-Haul: you do haul; you haul your murderous will and the debris of its acts, the burden of what you've done. And what you want, finally, is rest.

The male will, patriarchy, the Holocaust, violence against the helpless: surely these are worthy topics for a BYU professor.

President Lee didn't, finally, agree with Bruce's and my readings of these stories, but neither did he disagree. I ended the discussion by pointing out that Brian's stories require an active reader with specialized skill and that there is no reason to expect everyone to understand them. You are a legal scholar, I said, trained to read and understand texts to which I have little access. But why should you expect to be able to understand a complicated, subtle piece of literature? If you have questions about evolution, you consult a professor of biology. And if you want to understand a difficult piece of literature, you consult scholars of literature. What has happened here is that readers in Salt Lake and in your administration have made decisions about Brian Evenson's future at BYU in response to an anonymous letter and without the benefit of expert witnesses. It is, as Bert Wilson has told you, "a tyranny of crackpots." That unsettles everyone at the university who works on sensitive issues.

That's the first part of my talk. In the second I want to turn to my own experience with what is, for me, the most troubling story of the book: "The Munich Window."

Many of you know the story, told from the perspective of a man who, after a suspicious accident in which his wife leapt to her death from the window of their Dresden apartment, "found it expedient to leave Germany for warmer, more hospitable climes." Eighteen years later he is forced to return to Germany after his surviving daughter threatens to take legal action to have him extradited back to Germany to face charges of murder and child sexual abuse. In writing the story he calls "A Persecution," the obsessively clean and self-righteous man ("I had never fallen into the vice of drinking alcoholic beverages") recounts his version of the encounter with his daughter and her therapist, a series of violent incidents during which he ultimately kills the therapist and then psychologically bullies his daughter until she gives up the evidence she has against him and jumps from a Munich window to her death. The narrator tells this self-incriminating story in the firm belief that he is vindicating himself. As he finishes telling the story, immediately after forcing his daughter to decide to jump, he exclaims: "I am blameless. *Alis volabat propriis*. She jumped entirely of her own volition. Just like her mother" (42).

Like many of Brian Evenson's stories, "A Munich Window" can be read on several levels. The story is, for example, an allegory of Germany after the war, of the founders of the new republic. The people who take in the man's daughter when he abandons her to flee Germany are named "Grunders," "founders," and the man is contemptuous of what they have made of her in the intervening eighteen years.

But this story has reached me on a level more profound than historical allegory. I first read "A Munich Window" one night just before falling asleep. Several hours later I woke up from a horrible dream in which I myself was committing the crimes of the story. In the dream, fighting to retain some sense of myself as a decent person, I kept reminding myself that there was a narrator involved, that the events were just "said" to have happened. But every time I succeeded in widening the gap between myself and the vicious actions described by the narrator, some inexorable force pressed me and the story back together, squeezing out the buffering narrator. I woke up in the middle of the struggle and, even awake, found myself trying to figure out how to reinsert the narrator between myself and the story.

Why was I so disturbed? It has to be, I think, because on some level I identified with the narrator. I haven't driven my wife to suicide, nor have I sexually abused my children. But I am a man, I have a wife and daughter, and I do participate in the fatherhood and patriarchy the narrator claims as his own realms of action when he forbids the therapist to tell him how a father should act. She knows nothing about fatherhood and patriarchy, he says. Her response is to show him the pornographic photos he has taken of his daughter and to ask incredulously: "Nothing about? Nothing about?" (33).

When I watch the narrator oppose his powerful linear thinking to what he calls his daughter's instinct, when I see him magnify her faults and ignore his own, when I witness his attempt to force his daughter to see the world as he sees it, and finally, when I observe his use of masculine physical strength against the women in the story, I am left burning with shame. That's me. That's the way I and the other men of our society have been socialized to act. Why should I suppose I am immune to the abuses of authority against which Section 121 of the *Doctrine & Covenants* warns me?

Like the prophets and the feminists who have taught us to see and beware of the debilitating power structures we all are caught up in, the analyst in the story makes explicit the evils of the narrator's patriarchal, pornographic fatherhood. His response is to force her into the train's lavatory and to dispose of her. He gets rid of the incriminating evidence, bullies his daughter into suicide, and disavows any blame. As the shocked, shamed, dismayed reader of his text, however, I am left speaking words diametrically opposed to his protestations of innocence: *Mea culpa*, I gasp, I am guilty. Speaking those words, I can begin to heal. Driven to confess by the narrator's unwillingness to confess, I can make restitution.

Reading the narrator's last words, "I am blameless. . . . She jumped entirely of her own volition. Just like her mother," I am reminded of BYU spokesperson Brent Harker's statement on learning that Brian had accepted a position at Oklahoma State: "He has chosen to take his own destiny in his hands." The university, of course, is blameless. Harker added, "The university's sense of mission and Brian's sense of mission were quite divergent." That feels true to me. Unfortunately, it is Brian's sense of mission I identify with, and it is not the university that is leaving.

To conclude: Brigham Young University is, at the moment, in a schizophrenic position. On the one hand: "The Feast of Herod" hangs in the library; difficult, challenging, disturbing, and challenging literature and art and psychology and law and sociology and genetics are taught daily in every department on campus; the bookstore and library are crammed with challenging and disturbing books; and there are thousands of faculty and students who are anxious to engage in the risky and rewarding business that is university education. Unfortunately, writers of anonymous letters are dictating the university's agenda. Laurel Thatcher Ulrich cannot speak on campus, and for widely varied but related reasons, Hal Miller, Dan Blickman, Tom Delong, Bill Evenson (for a time), Meg Wheatly, Tom Matheson, Bill Davis, Tomi Ann Roberts, Cecilia Konchar Farr, David Knowlton, Martha Bradley, Martha Nibley Beck, Reba Keele, and others have left BYU, seeing it as a university without true academic commitment, anxious to leave an institution that stifles creativity and initiative.

And now Brian Evenson, having written the very story that could heal us, is forced from our community. We are left to write an official text blaming the victims and exonerating ourselves, a text that, against our wishes, will reveal our own insanity and inhumanity.

Sienna Wall

Grey Hill

SIX

Clipped and Controlled: A Contemporary Look at BYU

Originally by "Anonymous"

Sunstone, September 1996

In the spring of 1996, *Sunstone* editor Elbert Peck asked me to write about the current state of affairs at BYU. To broaden the scope of the essay, I drew on the work of several colleagues. The section about women at BYU, for instance, came in part from a report Susan Howe and others had drafted for the accreditation visit that resulted in a March, 1996 report reaccrediting BYU. (The head of the accreditation team, a Jesuit from Gonzaga University, met privately with the protesting faculty group and in the final report largely downplayed the women's concerns.)

Because of the specificity of some of my assertions, Elbert asked a former BYU administrator and faculty member to review the essay. The response began with these thoughts:

> Thank you for letting me review this piece. Like a number of others, I have been pained by what is happening. The article provides what the author clearly recognizes as a "sketchy" chronicle. However, the piece is probably worth doing if only because many friends of the university have puzzled over what has seemed to be a general "silence" in response to the dismantling that is underway. . . .
>
> [I left the university over] what were some clear philosophical differences regarding the direction the university was taking. These differences related most specifically to questions regarding the role of research and graduate education at BYU, and faculty issues that included hiring, evaluation, trust, and the protection of basic tenets of academic freedom. . . .

The reviewer pointed to two sections of the essay that were problematic (". . . the reference is only marginally descriptive of what really happened" and ". . . the paragraph does not provide a very accurate account of the sequence of events that led to that action"). I revised the essay in response and sent a new draft to Elbert, who invited me to the *Sunstone* offices in Salt Lake to talk through final revisions. He had a visitor when I arrived, so I sat in the lobby where various religious-studies journals were displayed. A volume of *First Things* caught my eye. BYU administrators (including Provost Bruce Hafen, who was member of that journal's editorial board) had been citing a series of articles in *First Things* about the secularization of religious universities in support of their continuing focus on the role of faith as opposed to reason at BYU. I was following the debate and had gone to the BYU Law Library several times to read the January issue but had failed to find it with the other issues. A librarian helped me look, to no avail. But here was a copy. Waiting for Elbert, I read Richard John Neuhaus's essay "The Christian University: Eleven Theses" and then Gertrud Himmelfarb's "The Christian University: A Call to Counterrevolution." I hadn't read far in Himmelfarb's work when I began to hear echoes of Merrill Bateman's recent inaugural address in which he attacked moral relativism and vowed not to allow that to infect BYU.

Elbert and I worked through minor changes to the essay. I borrowed the issue of *First Things* and at home found a printed copy of the inaugural speech. When I compared them I found that Bateman had plagiarized Himmelfarb's work. I added evidence of the plagiarism to the end of the essay and told Elbert that although I had always published under my name, this was a game changer. We agreed that the essay would appear anonymously. Unfortunately, the resulting uproar over the plagiarism deflected attention from critical issues documented in the rest of the piece.

Near the end of August, Bateman spoke at his first University Conference as president. He admitted that he had not attributed the sections on moral relativism during the inaugural speech but said the printed version had cited Himmelfarb, if somewhat misleadingly. Then he attacked the messenger:

> Five years ago the First Presidency and the Quorum of the Twelve issued a statement counseling members not to participate in symposia where presentations injure the Church or are not appropriate ("Church Leaders Issue Statement Counseling Members," Public Communications Department, The Church of Jesus Christ of Latter-day Saints, 23 August 1991). I believe the publication of an anonymous article by a symposia [sic] group denigrating members of the Twelve and advocating the transformation of BYU into a secular un versity supports the wisdom of that statement.

During the Church's October conference two months later, Boyd Packer uttered a grave curse on the anonymous author:

> Some few within the church, openly or perhaps far worse, in the darkness of anonymity, reproach their leaders in the wards and stakes and the church, seeking to make them "an offender for a word," as Isaiah said. To them the Lord said, "Cursed are all those that shall lift up the heel against mine anointed."

A critical voice in my *Immortal for Quite Some Time* asks whether the apostle's "curse feels threatening?" No, I answer, "the evil eye works only if the other person is superstitious."

Sunstone introduced the essay with these two paragraphs:

> Over the last few years, BYU has had well-documented conflicts over academic freedom—Evenson's violent fiction, the Knowlton, Farr, and Houston firings. Many less-publicized stories of the policing of a theological correctness circulate around campus—faithful, tenure-track candidates being rejected for a past period of Church inactivity or for using Marxist, feminist, or postmodern methodologies; faculty being "called in" for statements made in public; other respected faculty being encouraged to leave the university because they don't fit in with its direction. So it should come as no surprise that faculty and staff morale is low—even the university's self-study and the Northwest Accreditation Association have recently commented on it.
>
> People unfamiliar with these current conditions often ask if things really are all that different—after all, hasn't BYU always had academic freedom problems? Well, while there have always been incidents of faculty censorship, the systematic nature of the current campaign is different and does seem designed to change the overall direction of the university—to one of super-orthodoxy without any tolerance for discussion of differing religious viewpoints. In the essay that follows, titled after the grounds crew mission statement charge to keep the campus "clipped and controlled," one faculty member shares her/his perspective of how BYU is now doing the same to the faculty.

Three times in the past five years, faculty at Brigham Young University have found unannounced changes in their contracts:

1992 contracts required for the first time that "Faculty who are members of BYU's sponsoring Church also accept the spiritual and temporal expectations of wholehearted Church membership." 1993 contracts tightened the requirement: "LDS faculty also accept as a condition of employment the standards of conduct consistent with qualifying for temple privileges." On 8 February 1996, soon after taking office, BYU President Merrill Bateman announced that: "The commissioner [of Church Education] will annually write a letter to the ecclesiastical leader of each Church member employed at BYU and all other Church Educational System entities, asking whether the person is currently eligible for a recommend. As in the past, a reasonable but limited time may be allowed when needed to restore eligibility." *Sunstone* recently reported on the response to the most recent change ("Annual Worthiness Review Now Required for All BYU Faculty, *Sunstone*, June 1996). Along with these successive changes in contracts, there have been other new documents codifying university procedures, including the "Statement on Academic Freedom at BYU April 1, 1993" (the date struck some as ominous), one section of which lays out things faculty are not free to do while employed at BYU:

> Reasonable Limitations: It follows that the exercise of individual and institutional academic freedom must be a matter of reasonable limitations. In general, at BYU a limitation is reasonable when the faculty behavior or expression SERIOUSLY AND ADVERSELY affects the University mission or the Church.... Examples would include expression with students or in public that: contradicts or opposes, rather than analyzes or discusses, fundamental Church doctrine or policy; deliberately attacks or derides the Church or its general leaders; or violates the Honor Code because the expression is dishonest, illegal, unchaste, profane, or unduly disrespectful of others.... The ultimate responsibility to determine harm to the University mission or the Church, however, remains vested in the University's governing bodies including the University president

and central administration and, finally, the Board of Trustees.

These changes in documents governing faculty belief and behavior at BYU are facts. Their positive and/or negative effect on the university is a matter of interpretation. What follows is a sketchy, anecdotal chronicle and commentary, a counterweight to the one-sided accounts BYU's office of public relations presents to the public. This by no means pretends to be an exhaustive chronicle of every incident, but it does provide a sense of the on-going culture wars at BYU. It is drawn from many sources, each of which has its own context, both broader and more specific than the one I provide. I am especially indebted to the work done by Bryan Waterman and Brian Kagel (*The Lord's University: Freedom and Authority at Brigham Young University, 1985–1995*), to the many documents [formerly] available on the web site of the BYU chapter of the American Association of University Professors, thoughtful analyses of the directions BYU is taking by Omar Kader ("Free Expression: The LDS Church and Brigham Young University," *Dialogue: A Journal of Mormon Thought*, 26:3 [fall 1993]), Scott Abbott ("One Lord, One Faith, Two Universities: Tensions Between Religion' and Thought' at BYU," *Sunstone*, Sept. 1992), Paul Richards ("Academic Freedom at BYU: An Administrator's Perspective," remarks delivered 16 September 1993 at a B. H. Roberts Society meeting in Salt Lake City), and others in the pages of *Sunstone, Dialogue, Student Review*, and elsewhere, and to interviews with many members of the BYU faculty and administration. I, too, am an employee of BYU. I write this critique out of a sense of loyalty and while feeling a profound loss. As late as four or five years ago, BYU was still moving steadily to fulfill its unique promise as a Mormon university That momentum has been squandered. Because BYU's administration has been active in punishing the messengers who point out stages of the university's demise, I write anonymously, feeling both cowardly and wise as I do so (cowardly, because others at equal risk have spoken out publicly; wise, because when I leave BYU I wish to do so on my own terms).

A Bias Against Women's Studies

> "It's okay to teach about feminism but not to advocate it."
> —Merrill Bateman

A university is complex, and it is difficult to know where to begin this story. Perhaps the following document on the treatment of women at BYU prepared by a committee of the BYU chapter of the AAUP during the winter semester of 1996 and [formerly] available on its web site, presents the range of problems as well as anything else.

Limitations on the Academic Freedom of Women at Brigham Young University
March 1996

Brigham Young University has a history of suppressing scholarship and artistic expressions representing the experience of women. The following list provides examples of some of the ways in which university officials have acted over the past several years to silence women faculty and staff and suppress their scholarship.

In 1992 the administration refused to hire candidate Barbara Bishop for a faculty appointment in the English Department, although she was the choice of the section, [department] chair, and college dean for the position and had the full support of her local ecclesiastical leaders. At the time she even headed the Primary in her ward. The reason the administration gave for not approving her hire was that 17 faculty members in the English Department (of a faculty of 75) did not vote in favor of hiring her. Bishop's scholarship dealt with the works of African American writer Zora Neal Hurston and other American women writers.

In 1992, the LDS Church celebrated the sesquicentennial of the Relief Society. In conjunction with that celebration, Professor Marie Cornwall, then the head of the BYU Women's Research Institute, organized a scholarly conference on the Relief Society. Because speakers at that conference criticized as well as praised the Relief Society, Professor Cornwall was called in and censured by University Provost Bruce Hafen for planning this conference and carrying it out.

In 1992, the organizing committee of the BYU Women's Conference chose as the keynote speaker for the 1993 conference Laurel Thatcher Ulrich, faithful Mormon woman, recent Pulitzer Prize-winning author of *A Midwife's Tale: The Life of Martha Ballard*, and winner of a MacArthur Grant. Brigham Young University's board of trustees did not approve Ulrich to be a speaker for the women's conference. Although both she and her ecclesiastical leaders tried to find out why she was not approved, she was never given a reason. Nonetheless, the Church Museum of Art and History continued to display a copy of Ulrich's Pulitzer Prize in its display on the Relief Society.

In 1993, the board of trustees fired the chair of the BYU women's conference, Carol Lee Hawkins, from her position, even though during the six years she directed the conference, attendance almost doubled and the conference received an approval rating from participants who completed the exit questionnaire of over 90 percent. To explain the firing, the Board suggested only that a change of assignment was a good thing from time to time, as if this position were a Church assignment rather than a paid university administrative position and Hawkins's employment. Just after Carol Lee Hawkins was fired, a group of women's studies faculty from across the university met with University Provost Bruce Hafen and asked him about that action. He answered that Hawkins had not been fired, that she had indicated that she wanted a change in assignment, and that she was just moving to another position in the university. Hafen did nothing to help Hawkins secure another position.

In the summer of 1993, Provost Bruce Hafen tried to keep faithful Mormon woman and historian Claudia Bushman from speaking in a week-long faculty seminar sponsored by the Dean of Honors and General Education, although her husband Professor Richard Bushman was approved to speak. When Hafen learned that the Bushmans had both already been invited to participate, he required that Honors Dean Harold Miller only advertise Richard Bushman.

In 1993 the university terminated Professor Cecilia Konchar Farr after her third-year review. Konchar Farr is a feminist activist who worked to educate people about violence against women, who helped establish the feminist activist student club VOICE on campus, and who took a public pro-choice position, although she also said in her speech that she did not favor abortion and fully supported the LDS First Presidency's position on abortion. She also had the full support of her bishop and stake president as a faithful Mormon, worthy to participate in all Church ordinances. At first the university tried to represent Konchar Farr as an inadequate scholar and teacher, switched to unsatisfactory citizenship after an ad-hoc academic freedom committee published a comparison of her publications with those of others who had recently been promoted, and finally, after the appeal hearing, reached an agreement by which both sides were to say only that there were "irreconcilable differences" between them.

In 1994 candidate Marian Bishop Mumford was selected by the English Department, with the full approval of the department chair and the dean of the College of Humanities, for hire to the faculty of the BYU English Department. Her Ph.D. dissertation was an examination of women's journals, including the journal of Anne Frank, to demonstrate that women construct themselves most authentically in their journals because they consider themselves to be the sole audience. A part of that study was to examine the ways in which Anne Frank wrote about her body as a way to give herself identity, at least in language, in a culture that literally erased her from existence. Acting under the instructions of

Provost Bruce Hafen, Chair Neal Lambert told Bishop Mumford that she would be hired only if she agreed to discontinue her current scholarship. The candidate declined to come to Brigham Young University under those circumstances.

In 1994 and 1995 Joni Clarke was selected from a large pool of applicants as one of the two best candidates for an American literature faculty position in the English Department. She had the full support of her bishop and stake president and also associate academic vice president Alan Wilkins, who called her and interviewed her for over an hour to determine her worthiness to teach at BYU. Her research deals with Native American texts, particularly those by women. Provost Bruce Hafen did not approve her to be considered for hire.

In 1995 Dorice Elliot was also selected from a large pool of applicants as one of the two best candidates for a British literature faculty position in the English Department. Her research deals with 19th century British literature by women. She is greatly admired by her ecclesiastical leaders because of her work as the Relief Society president in her congregation. Provost Bruce Hafen did not approve her to be considered for hire.

The administration does not give reasons for its actions, but we may perhaps look at this as part of the pattern of exclusion or silencing of those who want to study women's experience from women's perspective.

In 1995 Professors Karen E. Gerdes and Martha N. Beck were forbidden to publish the results of their study of the experiences of Mormon women survivors of childhood sexual abuse who asked for help from their Mormon ecclesiastical leaders. In the majority of cases, the advice these victims received was damaging rather than helpful. Both professors have since left the university; the study appeared in the Spring 1996 issue of *Affilia, Journal of Women and Social Work* (Vol. 11, No. 1).

In April 1996 Katherine Kennedy was chosen for an English Department faculty appointment in Romanticism, the unanimous choice of the later-British literature section and with almost unanimous support from the department. Kennedy was supported for hire by the dean and even the general authority who interviewed her, as well as by her local ecclesiastical leaders. But the administration rejected her. Kennedy's research examines images of motherhood, including breast-feeding, in British Romantic poetry by women. Regarding the decision not to hire Kennedy, University Academic Vice President Alan Wilkins explained to the Department Advisory Council that the English Department could assume there was something about Kennedy's feminism that the administration did not approve of.

There is only one university lecture named after a woman, the Alice Louise Reynolds lecture. Money was raised to endow this lecture by Helen Stark, a strong feminist and well-known member of the Mormon community She herself contributed approximately $15,000 to the endowment fund. Stark died two years ago at the age of 89. In 1995 the committee selected Elouise Bell, a prominent, woman full [BYU] professor to deliver that lecture. The administration not only rejected Bell as the speaker; it informed the committee that Roger R. Keller, a male associate professor from the Department of Religion, would be the speaker. In 1996 the Alice Louise Reynolds lecture was not held.

For several years, women candidates for faculty employment at Brigham Young University have been asked this question by the academic vice president: "If a general authority asked you not to publish your research, what would you do?" It has been suggested to the candidates that they must agree not to publish in such a case. This condition of employment undermines the position of new women faculty members at Brigham Young University. To be hired, they apparently must agree to let male ecclesiastical leaders who are not trained in their disciplines have final authority over the publication of their scholarship. They are offered no review process to determine the fairness or accuracy of the authority's request. Again, women are instructed that they must suppress their own perspectives on their own experience or research if a male authority so directs them.

These accounts of women at BYU can be multiplied and amplified. In interviews with general authorities and BYU administrators, single women are being asked repeatedly and pointedly whether they are lesbians. Elder Boyd Packer, speaking to the All-Church Coordinating Council on 18 May 1993, made the position of women scholars at BYU doubly tenuous when he claimed that "There are three areas where members of the Church, influenced by social and political unrest, are being caught up and led away... The dangers I speak of come from the gay-lesbian movement, the feminist movement (both of which are relatively new), and the ever-present challenge from the so-called scholars or intellectuals." Provost Bruce Hafen paternally declared the kind of feminism approved of by BYU as "equity feminism." President Merrill Bateman told a gathering of BYU women faculty that "perhaps we have gone too far in encouraging women with children to work outside the home." He explained to the women that it is okay to teach about feminism, but not to advocate feminism; and to help them understand, he made an analogy to evolution, which he said is also okay to teach about at BYU but not to advocate.

Actions and Reactions
Protest letters, academic creeds, resignations

This general pattern of silencing and controlling women is part of a larger picture in which both women and men are finding it increasingly difficult to do the things they thought they were hired to do. The dismissal of Cecilia Konchar Farr coincided with that of David Knowlton, assistant professor of anthropology, also up for his third-year review, and, like Konchar Farr, an outspoken and popular teacher who wrote about Mormon topics for *Sunstone*. In response to both incidents, thirty-three members of the BYU faculty published a letter in the Salt Lake Tribune in which they pointed out that

> When we find ourselves threatened by the voices and ideas of others, we must ask ourselves why we

are threatened and scrutinize our own behaviors and motives. It is always appropriate to question and challenge opposing ideas. It is not appropriate to denigrate, attack or attempt to silence a person who holds alternative ideas. Such behavior threatens the very nature of our university, which requires diversity without rancor among scholars dedicated to faithful intellectual pursuit. (5 July 1993)

A few months earlier, shortly after the First Presidency's 1991 statement encouraging members of the Church not to take part in symposia that sponsor discussion of Church doctrines, members of the BYU sociology department drafted a letter to President Rex Lee that detailed ways the prohibition would keep them from pursuing scholarly interests important to themselves and the Church:

> We wish to express concern over the possibility that disciplinary action, whether through ecclesiastical or university channels, might be taken against BYU faculty members for scholarly discussion of Mormonism....
>
> Some social scientists who gave presentations at the last *Sunstone* Symposium have been called in by their stake presidents and questioned about their participation. One presently faces an interview with a general authority.... Such actions must be viewed as a constraint on academic freedom, especially for LDS Church members whose employment depends on church standing. (See "BYU Memo Highlights Academic Freedom Issue," *Sunstone*, Feb. 1992)

The sociologists' concern about ecclesiastical intervention in university matters was heightened by rumors of a "hit list" of faculty whom a member or members of BYU's board of trustees wanted removed. Provost Bruce Hafen denied repeatedly that there was such a list ("Academic Hit List Rumors Untrue, Provost Assures," *Daily Universe*, 22 July 1992). Insiders later said he was splitting hairs, that he had been told on the phone to fire certain people but that he hadn't been given a *written* list.

Omar Kader, formerly at BYU, and Scott Abbott, a current faculty member, read papers at the 1992 *Sunstone* Symposium about BYU. Kader was pessimistic about the possibilities of a Church university and suggested the Church divest itself of BYU. Abbott was more optimistic, although he detailed serious problems with the general intellectual climate generated by Church and university leaders. For his trouble, Abbott's stake president took his temple recommend.

In a case illustrating board and administration intervention into what are normally department and college affairs, George Schoemaker, after two one-year appointments in the English department, was recommended for a tenure-track position by the department but was turned down by Provost Hafen and Church Commissioner of Education Henry B. Eyring because of a letter one of Schoemaker's students wrote to a general authority about a book used in his class, Margaret Atwood's *Surfacing*, and because they disapproved of his avowed feminism, his speaking at *Sunstone*, and his role in forming the Ad-Hoc Committee on Academic Freedom that defended Konchar Farr and Knowlton. From this time on, as partially documented in the AAUP's report on women at BYU cited above, the English department has been in virtual receivership, with Hafen or an academic vice president or a member of the board of trustees making all the hiring decisions.

One of the least publicized changes at BYU during this time was the dismantling of Honors and General Education as the intellectual center of the university. Under Dean Harold Miller and several stellar associate deans, Honors and GE sponsored eclectic and well-attended concert and lecture series, funded innovative classes (most notably a growing set of classes that had students work for two semesters on some combination of the culture, history, language, geology, botany, etc. of a city or country, and then, funded by Honors and GE, travel to the place—Bolivia and Vienna were two early sites—to conduct additional research and/or to do a service project), and each summer hosted one or two guest lecturers for weeklong faculty seminars on philosophy and history, people like Terry Eagleton, Richard Rorty, Martha Nussbaum, Alan Bloom, and Richard and Claudia Bushman. In 1993, a new dean, Paul Cox, was appointed, and Honors and GE underwent several debilitating changes. Funding was dropped for the summer capstone experiences of the two-semester classes. Service learning was declared undesirable at BYU. The concert and lecture series were discontinued in favor of Sunday firesides. The faculty seminars went by the board, replaced several summers later only by nuts-and-bolts seminars on teaching. To complete the retrenchment, volunteers for *Student Review*, an independent student newspaper not controlled by the administration, were no longer allowed to meet in the Maeser Building (home of Honors and GE), copies of *Student Review* were removed from the Honors reading room, and the Honors Student Council was disbanded. Miller left the university to take a job as provost of Waterford School in Salt Lake City.

Several of these cases drew the attention of the academic community at large. Critical articles appeared in the *Chronicle of Higher Education*, and LDS faculty at other universities recorded their displeasure. Tom Hales, for example, then a University of Chicago assistant professor of mathematics being courted by the BYU math department and son of a member of the BYU board of trustees, wrote to President Rex Lee about academic freedom at BYU:

> There is widespread recognition that the free search for truth and its free exposition are essential to the academic enterprise. My professional code of ethics calls for me to oppose any policy that endangers those freedoms. Professors should be accorded greater freedoms and protections than ordinary citizens. In return they accept a higher standard of conduct. To cast a teacher as an official spokesperson or representative of the Church of Jesus Christ is to betray a fundamental

misunderstanding of the nature of the academic profession.

The issues that I have raised here are not hypothetical. It has been amply documented . . . that there have been certain abuses of procedure in recent months. (3 May 1993.)

Largely because of his concerns about academic freedom. Hales decided not to come to BYU, part of a growing group of disillusioned Mormon scholars who are desperately needed at BYU to replace the large percentage of the faculty that retires this decade. And within BYU, morale was declining precipitously.

At the close of his 1993 Distinguished Faculty Lecture ("Mathematical Parables," copy from the math department), for instance, J. W Cannon, a BYU mathematician, turned to the situation at BYU:

> Unfortunately, at BYU we occasionally find a large streak of fear towards those who are different, toward those who disagree with us, fear that they will corrupt us, fear that BYU will lose its uniqueness. We fear that secular truth will destroy moral truth. . . .
>
> Here is my personal academic creed:
>
> I will act with courage and not from fear—fear of what others may expect or think, fear of my own inadequacies.
>
> I will speak freely, openly, publicly I will remember what we have all experienced, namely, that our knowledge of truth, even revealed truth, proceeds by approximation according to our ability and experience and that difficult issues can be understood and resolved only in an atmosphere where the evidence—physical, spiritual, or intellectual—can be freely and openly discussed.
>
> I will learn from those who do not agree with me. In particular, I will not impute bad motives to those who do not agree with me. I will instead examine their evidence, their arguments, and their conclusions and weigh each thoughtfully and carefully. . . .

> I will not presume that because I control someone's wage that I have bought their loyalty. I will remember that loyalty can be earned but not bought, and that a wage buys only a share in people's time....

Discouraged faculty began to leave BYU in response to the changing climate, including:

- Martha Bradley, history
- Tomi-Ann Roberts, psychology (like Konchar Farr, a faculty sponsor of VOICE)
- William Davis, German (after defending Konchar Farr, Roberts, and VOICE in the media)
- Harold Miller, psychology and dean of Honors and General Education
- William Evenson, physics and dean of Math and Science, since returned to BYU
- Bonnie Mitchell, sociology
- Karen Gerdes, social work
- Martha Nibley Beck, sociology
- Stan Albrecht, sociology and former academic vice president

New Cases
Dismissals and intimidations

In retrospect, 1992 and 1993 were watershed years for BYU. Marked ideologically by Elder Packer's three-pronged attack on feminists, homosexuals, and intellectuals and his personal demands of BYU administrators and department chairs that they take specific action to enforce that ideology, these administrators saw not only the loss of important members of the faculty and decisions by others not to join the faculty but also that the demands involved immense amounts of time and energy and morale as supporters of the controversial measures were called on to defend the university's actions and critics sacrificed time and risked reputations in a loyal fight for a university worthy of the name. As university regulations and procedures, most specifically the routinely gentle, third-year, tenure-track review, were used to mask and legitimate orders by members of the Board of Trustees, the already tenuous process of faculty review in hiring was called into question and became an exercise in futility for many departments. The new academic-freedom document was immediately proven a sham.

In 1994 and 1995, the general trend toward more administrative control over departments and individuals continued, sparking the reestablishment of a BYU chapter of the AAUP in late 1994. Perhaps the most notable attenuation of academic freedom during this time occurred in the case of Brian Evenson. The following account is largely taken from a report written by Evenson's father, William E. Evenson, professor of physics and former academic vice president and college dean, for an AAUP evaluation:

> Brian Evenson joined the Brigham Young University English Department faculty in January, 1994 as assistant professor. In August, 1994, Evenson's book of short stories, *Altmann's Tongue*, was published by Alfred A. Knopf.
>
> On October 4, 1994, an anonymous student wrote a letter of complaint to an LDS Church leader or leaders about the violent images in the book and their incompatibility (in her view) with the teachings of the LDS Church.
>
> On November 15, 1994, the English Department Chair, C. Jay Fox, and the Creative Writing Section Head, Douglas H. Thayer, met with Evenson and asked him to respond to the anonymous letter by the end of the week. As a memo from Fox to Academic Vice President Todd A. Britsch, January 16, 1995, indicates, this discussion was initiated as the result of a meeting with the LDS Church Commissioner of Education and LDS Church General Authority, Elder Henry B. Eyring: "I met with Brian just a few days following the meeting

with Elder Eyring on Nov. 9.... The bottom line is that he knows that this book is unacceptable coming from a BYU faculty member and that further publications like it will bring repercussions...."

In January, 1995, Evenson was called in by his LDS Church stake president at the behest of the LDS area president and asked about the book.

Representatives of BYU's AAUP Chapter, including several literary scholars, met with Rex Lee to discuss what they thought were misrepresentations of Evenson's book. They pointed out, for example, that the title story "Altmann's Tongue," about justifications of violence, referred to the name Klaus Barbie, the Nazi "Butcher of Lyon," hid under in South America. Members of the group say that Lee was surprised and seemed to understand; but he was quoted soon thereafter in the *Daily Universe* to the effect that Evenson's prose was violent and evil and unacceptable at BYU.

On March 6, 1995, Evenson, accompanied by his father, met with BYU President Rex E. Lee, Provost Bruce C. Hafen, Jones, and Fox. Hafen and the others in that meeting denied that the anonymous letter was the source of the problem; it was a broader issue of appropriateness. They also denied that there had been any concerns raised by Church leaders, asserting that all the concerns came from within the university. In that meeting, Hafen put Evenson "on notice" that his work was not appropriate for a Church university even though he would not indicate in what way the work violated university policies.

When Evenson ... found that nothing he could say would affect the uninformed judgment of his work that would control his opportunities at BYU, he chose to leave and took a position at Oklahoma State University in August, 1995.

As Evenson's case was approaching its end, Larry Young, an assistant professor of sociology who was being evaluated for tenure and promotion, was called in by Associate Academic

Vice President Alan Wilkins and questioned about a "pattern of behavior" that concerned the administration. In the initial meeting, Wilkins identified three specific issues: Young had spoken at *Sunstone* symposiums, he was said to have worn an earing, and his scholarship in the sociology of religion made it impossible to determine "where his heart was at" with respect to the LDS church. As an illustration of the final area of concern, Wilkins noted Young's chapter in the recently published book *Contemporary Mormonism: Social Science Perspectives* (University of Illinois). Wilkins noted that while Young's reference to the hegemonic nature of Mormon authority might be factually correct, it placed the Church in a negative light.

Wilkins also charged Young with sloppy scholarship with respect to quantitative analysis in the chapter—suggesting that Young sought to misconstrue facts concerning international Church activity rates in an effort to raise controversy. Young noted that his work on the Roman Catholic clergy decline had given him prior experience with being charged with having a hidden agenda on politically sensitive religious issues but that the methodological rigor of his work had always held up under such attacks. Young strongly challenged Wilkins assessment, asking for examples of supposed inaccuracies in the findings presented or alternative strategies to more effectively address the issue discussed. The matter was dropped.

Not at issue was the quality of Young's scholarship. Indeed, BYU had actively recruited Young prior to his entering the job market from his Ph.D. program and he had turned down job offers from other universities during his early years at BYU. In addition, his work on contemporary Catholicism and social scientific theories of religion have been published by the leading journals in his discipline and by academic presses ranging from the University of Wisconsin and the University of Illinois to Routledge and Oxford Universities. When Young made it clear that he would not accept a year or two delay in the promotion and tenure decision, he was promoted to associate professor within a matter of a few days of the initial meeting with Wilkins, but without continuing status (tenure).

Also not at issue in Young's case was the support of his ecclesiastical leaders, who had been questioned by Wilkins during the week following the initial meeting with Young. Young's bishop voiced strong support and appreciation for Young's contributions to his ward and neighborhood. Throughout the four-month investigation that ensued, Young was told that his job at BYU was hanging in the balance and the university was uncertain as to whether it should make a long-term commitment to him. At the same time, the administration was not saying that Young had done anything wrong and would not cite any offenses. Nevertheless, Young was asked to write a memo justifying anything he had ever written for *Sunstone* and for *Dialogue: A Journal of Mormon Thought*.

During the next several weeks, Young met repeatedly with Wilkins in an effort to obtain a decision concerning tenure. At the same time, Young told representatives from the AAUP, of which he was a member, that he felt that, given the university's animosity toward the BYU chapter, he would be more effective in mounting a defense of his "heart" by working independently of the AAUP. In addition, Young asked several reporters from local newspapers and television stations who approached him concerning the investigation to ignore the story while it was still unresolved.

Young's primary defense came from senior members of his department, the dean of his college (Clayne Pope) and individuals from the Research Information Division and Church Education System of the LDS church. Young had provided volunteer consultation to individuals in the Research Information Division concerning ongoing research projects and had taught graduate seminars and served on graduate committees of several Church Education System employees who had come to BYU to earn their Ph.D.s in sociology. In addition, while Young said that he felt extremely compromised when asked to exhibit his spirituality and testimony in order to secure employment, he gave the administration a copy of a sacrament meeting talk he had given on the previous Easter Sunday in an effort to give them a sense of his spirituality that was not tainted by the investigation. Finally, he said that during every meeting with the administrators he sought to communicate his love for Christ and his students. When he asked the administration for clarification concerning how the investigation process related to university procedures and policy, he was told that the conversations being held with him and others, as well as the information collection process, stood outside of university policy—in large measure because nothing Young had done could be identified as violating the university's academic freedom document or other policies, and no complaints from students or faculty had ever been lodged against Young. Nevertheless, Young was repeatedly told that the university was unwilling to grant him tenure and that they might very well dismiss him.

At one point, Wilkins suggested to Young that one area of concern was Young's growing national stature in the sociology of religion. Young had recently been elected to the council of the sociology of religion section of the American Sociological Association, and he was frequently asked to comment on contemporary religious issues by local and national media. Wilkins indicated that one of the administration's concerns was that Young's academic stature gave him the legitimacy to discuss matters of religion in a secular fashion that could be misconstrued by the general public or manipulated and sensationalized by the press. In addition, Wilkins indicated that the administration was nervous about what the tone of Young's writings would be after he had obtained tenure.

Finally, in early August, separate interviews were scheduled with Academic Vice President Todd Britsch, Provost Bruce Hafen, and Commissioner and now Apostle Henry B. Eyring. Young reported that his session with Vice President Britsch went well. He said he shared his feelings of both sadness and grief over the process and his perceptions of the costs being inflicted on the university as a whole. At times, both Britsch and Young were in tears. During the hour with Provost Hafen, Young reported that he was asked seven different times if "knowing what you now know, do you feel like you still belong at BYU!" In addition, Young reported that he was asked a number of questions by Provost Hafen that he felt were inappropriate for anyone but an ecclesiastical leader to ask, especially given university procedures for contacting Church leaders. Nevertheless, Young felt compelled to treat Hafen as an ecclesiastical leader and provide answers since his job was hanging in the balance and the investigation clearly was focusing on Young's religious values and beliefs. Finally, Young reported that his interview with Elder Eyring was enjoyable and spirit-filled. Young was reported to have said, "When I told him that I loved Christ and I loved my students, I believe that Elder Eyring felt the genuineness and sincerity of my words." The morning following Young's appointment with Elder Eyring, he was finally awarded tenure.

During this time, at least three senior professors were asked by Rex Lee or Merrill Bateman to resign from the BYU faculty, including Samuel Rushforth (Botany) and two others. They were all told that the university was taking a new direction and that they would no longer be happy at BYU. None of the three has, as yet, resigned.

In June 1996, assistant professor of English Gail Turley Houston was denied promotion and tenure. This time, in contrast to the Konchar Farr and Knowlton cases three years earlier, the administration did not try to make a case against her scholarship but faulted her for politicizing the classroom and speaking against established Church doctrines:

> The genesis of our grave concerns and ultimate recommendations to deny continuing faculty status and rank advancement was the number and severity of occasions when your actions and words on and off campus, even following your third-year review, were perceived as harmful to tenets held by the Church and

> the university We feel that not only have these activities failed to strengthen the moral vigor of the university, they have enervated its very fiber.

The BYU chapter of the AAUP mounted a defense of Houston, most notably with the documents pertaining to the case they made public on their web site. In their annotated version of the letter denying tenure, they state:

> As we see it, it is BYU's mission to encourage better and deeper thinking about matters crucial to us all, including how our culture supports and inhibits women as they construct their lives. The debates and discussions necessary for progress are impossible in an environment in which every sentence spoken by a faculty member is evaluated for doctrinal purity, in which fear becomes the major motivation, in which timidity becomes a virtue, in which risk and discovery are impossible. "Trust," President Hinckley said, "comes from the top down." And without trust, this university will not fulfill its mission.

Although Houston has accepted a position at the University of New Mexico, she is appealing her case. Unfortunately, under BYU regulations, the same administrators who denied tenure in the first place also hear the appeal.

In fairness to now former Provost Bruce Hafen, who in so many accounts is the villain, it is important to recognize that in most of these cases he was simply following instructions (overt or implied). Associates of his report that a number of actions attributed to him were extremely painful for him, but his first loyalty was always to the Brethren. Reportedly, it is his belief that one can argue and defend a position, but that once the Brethren signal a different course, the only acceptable choice is to carry it out. Hafen was sustained as a seventy at the April 1996 general conference and left the university this summer to serve in an area presidency.

Considering the change in university presidents and Hafen's departure, the persistence and escalation of religious scrutiny of current and prospective faculty make it very clear that this campaign is directed from outside the university from individuals the faculty have no access to.

First Things Last
Can one be a loyal general authority and a good university president?

I shall end this chronicle, a tragic story for those, like myself, who have spent their lives and careers in the service of our Church's university, with a selective account of Merrill Bateman's first seven months as president of the university.

In an early interview, President Bateman declared that at BYU there would be no room for "advocates for the adversary." In subsequent months, he has continued this kind of divisive, suspicious thinking, routinely asking his vice presidents, for example, when discussion turns to a member of the faculty: "Is she one of us?" Clearly, Bateman came to BYU with marching orders. An instructive incident occurred during the week the university hosted a large group of prospective donors to the "Lighting the Way" capital campaign in early April 1996. On a Monday, the women's group VOICE hung its annual "Clothesline" in the garden court of the Wilkinson Center, part of a national art therapy campaign where victims of abuse express their private feelings in public. The display had rows of T-shirts bearing descriptions of violence done to women, statements of personal hurt, a few of which implicated bishops and stake presidents. According to the 4 August *Salt Lake Tribune*, one T-shirt said, "SUICIDE can seem better than living (?) through a temple marriage!" The project was approved at various levels by the appropriate administrators, who asked that several of the shirts not be included, and VOICE members complied. On Friday morning, the last day of the weeklong exhibit, reportedly after a flood of protesting letters, calls, and faxes from the conservative Eagle Forum and the conservative student "Dittohead Club," Bateman burst into the courtyard and instructed faculty advisors Tim Heaton and Brandie Siegfried to have the exhibit taken down immediately When Siegfried invited him to walk through the exhibit, he refused. Instead, he focused on two offending T-shirts, including the one quoted above. Sigfried asked him to try to understand their purpose. She pointed out the educational panels that explained the shirts and the reasons for the explicit language. She noted the group's stated support for the Church, even if they felt abused by a specific leader exercising unrighteous dominion. Bateman, who had never met Siegfried before, told her that he could see through the scheme and that he knew what her real agenda was. Some of the women students began to cry. Alton Wade, Student Life vice president, drew Bateman aside. Finally, an agreement was reached to leave up the Clothesline for the few remaining hours, after removing all shirts referring to bishops and stake presidents. Several students and faculty members who were present or who heard about the incident secondhand wrote letters of protest to Bateman, accusing him of revisiting the same patriarchal violence on the women from which they were trying to heal. Siegfried will be up for her third-year review in 1996–97.

One of Bateman's recurring themes as he has spoken about BYU has been moral relativism. Although he has said such silly things as that moral relativism will bring us to the brink of chaos as it introduces "approximate spelling" and does away with college entrance exams (speech to the Provo/Orem Chamber of Commerce, reported in the *Daily Herald*, 8 June 1996), he has other issues as well, best illustrated perhaps in the address he gave at his inauguration, "Inaugural Response." One of the ironies of the speech is that during the very days his administration was deciding to fire Gail Houston for politicizing her classes as a feminist, Bateman gave a politically charged speech, one section of which is the following simple-minded and self-serving account of the complex web of twentieth-century thought:

The second concern is the moral relativism spreading throughout higher education both in America and abroad. Although higher education was secularized during the past century, there was still faith in reason and knowledge through the 1960s and into the 1970s. Absolute religious truths had been largely rejected by the world long before the 1970s, but scientific absolutes were still in vogue. During the past two decades, however, a number of well-known educators have begun to denigrate truth, knowledge, and objectivity. The driving theory is a radical relativism and skepticism that rejects any idea of truth or knowledge. There is no God. There are no absolute truths—only that which is politically useful. Those associated with this movement refuse even to aspire to truth on the basis that it is unattainable and undesirable—the latter because the search for truth is assumed to be authoritarian and repressive by nature. The movement is a by-product of the politicization process that began after World War II. The premise is no truth, no facts, no objectivity—only will and power. The slogan is that "everything is political" (Gertrude Himmelfarb, "A Call to Counterrevolution," *First Things*, no. 59 January 1996 1:18). The result is characterized by Dostoyevsky's Ivan Karamazov, who in effect said, "If God does not exist, everything is permitted."

If university scholars reject the notion of "truth," there is no basis for intellectual and moral integrity. Secularism becomes a creed that is no longer neutral but hostile to religion. The university becomes a politicized institution that is at the mercy and whims of various interest groups. Tolerance is encouraged unless one's ideas are different. The word diversity is becoming a code word for uniformity. Universities are encouraged to be diverse from within but not from without.

Some may bristle at my calling this account "simple-minded" (the late Alan Bloom, for example, whose book *The Closing of the American Mind* blames all our societal ills on Nietzsche's influence on our universities, or anti-intellectual right-wing Irving Kristol, or ex-college professor Newt Gingrich), but when an ex-CEO of Mars Candy Company becomes a university president and mouths reactionary slogans of the religious right, having never read the thought he so blithely and second-handedly dismisses, it is not simply simple minded, but destructive to our university.

A sadder irony, however, is that this section of Bateman's speech is, to put it bluntly, plagiarized. It is not a word-for-word lifting of text, but it is a sequential summary of another person's ideas and writing without attribution. While heaping scorn on the moral relativists who bring us approximate spelling and university politics, Bateman, in his inaugural address, disregarded one of the most fundamental tenets of academic life: proper attribution, something for which faculty at most universities are summarily dismissed. Although he carefully cited Eugene Bramhall, John Taylor, Ernest L. Wilkinson, Franklin S. Hams, J. Reuben Clark, and "the editor of a Catholic publication," no reader of the printed version of the talk or member of the audience who heard it delivered could possibly know that Gertrude Himmelfarb was the author of the entire section on moral relativism. The printed version attributes the words "everything is political" to Himmelfarb, but Bateman failed to note that the rest of the discussion is her intellectual property as well. For a detailed look, compare the parallels in Table 1 between Himmelfarb's address, given at the inauguration of Baylor University's new president in September 1995, and Bateman's.

Table 1 Parallels between Gertrude Himmelfarb's "The Christian Univeristy: A Call to Counterrevolution" and Merrill Bateman's "Inaugural Response"

Gertrude Himmelfarb "The Christian University: A Call to Counterrevolution"	Merrill Bateman "Inaugural Response"
A secularization of the university took place in the twentieth century. (16)	Although higher education was secularized during the past century . . .
[The dogma that had sustained the university for centuries was] the faith in reason and knowledge, in the rational, dispassionate search for truth. (18)	There was still faith in reason and knowledge through the 1960s and into the 1970s.
Today many eminent professors . . . disparage the ideas of truth, knowledge, and objectivity. (18)	A number of well-known educators have begun to denigrate truth, knowledge, and objectivity.
The animating spirit of postmodernism is a radical relativism and skepticism that rejects any idea of truth, knowledge, or objectivity. (18)	The driving theory is a radical relativism and skepticism that rejects any idea of truth or knowledge.
[Postmodernism] refuses even to aspire to such ideas, on the ground that they are not only unattainable but undesirable—that they are by their very nature, authoritarian and repressive. (18)	[They] refuse even to aspire to truth on the basis that it is unattainable and undesirable—the latter because the search for truth is assumed to be authoritarian and repressive by nature.
After World War II . . . the socially conscious university inevitably became a highly politicized one. (17)	The movement is a by-product of the politicization process that began after World War II.

BYU's "Academic Honesty Policy" states that

> Intentional plagiarism is a form of intellectual theft that is in violation of the Honor Code and may subject the student to appropriate disciplinary action. . . . Inadvertent plagiarism, while not in violation of the Honor Code, is nevertheless a form of intellectual carelessness which is unacceptable in the academic community. Plagiarism of any kind is completely contrary to the established practices of higher education where all members of the University are expected to acknowledge the original intellectual work of others that is included in one's own work.

Undoubtedly, the public-relations apparatus of the university will explain this flagrant violation of university policy as an unfortunate oversight or as the mistake of an editor or as a computer glitch or as the result of mixed up notes (excuses that students invariably try when accused of plagiarism). The messenger, sadly *Sunstone*, will certainly be reviled. And in the process, students may learn a debilitating cynicism.

I don't want to blow this lapse of judgment out of proportion; nevertheless, it does seem emblematic of what is happening at the university. I am willing to accept that President Bateman's ethical breech was without malice, perhaps even innocent. Surely such appropriation is done daily in his business world where executives, or their staff, routinely slap together talks for chamber-of-commerce type gatherings. But it is easier to excuse such innocent behavior in a college freshman than a university president. At any university, especially one which so consciously strives to meet the high standards of the Academy while maintaining its unique religious mission, it is surprising that its president is, at best, naive about a fundamental ethical tenet of both the academic and the religious communities. Such actions make me and many other members of the faculty worried about the administration's ability to understand our concerns about the continuing vitality of intellectual life at BYU.

The following words, which ring so false as they were applied to Gail Houston, seem made for this case of plagiarism by our university president: "We feel that not only have these activities failed to strengthen the moral vigor of the university they have enervated its very fiber." First things have been put last.

The Future
Some say that without vigilant care, BYU will follow other former religious universities on the path to secularism. But over-zealousness can also lead to the same result.

We now have a university administration, led by a general authority, that is very competent in implementing the will of the board of trustees, but clumsy when it comes to the dynamics of a university where differing views must be hosted and tolerated and where academic standards are modeled and policed.

One of the most disturbing things about these recent events is that they are cumulative. A few years ago, BYU had reached a stature that allowed it to play on a relatively level field with the better universities in this country One of the best measures of this was that we were no longer competing with second-rate state universities for the faculty we really wanted to hire, but with Chicago, Michigan, Yale, and Columbia. And, in many instances, when we went head-to-head with these institutions, we won. I fear that that status is diminishing. A few years ago, some faculty could express dismay over restrictions on participating in "certain forums," but now there is a general pattern of intimidation for anything that does not reflect the full party line. If a faculty member can be "called in" because his name appears in the local newspaper in the context of defending a valued colleague who is being dismissed without apparent cause, or for commenting on a "creationist" speech given at a local Protestant church, or if one's work becomes an issue because of postmodern or feminist methodologies or content, then it is difficult to still qualify for the title "university." And if this intimidation is done primarily in the name of religion, then our religion becomes narrow and petty, suspicious and fearful, focusing on means instead of ends.

BYU wants to be a "religious university," a "Mormon university," but in over-stressing a narrow view of the religious and Mormon half, we may lose the designation "university." I can think of no better way to end my litany of despair than to turn to a *First Things* article that appeared with the spate of articles on the secularization of American universities so often cited by BYU administrators and members of the board of trustees—James Burtchael's "The Decline and Fall of the Christian College" (April 1991). Burtchael gives several reasons for Vanderbilt University's gradual transformation from a Methodist-supported institution into the secular university it is today (cited also in Scott Abbott's article on BYU), words that feel prescient in light of the situation at BYU today:

> There was a period of great intellectual turbulence, when fresh findings and methods and disciplines raised fearful philosophical challenges to theology. Spokesmen for the church's concerns, by a compound of incapacity and animosity, exacerbated the apparent hostility between the church and rigorous scholarship....
>
> The ... angry General Conference ... had narrowed its view of what it meant to be Methodist to things like a religious test for all faculty and disciplinary control over students. Absent any larger vision of Christian education, this program was unrelievedly negative, and assured the educational reformers that the church had no stomach for ambitious scholarship. And finally, as a result, an effective bond to the Methodist Church instinctively evoked references to bigotry, exclusion, narrowness, sectarianism, and selfishness.

And finally, as a result, "an effective bond to the Methodist Church instinctively evoked references to bigotry, exclusion, narrowness, sectarianism, and selfishness."

West Zion II

Sandstone

SEVEN

On Ecclesiastical Endorsement at Brigham Young University

Sunstone Magazine, Issue 105, April 1997

After publication of his prize-winning book *Mormons and Jews*, Steven Epperson was hired by the BYU History Department to teach American religious history, replacing Martha Bradley, who had replaced Michael Quinn. Under pressure for his publications on post-Manifesto plural marriages and for his new book *Early Mormonism and the Magical World View*, Quinn resigned from his tenured position and published, as he left, an essay called "A Marketplace of Ideas, a House of Faith, and a Prison of Conformity." Bradley, who was editor of *Dialogue* when she left BYU, resigned from her position on the grounds that she needed "to live in a society that values diversity. You would think the university would be the one sure place for that." Brigham Young University, it turned out, was not an institution that valued Steven's perspectives any more than it had Bradley's or Quinn's.

> Religion is being destroyed by the Inquisition, for to see a man burned because he believes he has acted rightly is painful to people, it exasperates them.
> —William of Orange

During Gail Houston's August 1996 appeal of Brigham Young University's decision to deny her tenure despite overwhelmingly positive English Department and College Committee votes, Associate Academic Vice President James Gordon testified that procedurally the University could not be faulted. Houston broke into his technical testimony to remind Gordon and the appeal panel that the hearing was about more than technicalities, that she was a woman with a family, that she was being forced from a position at a University where she had served with dedication, that the decision, in short, was existentially important to her. Gordon's responded to the panel that in her outburst she had exhibited the behavior that had led to her dismissal: "From the moment she arrived on campus we have been unable to control her."

On October 22, 1996, Steven Epperson, an assistant professor of history at BYU since 1993, was told that his services would no longer be required as of the end of August 1997. This made him an early casualty of the policy announced by BYU President Merrill Bateman on February 8, 1996, according to which the bishop "of each Church member employed at BYU" would be asked to certify annually "whether the person is currently eligible for a [temple] recommend."

The University has the legal right to establish regulations like the one demanding that all faculty must undergo ecclesiastical endorsement and Epperson's bishop, for reasons I will enumerate later, would not certify him. Similarly, James Gordon may have been right when he asserted the University correctly carried out its own policies in Gail Houston's case (although the American Association of University Professors has argued otherwise and is currently investigating BYU for academic freedom violations). But when Houston appealed for a wiser, more charitable judgment, when she asked that Gordon, for the University, look into her face and discern there more than the features of a feminist who had supposedly "enervated the moral fiber" of the University, she showed us a way out of the sanctimonious edifice we have constructed for ourselves, or have allowed to be constructed.

In this spirit, I would like you to consider the following portrait of Steven Epperson. My rendering will not do him justice; but it is fuller and more honest than the meager sketch passed from his bishop to BYU administrators. I have known Steven and his family for nearly twenty years. We have collaborated. We are friends.

Steven was born in Salt Lake City in 1954. After high school he enrolled as a student at Brown University. He served a mission in France from 1974 to 1976. A section from his poem "Tangled Woods and Parisian Light" (*Sunstone*, April 1991) evokes an experience from that time, contrasting the quiet message of two missionaries with the violence of a political demonstration:

> A boy clung to his father's leg
> Eyes on the street wide and wincing,
> The man cradled his son's head listening
> While the other pair spoke in low voices,
> Searching for words in an alien tongue.
>
> A dog was strung up on a lamp post,
> A placard hung round its attenuated neck,
> Its hanging tongue the same deep crimson
> As the shrill apocalyptic text
> Which it bore upon its broken chest.
>
> The two bent nearer the father and the son
> As if to shield them from the proximate menace,
> Continuing the tale of a youth
> And the questions he bore into a tangled wood.
>
> The seried ranks of acolytes bore the epicenter of the
>   quake away
> Leaving clustered knots of onlookers among the rubble
> To register the aftershocks, the emptied vials of wrath—
> The simplicity of the shouted syllogisms

The utter directness of the violence
The thrill of the extraordinary gesture.

The tale neared its end:
"The woods shone.
The boy returned through the fields,
A live ember of divine words in his hand.
And thus his story began."

Steven graduated from Brown in religious studies in 1979. He married Diana Girsdansky, whom he had met in the Providence Ward. After he had earned an M.A. from the University of Chicago Divinity School, Steven moved with Diana and their children to Princeton, New Jersey, where they spent a year before beginning a Ph.D. program in religious studies at Temple University in Philadelphia. I still remember the first priesthood meeting I sat through with the young man whose earnest voice and careful thinking made us all look forward to the year he would spend as a member of the Princeton Ward. At Temple, Steven studied with Paul van Buren, now director of the Center of Ethics and Religious Pluralism at the Shalom Institute in Jerusalem, and worked with Mormon historian Richard Bushman, then at the University of Delaware. For a personal description of Steven's years in Philadelphia, see our "House of the Temple, House of the Lord: A View from Philadelphia."

The Eppersons moved from Philadelphia to Salt Lake City, where Steven became history curator at the Museum of Church History and Art. He helped develop the permanent exhibition of Church history now displayed on the museum's main floor and with others curated various exhibitions on Church history and art, including "The Mountain of the House of the Lord," an exhibit commemorating the centennial of the Salt Lake Temple. In 1993 Steven began teaching as an assistant professor in BYU's history department.

When BYU's new policy required Steven's Bishop, Andrew Clark, to certify his temple worthiness, Clark refused, on the grounds that Steven was not attending Sunday school or priesthood meeting, nor was he currently paying tithing. Some background on both counts will be helpful.

Although he was still paying fast offerings, Steven was in fact paying no tithing at the time. Diana was starting up the Children's Music Conservatory, a public, non-profit, and initially expensive undertaking, and their best estimate was that after the Music Conservatory's summer camp in June it would begin to break even and they would be repaid the money they had paid out. Hannah, the Epperson's daughter, and Diana were not attending church. The family was going off in different directions, Steven reports, and there was some tension and disagreement. Uncomfortable with that state of affairs, they followed Hannah's advice and sought a Sunday activity they could do together as a family. Eventually they began going to Pioneer Park to join other Salt Lake residents in feeding the homeless. This was a deliberate and thoughtful attempt to keep the family together and focused on Sunday-related issues and service. Between November 1995 and April 1996, Steven raced back from Pioneer Park to attend sacrament meeting in his ward.

On May fifth, several months after Bishop Clark's initial refusal to certify Steven temple worthy, Steven was contacted by Associate Vice President James Gordon. Steven then met with Clark. He offered, despite the family problems it would cause, to attend priesthood and Sunday school in a neighboring ward at a more convenient time, and explained he would pay tithing again after the Conservatory's summer camp. On the same day, Clark refused to approve Nick, the Epperson's youngest son, for ordination to the priesthood—because he would not promise to attend all of his meetings. Nick said he would be with his family half of the month and attend meetings the other half; this wasn't good enough for Clark. On May 10, Steven had a follow-up telephone conversation with Clark, who told him that July-September was an insufficient period to judge whether he was a sincere tithe payer, and that no other church meetings would fill the requirement. Steven was a member of the 18th Ward. Period. Clark lectured Steven on principles of "priesthood leadership," explaining that Steven should lead and expect his family to follow as he "laid out the program."

All Steven could hope for at this point was that the BYU administration would try to understand that his predicament was the result of the inflexibility of his local leaders, and perhaps intervene. On May 17, Steven met with Gordon and told him that Clark had rebuffed his good faith effort to begin paying tithing at the end of June and to attend priesthood and Sunday school in another ward. He asked Gordon to speak with his bishop to try to achieve a compromise. Gordon said he could do nothing.

Finally, in mid-October, Gordon asked Steven if he could speak with his bishop. Steven agreed, asking only that Gordon give him a full report of what Clark said so that he could verify the information. On October 22, Steven was summoned to Gordon's office to discuss, Steven thought, what the bishop had said. Gordon gave a short report of his conversation with Clark. Steven responded. The letter of dismissal, which Gordon subsequently handed to Steven, was lying on the desk while they spoke. The administration had decided, the letter said, to terminate Steven's contract as of August 1997.

I tell this story not to argue that Steven was doing something better than going to church, nor to argue that his stubbornness in the face of what he saw as un-Christian inflexibility was the most politic choice, but rather to point out that routine church activity (as opposed to deeply held values) may be subject to circumstances. What is possible one year becomes more complicated the next; sometimes family dynamics require innovative strategies. Do thirty years of devotion, tithe paying, a mission, temple marriage, and church work mean nothing in the face of a year of well-meant but slightly altered church activity?

Where does this kind of insistence on the letter of administrative procedure get us? Will more people comply with its demands than before the new policy? And more to the point, will BYU faculty and staff now be more spiritual? Or do others respond to coercion the way I do? My nature is to do well the things I choose and to despise and evade what I am forced to do. Or, if I decide to knuckle under even while disagreeing with the requirement, I experience a diminished sense of dignity. Emphasizing the letter over the spirit shifts a people's sense of morality from heartfelt individual commitment to superficial observance of outward requirements. And the arbitrariness of the policy is staggering. In contrast to Steven's case, one Tooele County bishop has called a ward member who finds church attendance distasteful to serve breakfast to the homeless in Salt Lake City.

Steven Epperson stands for others who are currently under investigation by the BYU administration (on December 13, 1996, Merrill Bateman told BYU Humanities faculty that these number approximately 100) and who may be asked to leave, one by one, in the coming months. By insisting on the letter of its new policy, by weeding out members of the staff and faculty who cannot satisfy individual bishops' personal interpretations of the standard of temple worthiness, no matter how idiosyncratic, what does the University lose?

In Steven, it loses one of the fine apologists for our religion. As an invited speaker at conferences in Jerusalem, Baltimore, the former Soviet Union, and elsewhere, Steven has argued our case eloquently. Thinking people in many parts of the globe hold us in higher esteem as a people because he confesses our creed. Jacob Neusner, distinguished research professor of religious studies at the University of South Florida, begins his review of Steven's book *Mormons and Jews: Early Mormon Theologies of Israel* (Signature Books, 1992) with the words "Brilliantly conceived and elegantly executed," and then writes of "the doctrines Epperson lays out with the authority of scholarship and the passion of faith. He writes with craft and care; he speaks with humility; in the framework of his subject and his sources, he has given us a small masterpiece" (*Sunstone*, December 1994, 71–73).

Neusner continues with an anecdote that illustrates the service Epperson has performed for the Church:

> A personal word may prove illuminating. The first time I lectured at Brigham Young University, my topic, Pharisaism in the first century, spelled out in four academic lectures, interested only a few. The question periods after each lecture provided an exercise in practical missiology for young Mormons. I was the designated candidate, they, the aggressive proselytizers, and the protracted question periods, for four successive days, concerned only, what does a Jew say to this argument? And how can we devise a compelling answer to that negative response? In the end I wondered why my hosts had gone to so much trouble to bring me to undergo so sustained and demeaning a public roast. I left with the impression that all the Mormons wanted to know about the Jews was why we were not Mormons. When the Mormons sought permission to build their center in Jerusalem, I therefore took note, in the Jerusalem Post, that they have written a long record of persistent missions to Israel, the Jewish people, marked by an utter absence or regard for our religion, the Torah.
>
> But God does not leave us standing still. People change, and God changes us. So I hasten to add that subsequent visits to Provo have proved far more productive.... Epperson's definitive work, both the historical and the theological chapters, lays sturdy foundations for the construction of a two-way street, one that both religious communities, each a pilgrim people, stubborn in its faith, eternal in its quest to serve and love God with and through intelligence (which is God's glory), may share as they trek toward that common goal that Israelite prophecy has defined for us all.

Along with Steven's skill as an inter-faith interlocuter, we lose a talent for thinking creatively about our own beliefs and institutions. Consider, for example, his depiction of the temple and its possibilities:

> The temple is a paradox, an earthly home for a transcendent God. It cannot house his glory, yet he bids his children raise its walls, adorn its chambers, weave its veil. For he chooses just this place and not celestial spheres to disclose and veil his presence among the children of Israel. Signs of fellowship and wisdom, signs of sovereignty and orientation hewn upon the temple's sheer face betoken the knowledge and endowment bestowed within. Mortal hands and eyes are led by ones immortal to frame the fearful symmetry of his form, his house, his kingdom here on earth. We cannot place the crown upon his kingdom—cannot bind all wounds, sate all hunger, pacify all violence, wipe away all tears. Yet he bids, he demands a realm of equity and justice, now, from our flawed hearts and feeble hands.
>
> The House of the Lord is the matrix for the kingdom of God on earth. The temple transmutes city and wilderness: it pursues neither Eden, nor the heavenly Jerusalem. It sanctions neither a naive return to a romanticized past, nor the negation of the sensuous present, the real, for an abstract future. Rather, by a mysterious alchemy conjured through the conjunction of words from an improbable rite, it would bridge the rift between parents and children, the whole estranged family of Adam and Eve, and it would establish Enoch's city here, in this world, through unnumbered acts of charity and justice. (*Dialogue*, Fall 1987, p. 140)

We lose, in addition, a fine critical eye. Steven recently published, at the invitation of the editor of *BYU Studies*, a review essay of Robert Millett's and Joseph McConkie's *Our Destiny: The Call and Election of the House of Israel* (SLC: Bookcraft, 1993), a review that will help us, if we listen, move beyond morally ambiguous patterns of accepted thought. Steven points out, for instance, that

> .... the authors contend that since "literal blood descent" from Abraham delivers "the right to the gospel, the priesthood, and the glories of eternal life," "rights" by blood descent are crucial for the exercise of legitimate authority to establish and maintain the Church. They claim that such authority is rooted securely, since the church's early leaders "were all of one stock," sharing with Joseph Smith a "pure . . . blood strain from Ephraim"; they are "pure-blooded Israelite[s]." This teaching, the authors assert, is to be taken literally; it is "neither myth nor metaphor." ("Some Problems with Supersessionism in Mormon Thought," *BYU Studies* V. 34, No. 4, 1994–1995, 132)

Steven then demonstrates that assertions of pure blood lines are biological nonsense and points out that when the authors cite William J. Cameron as an authority and a "wise man" they are associating themselves with the thought and person of the editor of Henry Ford's *Dearborn Independent*, a virulently anti-Semitic weekly, with a man who was subsequently the editor of *Destiny*, the publication of the anti-Semitic Anglo-Saxon Federation of America. Cameron maintained, Epperson writes, "that Jesus was not a Jew. And the Jews, as we know them, are not the true sons of Israel. It was the Anglo-Saxons who descended from the ten lost tribes of Israel'" (133). Steven's review ends with a question: "Is it possible, just when the LDS community is emerging from ethnic, linguistic, and geographical parochialism to become a worldwide religion, that *Our Destiny* would unwittingly turn us back?" (Steven received a letter from Salt Lake lawyer Oscar McConkie threatening legal action for having called Joseph McConkie racist.) This critical review was the kind of activity you hope university professors will engage in; in the give and take of discussion ideas are sharpened and deepened and revealed for what they are. The political backlash that surely factored in the decision to fire Steven was antithetical to such discussion.

Epperson was hired at BYU, in part, because of the quality of his book *Mormons and Jews*, which won the Mormon History

Association's 1993 Francis Chipman Award for Best First Book and, in an earlier form, the MHA's William Grover and Winifred Foster Reese Best Dissertation Award. In the Fall of 1995, Steven underwent a routine third-year review in which departmental, college, and university committees judged whether he was making the progress in citizenship, teaching, and scholarship required of an assistant professor. During the process, the orthodoxy and quality of *Mormons and Jews* became the crucial questions in evaluating Steven as a professor, even though the book had been disallowed for consideration as productive scholarship during Steven's three trial years because it had been published prior to his arrival at BYU. Academic Vice President Alan Wilkins, after an hour-long discussion with Steven about the book's orthodoxy, asked "What would you do if the General Authorities asked you to suppress this, not to teach it, to recant? If they declared that this work wasn't doctrinally sound?" Steven replied that "that is their prerogative; they determine what is doctrinal for the Church. That's not what I do. I don't claim or teach this as doctrine. But I have done a professional job of recovering and representing to readers what is in the historical record."

In late September 1996, nearly half a year after the results of other third-year reviews were announced, James Gordon asked Steven if he could send copies of the book to two outside reviewers for evaluation. Steven agreed. Two weeks later, however, the evaluation was cut short with the letter announcing that Steven's bishop would not judge him temple worthy. That made things easier for BYU administrators and surely pleased Oscar McConkie. And it strikes me as suspicious.

Steven Epperson's case is serious enough if it stands alone. But there are professors and staff members in every department of the University whose lives are under scrutiny at the moment, whose years of devoted and skillful service are being discounted under the new ecclesiastical endorsement policy. And if, for various reasons—perhaps feeling themselves victims of unrighteous dominion, out of pride, from sheer obstinacy—they refuse to comply to whatever their particular bishop requires, however arbitrarily, we lose their services. I am not arguing for leniency for rapists and thieves and plagiarists. BYU has routinely fired staff, faculty, and administrators caught in acts of moral turpitude. Regardless of their skills, a morally solvent institution cannot afford to have such people around.

That is not, however, what is at stake here. The question is why the behaviors that we require of all members of our community, the laws by which we judge one another good or bad, must proliferate as they have. Why must we raise peccadillos (occasional church attendance or sporadic tithe paying) to mortal sins? There are obvious spiritual benefits to paying tithing, to take the latter example, and a Church university all of whose faculty and staff pay tithing may be an especially fine place. The sweetness of that utopia diminishes, however, when compliance is forced. The claims of free agency weigh heavy here.

No, one may argue, we are firing people who don't pay tithing or go to church so that we may employ only people who want to do so. And our new interviewing and screening procedures are aimed at ensuring such voluntary compliance. My answer is that you simply cannot ensure voluntary compliance. You can't even ensure involuntary compliance for that matter, for there are some bishops who refuse to play this spiritually destructive game. But "ensure" and "voluntary" don't belong in the same sentence. Remember the slogan during the Wilkinson presidency—free agency and how to enforce it. You can kick out some of the students who wear shorts above the knee and thus force most of the others to wear longer shorts. You can fire faculty members who, for whatever reasons, don't go to church enough to satisfy their bishop and thus put the fear of ecclesiastical non-endorsement into their colleagues. But why would you want to do that? Trust, President Hinckley reminded members of the BYU community on 13 October 1992, comes from the top down.

So, to review my argument: Forced compliance to proliferating policies has little spiritual benefit to the individual or to the university. The principle of free agency (over which the war in Heaven was fought) is of extreme importance both to individuals and to the university. In all cases of transgression except those so egregious that we would all see them as unacceptable, the transgressor might receive charitable counsel but ought never to be coerced to be "good" (by expulsion from school, if a student, or by firing from a job, if staff or faculty). "Teach them correct principles, and let them govern themselves," said our founding Prophet. Do we not believe him? And why do we ignore the clear words of Jesus Christ? "Ye blind guides, which strain at a gnat, and swallow a camel" (Matt. 23:24).

Letter from Steven Epperson to his Colleagues

My dear colleagues:

I have been informed by University administrators that my contract will not be renewed after its expiration in August, 1997. The immediate cause cited for that decision is my failure to obtain, over a reasonable period, the letter of ecclesiastical endorsement which we all must now secure annually in order to remain employed at BYU. It is, I believe, an unfortunate decision. But I will not appeal it or seek to have it set aside. Six months of interviews have served only to disclose how differently my bishop and I perceive my stewardship as husband, father, and priesthood holder. Six months of meetings have only disclosed how willing University administrators are to grant local ecclesiastical leaders inordinate power to determine who works and who does not work for this institution. I cannot imagine, as a condition for employment, submitting annually to the intrusive scrutiny of my private family life mandated by this ill-conceived policy.

It is very important to me, no matter what disagreements there may be between us on this policy issue, that all of you understand how appreciative I am of the confidence and fellowship you extended to me three and a half years ago when you voted to welcome me as a member of this department. I have never taken that trust lightly; I treasure it to this day. I hope only that you will not feel that your good will was misplaced. When I signed my letter of appointment in 1993, I had every expectation that my stay at BYU would be an enduring and productive one. I am sorry and disappointed, keenly disappointed, that my stay here will be so brief.

I sincerely wish all of you the very best of success in your research, teaching, and service here. We have a marvelous body of students—intelligent, well-meaninged, curious and decent—who need excellent teachers/scholars/saints to assist in their pursuit of knowledge and wisdom. May we be equal to them.

The contract I signed in July is good for the academic year 1996–97. I look forward to our continued professional and personal associations through this year and beyond.

Sincerely,

Steven Epperson
Department of History

Steven returned home after the final decision and apologized to his wife Diana for having lost his job. Steven, she said, we can be Americans again! Steven eventually became a Unitarian Minister, serving first in the South Valley, Salt Lake City parish, and since then as the parish minister in Vancouver, British Columbia. If you go to the Vancouver parish website (http://vancouverunitarians.ca/), you can read a sampling of Steven's sermons over the years, testimony to his wisdom and compassion.

And I, after nearly forty years of voluntary compliance to the Word of Wisdom, began to brew black tea in my BYU office.

Joanna Brooks' *Mormonism and White Supremacy: American Religion and the Problem of Racial Innocence* (Oxford University Press, 2020) offers a new context for evaluating Steven's review of McConkie's and Millet's book *Our Destiny* and BYU's subsequent investigation and decision to fire him. "This book," Brooks tells readers with her first sentence, "seeks to instigate soul-searching—academic, institutional, and personal—on the matter of how American Christianity has contributed to white supremacy." With its historical priesthood ban for supposed black-skinned descendants of Cain, Mormonism provides a disturbing case history. Brooks addresses the official silence on the issue after the 1978 revelation that extended the priesthood to Black men, a troubling unwillingness to wrestle with a racist past. "To maintain control over the narrative," she writes, "the institutional LDS Church and Mormon culture repressed internal critique and dissent. In place of critical self-examination, the LDS Church has used multiculturalism, rhetorical evasion, and duplicity to manage the legacy of Mormon anti-Black racism without taking responsibility for it."

Steven's review took up the responsibility his leaders were shirking. "Is it possible," he asked, "just when the LDS community is emerging from ethnic, linguistic, and geographical parochialism to become a world-wide religion, that *Our Destiny* would unwittingly turn us back?" The question was doubly potent given the status of the authors and of the press that published the book.

Deseret Book, as I write, still offers an eBook version of *Our Destiny* for sale. Joseph Fielding McConkie, BYU Professor of Religion and author of more than two dozen books, was the son of Amelia Smith McConkie (the daughter of President Joseph Fielding Smith) and of apostle Bruce McConkie. Robert Millet was Dean of Religious Education at BYU and author of a series of books that eventually numbered more than sixty.

That Mormon writers would claim literal blood descent from Abraham earned by valiance in pre-mortal life and giving them rights to the priesthood and thus prospects of hierarchical advantages in the next life is not surprising. Such racist claims had been made by many Church leaders since Brigham Young, including Joseph McConkie's father-in-law Joseph Fielding Smith, whose book *The Way to Perfection* spoke of the curse of Cain and of his descendants (people whose black skin marked them with the curse). Joseph McConkie's father, Bruce McConkie claimed in his *Mortal Messiah* that Jews were cursed for rejecting Christ (explaining the suffering of millions of Jews over the centuries). His *Mormon Doctrine* explained that Blacks were denied the priesthood because of lack of valiance in the pre-mortal existence.

But the 1978 revelation extending the priesthood to Black men should have ended that. Bruce McConkie said as much in a devotional address at BYU on August 18, 1978 titled "All Are Alike unto God":

> We have read these passages and their associated passages for many years. We . . . have said to ourselves, "Yes, it says that, but we must read out of it the taking of the gospel and the blessings of the temple to the Negro people, because they are denied certain things." . . . We spoke with a limited understanding and without the light and knowledge that now has come into the world.

Still, McConkie held on to the belief that Black men had been denied the priesthood until 1978 because God required it:

> And the other underlying principle is that in the eternal providences of the Lord, the time had come for extending the gospel to a race and a culture to whom it had previously been denied, at least as far as all of its blessings are concerned. So it was a matter of faith and righteousness and seeking on the one hand, and it was a matter of the divine timetable on the other hand. The time had arrived when the gospel, with all its blessings and obligations, should go to the Negro.

Our Destiny, fifteen years later, continued the racist story.

And now I'm wondering about the institutional non-response to *Our Destiny*.

Why didn't someone at Deseret Book, owned by the Church, say: no, we're no longer in the business of publishing racist ideas?

Why didn't the General Authority members of the BYU Board of Trustees say: no, we are trying to move on from our institutional racism and this book works against that?

And most interesting for Steven Epperson's case, why didn't BYU administrators, at the latest when Steven's review appeared in *BYU Studies* in 1996, call in the Dean of Religious Education and the Professor of Ancient Scripture and require them to recall their book and to publicly recant its racist ideas?

Instead, Joseph McConkie's uncle Oscar (senior partner representing the LDS Church for the firm Kirton McConkie) threatened legal action. Instead, BYU administrators submitted Steven's book *Mormons and Jews* for review and asked what he would do if it were found to be doctrinally unsound. Instead, BYU administrators summarily fired Steven because, they said, his Bishop would not endorse his worthiness.

They should have promoted him and awarded him tenure for his service.

Castle Valley

EIGHT

Telling Stories

**A Review of *Remembering Brad: On the Loss of a Son to AIDS*
by H. Wayne Schow Salt Lake City (Signature Books, 1995)
160 pages, $15.95**

Sunstone, July 1997

Wayne Schow lost his son Brad to AIDS. I lost my brother John to the same scourge. Eight years after John's death I was privileged to review Schow's powerful book about his son. By the time I wrote the review, I had filled several notebooks with what I called "fraternal meditations," a practice I continued until the University of Utah Press published *Immortal for Quite Some Time* in 2016. I was writing my way into a story I could hardly imagine, a story that included John and in which he, I hoped, would have included me. It became a story, as time wore on, that required resignation from my job at BYU and from the Church whose stories still, even now, structure my identity. For better and for worse.

> I was working on a kind of puzzle—matching one set of colored squares with another After much exertion, I left them for a minute. When I returned, I found that John had dumped them all out. I beat him severely.
>
> I was beating up on John, repeatedly and brutally. He brought in an accountant who was going to investigate every aspect of my financial life. I would have to provide endless, detailed documentation.
>
> —Dreams, from *Immortal for Quite Some Time*

After the Boise coroner called and said my brother John had died (of pneumocystis pneumonia, a byproduct of AIDS), I drove with family members to Boise to pick up his personal effects. Among them was a manila envelope in which I had sent him, a year earlier, a bad Xerox copy of a copy of a copy of a letter written by Wayne Schow to a general authority of the LDs church. In the letter, as I remember it, Schow explained what recent experiences with his gay son had taught him about possible sources of our various sexual orientations and he outlined the effects of current LDS beliefs on our gay brothers and sisters. I say "as I remember it" because the lengthy letter was no longer in the envelope. John and I never talked about Schow's ideas, so I have no sense of how he responded; but I have often wondered since whether the letter gave him a sense of solidarity with Church members like Schow—or did he think it was simply a waste of words, having decided two or three years after serving his mission in Italy to leave behind, as well as he could, the religion that had dominated the first two decades of his life? There is no way to know, of course, but, looking back I wish John and I had read and discussed Schow's letter and now *Remembering Brad*.

This wish is related to questions I have recently asked myself: Why am I so anxious that my children become readers? Why does it please me so much when I find them, as I have recently, curled up with McCarthy's *All the Pretty Horses* (Knopf, 1992), or Banks's *The Indian in the Cupboard* (Avon, 1980), or the Bible. The answer I tend to at the moment is that we hope our children will read because of the value of multiple stories. The best stories, some of which are scriptural, work as powerful patterns. A culture that severely limits the number and quality of its stories and that discourages individual interpretation of the stories it does tell is powerful in producing conformity, but it is unable to meet the needs of, or provide useful paradigms for, its even slightly marginal members. A culture that encourages the telling and retelling of its shared stories while inviting new stories provides opportunities for the other as well as the same.

I'm not suggesting that all stories are equally good. There are destructive stories, stories that bind rather than free us. Pornography, for example, sets up destructive paradigms, while good erotic art opens possibilities for fuller lives. Stories that celebrate violence as the ultimate problem-solver are bad for us, while violent stories like those in Brian Evenson's *Altmann's Tongue* (Knopf, 1995) can unmask the immorality of violence and enhance our humanity. Good stories inform us of possibilities, allow us to compare our lives with those of historical and fictional characters, provide information and skills with which we can make our livings. Well-educated, we know not only Steven Covey's prescriptive *Seven Habits of Highly Effective People* (Simon and Schuster, 1989), but have access to thousands of characters, including Dostoevsky's axe-murderer and the abused and doggedly heroic women of Smiley's *A Thousand Acres* (Knopf, 1991). Good stories suggest the complexities of Emma Bovary's life, confront us with the required and paradoxical perfections of the Sermon on the Mount, tell us that the universe is vast and yet open to comprehension, impart the sad wisdom of Blind Lemon Jefferson's "See That My Grave Is Kept Clear," and teach us that blended pine nuts, fresh basil, garlic, olive oil, and Parmesan cheese are very tasty on pasta. In short, we read good stories in large numbers because they enable better lives.

Schow's reflections "On the Loss of a Son to AIDS" join a growing list of works written as acts of mourning in an LDS context. The best of these is Terry Tempest Williams's *Refuge: An Unnatural*

History of Family and Place (Pantheon, 1991), an account of cancer in the family, U.S. atmospheric atomic tests, and the delicate and erotic balances of nature. Carol Lynn Pearson wrote eloquently about her experiences with her husband's homosexuality and his battle with AIDS in *Good-bye, I Love You* (Random House, 1986). In *Peculiar People: Mormons and Same-Sex Orientation* (Signature, 1991), Ron Schow, Wayne Schow, and Marybeth Raynes collect a wide variety of personal and professional accounts that widen our perspectives (if not answering all our questions) on "Mormons and Same-Sex Orientation." And now Wayne Schow's honest and compelling book invites and enables us to think again about family and religion and sexuality.

Remembering Brad is divided into seven parts (plus a section of photos of Brad and his family and friends): a prologue, in which the author describes how the book came to be; five chapters that, first, in the context of literary tragedy (Schow is a professor of English at Idaho State University), sketch Brad Schow's biography; second, present entries from Brad's journals (by far the longest section of the book); third, offer a series of letters written by Wayne Schow to his son while he was away from home; fourth, attempt once again to revisit the last months of Brad's life, focusing on the roles the family came to play in their Pocatello society; and, fifth, trace the process of grieving, including the Schow's productive and ongoing outreach to others concerned with and by same-sex issues. Finally, as an epilogue, Schow ventures a parable of a relationship between an institutional church and individuals.

A natural response to the death of a loved one is to romanticize that person's life, to forget their faults and magnify their strengths. We have, as a result, few honest funerals or family histories. Like the rest of us, Schow has tendencies in that direction, but he is self-conscious and honest enough to make of this book more than a simple-minded celebration of the brave and noble son by his wise and charitable father. Brad Schow died of a disease he contracted through risky and even self-destructive behavior, a fact of which both he and his father were only too aware. As Brad wrote to a friend, "I was diagnosed with AIDS in July of last year, the result of my profligate life in Los Angeles." His journal entries repeatedly reflect the manic-depressive nature of his profligacy, of which I shall give a single example:

> August 4, 1982: I think at times that L.A. must be the coolest city on earth. But it's like too much cocaine. It gets to the point where you need more and more of it to get you off, and I don't feel like I'm getting high any more. So many unhappy people. So much frustration, so much pressure to live the illusion of a life of wealth and status—to be ONE OF THE BEAUTIFUL PEOPLE, man!

And Wayne Schow's letters to his son record the anguish of a father intensely worried about his son's choices but unable to do more than give advice like the following (and then to wonder if he is doing the right thing):

> I have the impression that the gay life in L.A. is hedonistic to an extreme—and that brings with it not only the much publicized health dangers (which you would indeed be wise to take seriously) but also dangers to the psyche, the will, undermining your sense of purpose with a continuing and debilitating quest for sensations and nouveau experience. That way lie frustration and personal nihilism—which I am aware you do not want. I speak in general terms—and with no intent to preach.

Though realistic and moral, the Schows' stories are not strands of a black-and-white medieval morality play but feel more akin to the literary tragedies Wayne Schow describes:

> the tragic vision of life embodies more than simply misfortune and loss, more than victimization and pathos. . . . Tragedy has a powerful affirmative side. Misfortune notwithstanding, tragic vision ultimately makes us aware of impressive dimensions in human nature. Instead of plunging us into despair at the prospect of life's cruel uncertainties, tragedy in the strict

> sense reconciles us to existence because it makes us believe that we can be greater than our fall. . . .

Brad Schow's journals reveal him as an intense, conflicted, honest, seeking, flawed, loving young man. But the real power of this book is in his father's life, in the education Wayne Schow undergoes from the moment his son comes out to him. Brad's perilous experiments, illness, and death, Schow writes in retrospect,

> caught me by surprise and left me dubious. First of all because his strong-willed temperament and his broad-shouldered physique hardly fit the common stereotype. But there was a second and even more compelling reason for me to deny the validity of his assertion: I accepted the prevailing view of the church that homosexuality is a perverse 'choice' of lifestyle, an impulse that can be overcome. With sufficient time to sort out his experience, surely a decent young man like Brad would not ultimately make such a choice. My son a queer? No. I had known him too long, too well to believe he really wanted such an identity. I felt certain that if he were patient he would come to recognize his assumption as fallacious and develop normal heterosexual desire, leading to marriage and a family.

As the story progresses, Schow is able to make a move not unlike the one I made in sending his letter to my brother, only the text he sends is Andre Gide's story "The Prodigal Son": "You will, I'm sure, find Gide deeply perceptive, deeply sympathetic, and extraordinarily honest about the nature of individual experience. I think you are aware that Gide himself was homosexual. He was indeed a great writer."

Through this act Schow tells his son that although Brad is not living the story Schow would have chosen for him, he recognizes that there are other stories, and that it is still crucial that Brad pattern his life after good stories, honest stories, well-written stories. By the end of the book, Schow has profound doubts about some of the stories that have structured his own life. And while still suffering deeply, he is grateful for what he has learned: "Yet even if [my grief] could be dispelled by some deep healing, I think it should not be. I would be loath to lose it altogether. It stands as a reminder of the truth about this flawed condition of mortality . . . I have acquired that knowledge dearly, and I do not wish to forget at what cost."

The cost was and is too dear, and in a better world would not have to be paid. But this is not a better world, and we are left with the narrative consolations of the Bible's and Gide's prodigal son, with *Refuge* and *Remembering Brad*. I would have wished my brother the pleasures and sorrows of those four stories. In his apartment, after his death, I found the following depressing and yet not utterly unredeeming assortment:

- Cassette tapes: "The Best of Judas Priest"; Guns and Roses—"Appetite for Destruction"; Anthrax—"State of Euphoria"; "Foghat Live."
- Twenty-six paperback novels, most of them with the front cover torn off: "Do not buy this book if the cover has been torn off!" Eric V Lustbader dominates the pile, but there are others as well:
- *Neon Mirage* by Max Allan Collins: "Mob Justice . . . Another shotgun blast ate into the side of Ragen's once-proud Lincoln."
- *Vision of the Hunter* by John Tempest: "In his hands, his people's future. In her eyes, the promise of a love stronger than time."
- Burt Hirshfeld's *Moment of Power*: "The savage new shocker. . . ."
- *Superconscious Meditation* by Panda Arya, Ph.D.
- *Self Hypnosis: The Creative Use of Your Mind for Successful Living* by Charles Tebbetts.
- Louis L'Amour's *Education of a Wandering Man*.
- *The Magnificent Century* by Thomas B. Costain.
- *Home As Found* by J. Fenimore Cooper.

- Radclyffe Hall's *The Well of Loneliness*: "Banned in the U.S.... Foreword by Havelock Ellis."
- Hoyle's *Rules of Games*, Second Revised Edition.
- *Basic Documents Supplement to International Law: Cases and Materials.*
- A 1953, fifty-cent paperback edition of Edith Hamilton's *Mythology*.
- *ETCETERA: The Unpublished Poems of e. e. cummings.*
- The dust jacket of a Modern Library edition: *The Philosophy of Kant*. The book itself was missing.

Epilogue
14 August 1972, Wickenburg, Arizona

While we drill an exploratory oil and gas well a few miles north of town, I've taken a room in an old motel crammed into one elbow of a highway-railroad intersection. My next door neighbor is a wizened ex-contortionist who looked deeply into my eyes the first time I said hello and told me she would read my palm if I would come into her room. I begged off, claiming I had a vague palm. Her name is Maria, and in the relative cool of the evenings, she maneuvers a hose to sprinkle the tiny plot of grass and flowers in front of our rooms. She wears a sleeveless blouse, a pair of loose shorts, and sneakers with no socks. She has tied white rags around her deeply tanned left calf and her equally brown left bicep, white semaphores that accentuate the contrast between the almost theoretical lines of her emaciated limbs and their pronounced, protuberant, grotesque joints. Galls. Burls. One evening she saw me staring at her bulbous elbows and went into a practiced explanation of how her mother used to tie her up in knots when she was a baby so she would be limber. She made it clear that she had never regretted that turn in her life, it leading to her eventual greatness and the chance to mingle with the truly great people of this century. And she is resigned to living out her days in Wickenburg, where the desert heat eases her arthritic joints.

Salt Valley Hills

NINE

Sinister Virtue: The Effects of Cultural Despair on Academic Freedom at a Private Religious University

Presented at the American Association of University Professors Conference on Religious Institutions and Academic Freedom: Chicago, 1997 (unpublished)

In their brilliantly detailed book, *The Lord's University: Freedom and Authority at BYU*, Bryan Waterman and Brian Kagel open the chapter titled "A Collision of Cultures: The Bateman Administration and the AAUP" with a dream:

> At the end of October 1996, BYU botanist Sam Rushforth had a dream. In it he and his wife, Nancy, stood beside a sick horse. Sam held a giant syringe of medicine that could cure the animal's illness. Just as he stood poised to plunge the needle, Nancy stopped him. "Look, Sam," she said. "Move away from the horse's rear

end. Sure, you're going to cure this thing, but when you do it's going to blast manure all over everything."[1]

As I remember it, Nancy said "horse's ass" and "it's going to blast shit"—more appropriate appellations in the fevered atmosphere of the day. But either way, it was clear to us that BYU was sick, that we were trying our best to heal the university, and that the response was going to be anything but pleasant. Waterman and Kagel continue with my own explosive imagery:

> "I've been feeling that I'm holding on to a lit stick of dynamite," [Scott Abbott] would say in the seclusion of his office, a Question Authority sticker taped to the wall above his desk. "I'm trying to gauge just how long I can hold it before throwing it."

Just how did we come to dream such dreams and think in those violent terms? For a meticulously researched version of the academic freedom fights at BYU during those years, read *The Lord's University*. But for those unacquainted with the events, I'll review a few details here.

In 1993, when Cecilia Konchar Farr and David Knowlton were told their scholarship was insufficient to pass their third-year tenure reviews, George Schoemaker, a folklore specialist in the English Department, came to my office and recommended that we do something in their defense. We gathered a group of colleagues to form an Ad Hoc Committee on Academic Freedom and began to gather CVs of faculty members who had passed third-year reviews that year. It quickly became clear that more than a few had passed with scholarship substantially less robust than the work Cecilia and David had done. A letter from Provost Bruce Hafen intervening in the review process suggested that the real reason for the denial was that Cecilia had given a pro-choice speech at an abortion-rights rally and that David had published an essay about how negative perceptions of the Church in South America might be altered through changes in dress and architecture, an argument that

---

1. (Salt Lake City: Signature Books, 1998) 368.

pointed out the hegemony represented by the phallic shape of the new Church Office Building. Our administrators had attempted to mask their displeasure by claiming inadequate scholarship.

That disingenuous practice changed three years later when they fired Gail Houston at her tenure review for activities that not only "failed to strengthen the moral vigor of the university, they have enervated its very fiber." And what were these powerful activities? Gail had written about comfort she found through praying to her Mother in Heaven.

In 1995, Sam Rushforth and I organized an official BYU chapter of the American Association of University Professors as a bulwark against increasingly blatant infringements on academic freedom, including attempts to control English professor Brian Evenson's literary activities. Several of us met with President Rex Lee to discuss the role we hoped to play as a chapter and to protest the attacks being leveled at Brian. Bert Wilson, an eminent scholar of folklore, broadened the discussion to included other recent cases and opined that we "seem subject to the tyranny of crackpots." Gail Houston's firing at the behest of BYU's new president, Merrill Bateman, himself a General Authority, gave us cause to turn to national officers of the AAUP for help. After reviewing documents we sent, they agreed to send an investigating committee.

A couple of days before the AAUP representatives were scheduled to arrive for their investigation, I got an evening call from BYU Academic Vice President Alan Wilkins.

Scott, he said, there's been a sighting.

A sighting of what? I asked.

The AAUP investigators are already on campus, he answered; one was seen leaving Susan Howe's office in the English Department.

How did they know he or she was from the AAUP?

He was wearing a ponytail, Alan said.

I pointed out that I was scheduled to pick the investigators up at the airport when they arrived, that they wouldn't arrive for two days, and that he ought to consider the source of the rumor.

When Linda Pratt (University of Nebraska-Lincoln, English) and William Heywood (Cornell College, History) in fact arrived, I managed their meetings with President Bateman and more than one hundred members of the faculty and student body. As I noted in my *Immortal for Quite Some Time*, one event stood out:

> ... I escorted President Bateman and two of his dark-suited vice presidents out of the room where they had met with the investigators. As their stiff, retreating backs passed through the door, one of the investigators looked at me in disbelief and rolled her eyes far back into her head.
>
> Somehow the risks and experiments enabled by academic freedom have taken on the hue of moral relativism in the minds of an administration that supposes it acts unequivocally from an absolute moral center. It's too bad. When I was hired the two vice presidents who interviewed me were more interested in what I was reading outside my discipline than in the orthodoxy of my beliefs. I put a new sign on my office door: CURB YOUR DOGMA.

The AAUP report censuring the BYU administration was published in 1997. A couple of paragraphs near the end of the long report are telling:

> The case of Professor Houston, along with those of Professors Farr, Knowlton, Evenson, and Epperson, persuades the investigating committee that BYU's *Statement on Academic Freedom* provides little guidance to the faculty about specific limitations to academic freedom. Numerous other reports of interference with the work of creative artists on campus, constraints placed on academic research (particularly on the subject of Mormonism itself), hostility to feminism and postmodern theory, and control of professors' participation in symposia devoted to an independent study of Mormonism sustain the pattern seen in the cases that have been reviewed. The number of cases in itself indicates that the limitations on academic freedom at Brigham Young University are not adequately stated

to guide faculty members away from areas of conflict. Instead of being based on principles of intellectual freedom or doctrinal policies of the Church, academic freedom at BYU strikes the investigating committee as often subject to the political concerns of Church officials who worry about new philosophical perspectives that seem to challenge tenets of Mormonism and about outspoken faculty members whose extramural utterances might embarrass the Church. Vice President Wilkins, in conversations with Professor Houston shortly before the final decision not to retain her, referred to the problem of press coverage of her case and stated that the university lived in "a glass house" where, presumably, the rocks of criticism could shatter the image.

The issues in these cases extend beyond the damage to individual careers or the failure of policies designed to state limitations and protect academic freedom. The administration's efforts to protect the orthodoxy of the institution hinder faculty members from scholarship and teaching that is current within their disciplines. The humanities and social sciences have been under particular fire because the influence of postmodernist theory, feminism, and revisions of the canon have most directly affected scholarly work in these fields. Ironically, Brigham Young University is also a dangerous place in which to be a scholar of Mormonism, since findings that are perceived to disturb the Church may result in efforts to stop the research. Faculty members who resist the pressure to alter or stop their research are at risk of losing their positions, as in the case of Professor Knowlton. Beyond Mormon specialists, women who defend the civil rights of pro-choice advocates in extramural remarks are subject to nonretention, as in the case of Professor Farr. Artists who resist "correction" are also at risk, as in the case of Professor Evenson. Faculty members who encounter problems with their bishop may suffer nonreappointment, as in the case of Professor Epperson. Feminist faculty members who question the soundness of gender roles in the Church may be denied continuing status, even when they have

> a "temple recommend" from their bishop, as in the case of Professor Houston.
>
> Much more than an isolated violation of academic freedom, the investigating committee's inquiries into complaints at BYU have revealed a widespread pattern of infringements on academic freedom in a climate of oppression and fear of reprisals.

Subsequently, Alan Wilkins sent a memo to members of the BYU faculty pointing out that the AAUP often acted as a labor union [oh no!] and that it had historically disapproved of religious colleges and universities. It must have surprised him, then, when the AAUP announced its conference on Religious Institutions and Academic Freedom later that year. I was invited to speak at the conference and the BYU administration was invited to send someone as well. They declined, citing supposed bias. My Department Chair was informed that I was to receive no funding for the trip.

In Chicago, during the question-and-answer session after I delivered my paper, Keith Wilson, a BYU professor of religion, rose and told the audience that I was among a very small minority of the faculty who disagreed with the administration concerning academic freedom. Session moderator, the AAUP's Jordan Kurland, pointed out that the AAUP made its assessments of violations on the basis of facts and not on the basis of majority opinion.

In his study of the origins of what he calls "the German ideology," Fritz Stern explores

> the pathology of cultural criticism . . . of cultural despair. Lagarde, Langbehn, and Moeller van den Bruck . . . attacked, often incisively and justly, the deficiencies of German culture and the German spirit. . . .
> As moralists and as the guardians of what they thought was an ancient tradition, they attacked the progress of modernity—the growing power of liberalism and secularism. They enumerated the discontents of Germany's

> industrial civilization and warned against the loss of faith, of unity, of "values." *The Politics of Cultural Despair: A Study in the Rise of the Germanic Ideology*

Every civilization has its discontents, and moralists are always poised to attack liberalism and secularism and to decry lost faith, unity, and values. What follows is my analysis of this process as it has played out at BYU.

Brigham Young University's official "Statement on Academic Freedom" (1 April 1993) asserts that "Freedom of thought, belief, inquiry, and expression are crucial no less to the sacred than to the secular quest for truth. . . . [N]either testimony, nor righteousness, nor genuine understanding is possible unless it is freely discovered and voluntarily embraced. . . . Perhaps no condition is as important to creating a university as is the freedom of the individual faculty member 'to teach and research without interference.'"

At the end of January 1997, at the request of its BYU Chapter, a committee of the American Association of University Professors visited BYU to investigate the denial of tenure to Gail Houston, an assistant professor of English. Houston was denied tenure, the official letter stated, because of "the number and severity of occasions when your actions and words on and off campus . . . were perceived as harmful to tenets held by the Church and the university. We feel that not only have these activities failed to strengthen the moral vigor of the university, they have enervated its very fiber" (June 5, 1996 letter from the administration to Houston). In its initial response to this situation, the AAUP argued that "the university administration's willingness and ability to stand up for academic freedom is weak indeed." The final report, published in the September/October 1997 issue of *Academe*, states that "Brigham Young University, in establishing limitations upon academic freedom, fails to give adequate guidance to the faculty . . . infringements on academic freedom are distressingly common and . . . the climate for academic freedom is distressingly poor."

What has happened to make BYU administrators come to regard academic freedom, a virtue they themselves had vigorously espoused, as somehow sinister? The short answer is that successive BYU administrations have chosen to severely limit academic freedom at BYU because of their wholesale acceptance of a rhetoric of "cultural despair." Whatever its justification and effect on U.S. public and private universities, its effect on BYU has been to unsettle a precarious balance.

BYU has long attempted to balance the spiritual and the secular, most recently and most explicitly in the "Statement on Academic Freedom" cited above. The statement defends what it calls institutional academic freedom while asserting the necessity of individual academic freedom:

> Thus BYU defines itself as having a unique religious mission and as pursuing knowledge in a climate of belief.... To force religious institutions to comply with narrowly secular definitions of academic freedom is to further imperil the survival of these distinctive intellectual communities. . . . Nevertheless, institutional freedom is a prerogative that, if regarded as absolute, would invite abuse. Therefore, academic freedom must include not only the institution's freedom to claim a religious identity but also the individual's freedom to ask genuine, even difficult questions.

Based largely on an article by Michael W. McConnell ("Academic Freedom in Religious Colleges and Universities," *Law and Contemporary Problems* 53.3 [1990]: 227–301), the argument for institutional academic freedom, especially as tempered by careful qualification as above, found general acceptance among BYU faculty. Disagreement arose, however, over the "reasonable limitations" the document lays out, with objections voiced about the non-specific nature of the limitations and about the resulting openness to idiosyncratic interpretations, especially as the administration and Board of Trustees retained the right unilaterally to determine harm.

Unfortunately, since its adoption (without faculty vote) in 1993, the University administration has radically skewed the balance in favor of "institutional academic freedom" and against "individual academic freedom." There is not room here to cite all the examples (for more detailed accounts see the AAUP report in *Academe*, Martha Nussbaum's analysis in of BYU and Notre Dame in chapter eight of her *Cultivating Humanity: A Classical Defense of Reform in Liberal Education* (Harvard UP, 1997), and the anonymous "Clipped and Controlled," *Sunstone* 19:3 [1996]: 61–72). Several dozen members of the faculty have been forced to leave or have left on their own, departments have lost much of their ability to determine whom they will hire and promote, numbers of non-Mormon faculty have declined precipitously (it was already less than 5%), faculty have come under fire for writing about the Mormon Church (work that has been determined variously to be unduly critical, too ecumenical, or harmful to the Church's missionary effort), and there have been repercussions for a controversial book of short stories (judged immoral), for teaching feminism, postmodernism, and certain contemporary novels (i.e. Margaret Atwood's *Surfacing*), and for politicizing the classroom.

To justify the proliferating limits on academic freedom that have drawn AAUP attention, the BYU administration has turned repeatedly to the arguments and rhetoric of Alan Bloom's *The Closing of the American Mind*, to the 1990–1992 series of articles in the journal *First Things* about the secularization of American universities, and most recently to a speech by Gertrude Himmelfarb that appeared in *First Things*.

Not long after Alan Bloom published *The Closing of the American Mind* (1987), he spoke to an admiring audience at BYU. Subsequently, his book was named university book-of-the-month and was featured in great quantities and at a large discount at the BYU bookstore. We learned from Bloom "how higher education has failed democracy and impoverished the souls of today's students," that German thinkers like Nietzsche and Heidegger have imposed a sophisticated nihilism on our educational system, and that only drastic action can raise us out of the resulting swamp of moral relativism. At about the same time, the authors of the *First Things* articles (cited not only in our "Statement of Academic Freedom," but in every discussion of academic freedom at BYU since) taught us that the balance between the academic and the spiritual we had so carefully laid out is virtually impossible and that despite all indicators (the LDS Church supplies a large percentage of the university's budget, over 95% of all faculty are practicing Mormons, etc.), only extreme measures will keep us from secularization. Gertrude Himmelfarb's address on the occasion of the installation of the new president of Baylor University ("The Christian University: A Call to Counterrevolution." *First Things* 59 [1996]: 16–19), featuring alarmist rhetoric like "utterly disastrous for the university," "prescription for intellectual and moral nihilism," "profoundly subversive," "absolute relativism," and "a revulsion in society at large," inspired new BYU President Merrill Bateman, in his own inaugural address, to repeat her arguments (without attribution) and to call to arms against "the moral relativism spreading throughout higher education."

In the resulting climate, the necessary and potentially productive risks and experiments enabled by academic freedom have taken on the hue of moral relativism. As such they have engendered fear and have brought censure from an administration that supposes it acts unequivocally from an absolute moral center.

The development I have sketched here has an analogue in the recent history of Arab universities, as described by Edward Said in "Identity, Authority, and Freedom: The Potentate and the Traveler" (in *The Future of Academic Freedom*, ed. Louis Menand, University of Chicago Press [1996]: 214–228). Dominated for centuries by colonial powers, newly independent Arab countries turned to their universities to help shape national identity, and the result was a new flowering of the Arabic language, Arab history, and Arab culture in general. When, however, the universities became tools of the national security state, when "nationalism in the university [came] to represent not freedom but accommodation, not brilliance and daring but caution and fear, not the advancement of knowledge but self-preservation" (219), the educational enterprise was short-circuited. "For those of us just emerging from marginality and persecution," Said writes, "nationalism is a necessary thing: a long-deferred and long-denied identity needs to come out into the open and take its place among other human identities. But that is only the first step.... A single overmastering identity at the core of the academic enterprise ... is a confinement, a deprivation" (226–227).

On this model, BYU's argument for institutional academic freedom as necessary for preservation of identity makes good sense. Mormons (and perhaps society at large) are well served by a university in which the culture and values of Mormonism are taken seriously. However, Said notes, when "political conformity rather than intellectual excellence [is] made to serve as a criterion for promotion and appointment ... timidity, a studious lack of imagination, and careful conservatism [come] to rule intellectual practice" (219). And a university ceases to be a university.

As demonstrated by the case of BYU, at least by my reading of the situation there, the sanctification of supposed absolute values in the rhetoric of cultural despair by Bloom, Himmelfarb, et al. can, in a situation like ours, catalyze a movement away from academic freedom, the *sine qua non* of university life. When moral relativism as supposedly propounded by postmodernism becomes the major evil, when fear of secularization dominates all thinking, when identity thinking rules all decisions, academic freedom becomes a sinister virtue.

Toward Hite

TEN

Debating the Possibility of a Mormon University

Documents from My Appeal of the Administration's Denial of Promotion

1998 (unpublished)

My application for promotion from associate to full professor featured a robust section on service. I highlighted my AAUP activities, including my role in the AAUP investigation that had resulted in a stinging censure of the BYU administration. The application was not received well by the administrators in charge of tenure and promotion, although my department colleagues and the College advancement committee strongly recommended promotion. I filed an appeal with the help of Sam Rushforth, co-president of the BYU Chapter of the AAUP, a botanist with an international reputation and my dear friend. Vice President Jim Gordon, who had denied promotion in the first place, appointed the appeal committee. In a series of letters, Sam protested that obvious unfairness, appealing to Jim's common sense. Jim quoted policy and refused to comment on fairness. This was not meant to be a fair appeal. Knowing that, we were free to turn the appeal into forum on what a Mormon University ought to look like.

James D. Gordon III
Associate Academic Vice President
May 7, 1998

Dear Professor Abbott:

We regret to inform you that the University has decided not to grant you an advancement in rank to full professor. This decision was reached after consideration of the recommendations of the department and college committees, the Department Chair, the Dean, the University Faculty Council on Rank and Status, and the Academic Vice President. The final decision was made by the President. Below is a summary of the University Faculty Council's response to your file:

> "We regret that we cannot support your promotion to full professor. This decision was difficult to make and was reached only after a great deal of deliberation at several levels of review.
>
> "First, it should be made clear that this decision was not made on the basis of deficient teaching or scholarship. In teaching we note that you have received high student ratings, which are supported by the observations of your peers. Regarding scholarship, both external and internal reviewers rate your work as strong. In addition, you are viewed as making a positive contribution to the intellectual climate of the department.
>
> "With respect to citizenship, we believe that your zeal to change policy at BYU has driven you to actions and statements that have taken you beyond the bounds of propriety for a citizen of this University. Section 3.1.10

of the University Policy on Faculty Rank and Status states, 'A Faculty Rank and Status review . . . focuses not merely on the presence or absence of harm, but on the 'quality of the faculty member's overall <u>affirmative contribution</u> to the University.' We believe that the evidence argues that more affirmative contributions could have been made."

The specific combined reasons for the conclusions of the Dean, the Faculty Council on Rank and Status, the Academic Vice President, and the President that you are not ready to be advance to the rank of full professor are stated below.

Section 3.2.2 of the University Policy on Faculty Rank and Status provides:

> "As an institution supported by the Church of Jesus Christ of Latter-day Saints, Brigham Young University expects all of its personnel to adhere to the highest principles of personal behavior. . . . They should not denigrate fellow faculty members. . . . They should not abuse the moral climate of discourse on the campus. Although professionalism requires rigorous review and critique, faculty should always interact with colleagues . . . and other with civility. . . . At the very least, faculty members' relations with . . . colleagues must be professional, avoiding disruption, manipulation, and contention."

Appropriate methods for expressing disagreement with University policy and decisions exist. A faculty member may discuss issues with the administration and colleagues, follow the established grievance and appeal procedures, make suggestions to the Faculty Advisory Council, and express views publicly in a civil manner. However, the methods you have used are inconsistent with the citizenship expectations set forth in University policy. You have engaged in a pattern of contentious criticism of the University, Church leaders, faculty colleagues in another college in the University, and others that falls below the standards of civility for a BYU faculty member. Although you apologized for publicly criticizing Church leaders, your general pattern of behavior has continued. The emphasis of these activities has been to pressure the University to change policies of the Board of Trustees. Your behavior does not meet the standards of citizenship expected of a full professor at the University.

In addition, you have engaged in a pattern of publishing and presenting factually incorrect statements without citing references or verifying the statements, which falls below the standard of care in academic discourse. For example, you have stated that since the adoption of the academic freedom statement "several dozen members of the faculty have been forced to leave or have left on their own" (Scott Abbott, "Sinister Virtue: The Effects of Cultural Despair on Academic Freedom at a Private Religious University," presented October 25, 1997, Chicago, Illinois) and that "numbers of non-Mormon faculty have declined precipitously" (Id.). These statements are factually incorrect. Your false assertions and failures to cite references and verify your information are inconsistent with the standards of professionalism expected of a faculty member.

As the Faculty Council stated above, a rank advancement decision focuses not merely on whether a faculty member has harmed the University of the Church, but rather on the quality of the faculty member's overall affirmative contribution to the University. Your overall affirmative contribution to the University does not meet the level expected of a full professor. While your Dean concludes that you are not ready for advancement to full professor, he pledges his willingness to work with you so that you can soon merit promotion in every aspect of your work for the University.

We realize that this must be a disappointing decision for you. There is an appeal process that you may consider and initiate if you so choose. The details of that process are described in Section 12 of the University Policy on Faculty Rank and Status:

Professorial. We sympathize with your disappointment at this outcome and wish you well in your efforts in the future.

Sincerely,

James D. Gordon III, Associate Academic Vice President

Van C. Gessel, Dean

And so I appealed. As required by policy, I sent a summary of the appeal to the committee. The university representative, a professor of chemistry, sent me his eleven-page response, which he then read at the appeal hearing.

Response to Scott Abbott's
Appeal Summary of 30 October 1998
Prepared by Earl Woolley, University Representative,
15 January 1999

Scott Abbott was denied advancement to the rank of professor because of inadequate citizenship.... The appeal panel shall review the president's decision with the following presumptions:

> In considering the substantive merits of the faculty member's ... advancement in rank the panel shall presume that the president's decision is reasonable and justifiable. Therefore, the burden of persuasion lies with the faculty member who must demonstrate that the president's decision is without reasonable basis in light of all the information presented. (Section 12.9)

. . .

Reasons for the Decision

. . .

The issue in Abbott's application for promotion was not whether he violated BYU's Academic Freedom Statement, but rather whether his overall affirmative contribution in citizenship warranted advancement to full professor. The University Faculty Council on Rank and Status concluded, "We believe that the evidence argues that more affirmative contributions could have been made." (7 May 1998 Letter)

. . .

Abbott publicly criticized Elders Dallin H. Oaks, Neal A. Maxwell, and Boyd K. Packer of being "purveyors" of anti-intellectualism. . . . Abbott then stated, "Again I ask, why do they and so many others defend faith over reason in what our theology teaches is a false dichotomy?" (Sunstone 16:3, p. 20) In other words, Abbott argued that the teachings of these Apostles contradicted LDS theology.

. . .

The 1992 Sunstone article continues to be a probable source of damage to the university, as noted in Dean Gessel's letter:

> Scott wrote letters of apology to three of the apostles he referred to in his Sunstone article. But how many people today who pick up the September 1992 issue of that journal are aware of Scott's "retraction"? The potentially harmful statements are still in place, still bearing the potential of influencing readers to question the inspiration of individuals who are even today sustained as prophets, seers, and revelators, and to wonder how widespread is the perception among BYU faculty that the Church leaders are "out of touch." Without a public expression of apology—assuming that Scott feels apologetic—the article stands as written. It has become a public document, independent of its author, its ideas floating out there for all to ingest. (Dean Van Gessel, 29 November 1997)

. . .

Abbott stated that faculty hired in Religious Education are not teacher-scholars, that they are not qualified, and that they do fit the "unctuous" seminary teacher mold. "Unctuous" is defined as oily, insincerely smooth, or characterized by a smugly or ingratiatingly sentimental pretense of spirituality. These statements are public personal attacks that denigrate fellow BYU faculty members.

. . .

Abbott has also engaged in a pattern of contentious criticism against the University. As President of the local chapter of the American Association of University Professors, Abbott led the effort to have the national organization publicly censure BYU. Dean Van Gessel's letter states that

> . . . the university has been held up to national ridicule. The sad fact is that when this university is exposed to public humiliation, one cannot protect the Church from suffering as an accomplice. Were there a Hippocratic Oath governing university citizenship, I think it would open with the words, "First, do not harm." To cite but one palpable example of potential harm that has emerged from Scott's activities: if BYU is censured next summer by vote of the AAUP . . . the published job listings for the Modern Language Association, the primary source of academic employment information for the humanities, will print BYU's name as a censured institution in the preface of every edition and actively encourage candidates not to apply for jobs we might list. Scott has, thus, been directly involved in the process of discouraging qualified scholars from joining him at BYU. (Dean Van Gessel, 29 November 1997)

. . .

Efforts that bring to the University public censure, humiliation in the national press, damage to its reputation, and encouragement of scholars to not affiliate with it are inconsistent with the highest principles of personal behavior. These actions abuse the moral climate of discourse on campus, and they are beyond the bounds of civility for a BYU faculty member. To attempt to pressure this University to change its policies through public censure by an outside group is neither productive nor constructive criticism. Instead, it is disruptive, manipulative, and contentious criticism.

Abbott has also engaged in contentious criticism of the University regarding the temple conduct standard. ("On Ecclesiastical Endorsement at Brigham Young University, Sunstone 20: 1 April 1997, pp. 9–14) In connection with the temple conduct standard, he described BYU as a "sanctimonious edifice" (p. 9) and as a "formalistic, impatient, over-pious community." (p. 11) In a statement aimed at those responsible for the temple conduct standard, he wrote, "And why do we ignore the clear words of Jesus Christ? 'Ye blind guides, which strain at a gnat, and swallow a camel' (Matthew 23:24)." (p. 14)

Abbott's efforts to bring censure to the University by AAUP and his contentious criticisms are even more problematic given that the Academic Freedom Statement and the temple conduct standard were adopted by the Board of Trustees, which includes the First Presidency and several members of the Quorum of the Twelve Apostles. These are people whom we sustain as prophets, seers, and revelators, and they deem these policies important to the fulfillment of BYU's mission. Faculty may disagree publicly with University policies. However, faculty should use particular sensitivity and civility when they consider public criticism of the decisions of Church leaders. The Academic Freedom Statement provides that the faculty "assumes an obligation of dealing with sensitive issues sensitively and with a civility that becomes believers." (Section II.C.4)

Academic Vice President Alan L. Wilkins has stated:

> When we use outside agencies to try to pressure others against, say, a temple eligibility standard, we are on dangerous ground. These tactics invite the spirit of contention and damage our relationship with prophets of God.... They have ... prayerfully decided to ask us to accept this commitment as a minimum standard for worthiness of BYU employees who are members of the Church. To fight against this standard, especially publicly, is to fight with God's prophets and will certainly harm our attempts to become a Zion university. That is the world's approach to influence and change. Righteous attempts to influence in God's kingdom come from persuasion, gentleness, meekness, love unfeigned, prayer, fasting, and faith. And righteous influence attempts are made with humility before the Lord's anointed. ("Journeying Toward A Zion University," 1997 Annual University Conference, at 42).

...

In an address at an AAUP conference in 1997, Abbott stated:

> Unfortunately, since [the Academic Freedom Statement's] adoption (without faculty vote) in 1993, the University administration has radically skewed the balance in favor of "institutional academic freedom" and against "individual academic freedom." There is not room here to cite all the examples . . .; but in short: several dozen members of the faculty have been forced to leave or have left on their own. . . . ("Sinister Virtue: The Effects of Cultural Despair on Academic Freedom at a Private Religious University," a paper given by Abbott at the AAUP Conference on Religious Institutions and Academic Freedom, Chicago, IL, 24–26 October 1997)

Since "several" means at least three, Abbott publicly stated that at least 36 faculty members have left BYU since the Academic Freedom Statement was adopted. His statement implied that those faculty members left BYU for academic freedom reasons. Abbott should provide the names of at least 36 BYU faculty members who he can document have been forced to leave or have left BYU for academic freedom reasons between 1992 and 1997. Otherwise, it would appear that his public statement at the AAUP conference in 1997 was factually incorrect.

. . .

At the appeal hearing Abbott intends to assert the necessity of critical voices and his view of academic freedom at BYU. However, neither of these matters is the issue of the denial of advancement to professor.

. . .

Abbott's appeal must show that there was no reasonable basis for the President's decision. . . . [I]t is very difficult to argue that President Bateman's decision was without reasonable basis. Therefore, the President's decision should be sustained.

When the University representative was finished, Sam spoke as my faculty representative.

From time to time events of seeming modest import are revealed to be of larger substance and moment than previously thought. I suggest that the appeal hearing we attend today is such an event.

On the surface, we evaluate the application of Professor Scott Abbott for advancement from Associate Professor of German to Full Professor of German. I believe all of us would agree that Professor Abbott's scholarship and teaching are superb, even exemplary. . . .

There are those, however, who have taken exception with what is known at Brigham Young University as citizenship: the absence of causing ripples, no writing or speaking on controversial topics, no offering of any sort of eccentric point of view, no visibility on any issue that has the slightest potential for making a member of the administration or Board of Trustees nervous, no controversy, no speaking out, no mix of heady and intoxicating new ideas. Citizenship at Brigham Young University has come to mean sitting on university committees, being a boy-scout leader and performing weekly church duties. Clean and simple.

Requiring citizenship of this ilk vitiates a university. It is antithetical to academic excellence, chilling to a community of scholars engaged in study together, and stultifying to personal intellectual and moral growth.

Human beings are open learning systems. We learn our humanness, we are taught our morality, and we grow generation by generation in collective intellectual potential. And all of this is chancy and has the potential to fail. We rely on culture to provide us with much of the material to make us human. Being a human being is riskier than being another large mammal. We can abjectly fail to reach our human potential. This is the risk that every generation takes, a risk that every parent takes, a risk that all institutions take. There is no escaping it, learning to become human is difficult, risky, frightening in the possibility for failure.

There is nothing wrong with a conservative approach to teaching and learning. Many, perhaps most, of the concepts we learned as children may have potential to help us find our way now and in the future. But clearly not all of our cherished concepts about the world and how it works are useful. Some are outdated or even harmful. It is often the case that our notions about how the world works, or at least should work, are so much a part of us that we have little room for hearing or tolerating the views of others. And it is even more frightening when a person comes along and suggests that our well-worn system may have some problems, may not work as well as it might. We may become so frightened by challenges to our worldview that we become angry with the messenger who suggests new ways, offers new paradigms. Bertolt Brecht explored this problem in his play *Galileo*.

> PHILOSOPHER: May I pose the question: Why should we go out of our way to look for things that can only strike a discord in the ineffable harmony? . . .
> GALILEO (keeping his temper): "Truth is the daughter of Time, not Authority." Gentlemen, the sum of our knowledge is pitiful. It has been my singular good fortune to find a new instrument which brings a small patch of the universe a little bit closer. It is at your disposal.
> PHILOSOPHER: Where is all this leading?
> GALILEO: Are we, as scholars, concerned with where truth might lead us?
> PHILOSOPHER: Mr. Galilei, the truth might lead us anywhere!
> GALILEO: I can only beg you to look through my eyeglass.
> MATHEMATICIAN (wild): If I understand Mr. Galilei correctly, he is asking us to discard the teachings of two thousand years.
> GALILEO: For two thousand years we have been looking at the sky and didn't see the four moons of Jupiter, and they were there all the time. Why defend shaken teachings? You should be doing the shaking.

While it is clear that Professor Abbott has never challenged the underlying tenets of the Mormon Church, he has asked us to look at the world in a slightly eccentric way and consider that we may find new ways of being at our university, new ways that have the potential to make us a better and greater institution. He has pointed out to us that the ways we have acted in the past may be less than adequate. He has supported our colleagues at Brigham Young University who have been unjustly accused and fired for spurious reasons. Professor Abbott has worked tirelessly to establish a chapter of the American Association of University Professors on our campus—an organization that is dedicated to improving academic freedom, shared governance, and due process for faculty members. Professor Abbott has been guilty of suggesting that we have the potential to improve, to become better than we are, to begin finally to reach our full potential.

And for this work, Professor Abbott has been denied promotion.

At BYU contentious criticism and affirmative citizenship are code-words. They mean don't speak out on controversial matters unless you are on the safe side of the issue. They mean keeping your best and most eccentric ideas to yourself or at best shared with one or two trusted colleagues. They mean tenure, advancement or retirement are too important to make waves.

Biologist Lewis Thomas and others have pointed out that passing genetic information perfectly from generation to generation can be achieved with relative ease. The trick, it turns out, is not to pass unchanged information but to allow a certain amount of change to filter through, change that ultimately will be responsible for the evolution and survival of the species. And here's the deal. Just enough novel information must filter through to allow for necessary change without damaging the integrity of the extant gene pool.

A parallel situation exists in social systems. We must somehow design social systems that exhibit stability while at the same time allowing enough new information to filter through to ensure the long-term survival of the system. In modern culture, we have built several methods for embracing novel information. One of the most important is the invention of the modern university. The role of the university is to be a "disorder generator." The university is responsible for questioning everything we do in society and how we do it and for devising new strategies for living better lives.

This makes universities frightening places. Disorder and questioning the known are uncomfortable propositions. But without disorder and questioning, society stagnates, stultifies and risks extinction. And a university must have the internal strength to allow questioning and inquiry to exist. In fact, a healthy university encourages questioning and is not threatened when one of its members pushes sensitive, even uncomfortable boundaries. If an institution is not able to allow such questioning, it is not a university but something other, something less.

Brigham Young University is currently awash in fear. The firings of David Knowlton, Cecilia Konchar Farr, Gail Houston, and others have dampened the willingness of many of our colleagues to speak out. This is a dangerous and restrictive situation, a situation of great peril for a university.

Professor Abbott's work has been to ask us to question the ways we have behaved in the past and to look forward to better and more productive activities and interactions. It is only a diminished community of scholars and administrators that would be threatened by his voice. Instead of celebrating the life-giving diversity among our community, we single out Professor Abbott and others and suggest they should be punished.

Professor Abbott returned to Brigham Young University, leaving a tenured position at Vanderbilt, to devote himself to the growth and expanding excellence of our institution. Professor Abbott has worked for the betterment of this university in every way. He is a consummate academic. But equally important, he has been willing to see the future in new ways. He has been willing to examine the past and point out our errors, not for any spurious or malicious reason but because he thinks we can be better. Scott came to Brigham Young University because he holds a vision of our institution that is better than reality. And he has the courage and drive to work toward the realization of that alternative Brigham Young University. If we are not willing to hear voices like that offered by Professor Abbott, how can we grow?

I hope Scott's dreams of a better BYU are someday reached, but this will never occur unless and until we are able to tolerate, even celebrate the different voices we hear among us.

When Sam was finished, it was my turn.

We are meeting today in the Humanities Dean's Conference Room where two years ago I introduced you, Associate Academic Vice President Noel Reynolds, and you, Associate Academic Vice President Cheryl Brown, and others, including President Bateman, to the two investigators from the AAUP. You spoke in defense of BYU as a place where we have more academic freedom than academics do elsewhere. Three of you on this committee are on public record as opposing the conclusions I and nearly a hundred of our colleagues came to, conclusions subsequently reached by the AAUP, by Martha Nussbaum in her book *Cultivating Humanity*, and to some extent by the BYU Faculty Advisory Committee.

Imagine what it feels like to me to address an appeal to a committee several of whom are administrators in the office of the very Academic Vice President who decided I was not worthy of promotion.

I am a writer and a teacher. I write and teach mostly about German literature, about texts by Goethe, Schiller, Rilke, Peter Handke, and others. As a citizen of this University, it is also my responsibility to think about ways to improve the atmosphere here for learning and teaching. I felt that responsibility at Vanderbilt University, where I taught for seven years. I felt that responsibility at Princeton University, where I was a faculty member for two years.

I still remember my first faculty meeting at Princeton, held in Nassau Hall in a room that had been exposed to the elements by a British cannonball during the Revolutionary War. The meeting was opened by an invocation by the University Chaplain who asked the Lord (not without some gentle irony, knowing his audience) to "Bless us who labor here at Thy University." It made immediate sense to me, for any institution engaged in serious education is engaged in holy work. At that moment I committed myself to the moral responsibility of good thinking and good teaching and of being an active citizen of the academy.

As an appeal committee whose task is severely limited by BYU regulations, you are only authorized to decide whether, given our current policies, there was a "reasonable basis" for denial of promotion. I can perform that task for you. Given our current policies—policies, I should remind you, that the Faculty Advisory Council is attempting to improve—there was indeed a "reasonable basis" to deny promotion. But those policies are flawed. They are policies that over the past six years have cut away at the fundamental principles upon which any university must be built. They have slowed the momentum that you and I and our colleagues have worked hard to establish.

Even if you were to be moved by my arguments, even if you were to agree that some of our policies hinder us as we try to think well and teach well, even if you were to decide that I am not the misguided and dangerous zealot Jim Gordon says I am, it would make no difference. BYU regulations give you only an advisory say in the matter. President Bateman will make the final decision without having heard the arguments we are making here today, without having spoken with me. This is an exercise in pretending there is faculty governance at BYU. I'm not naive enough to think I'll win this appeal. There's no way in hell I could win this appeal. But as long as I am at BYU, as long as I am an educator, I'll continue to carry out the moral commitment I made in 1979 in Nassau Hall. Fairness matters. Academic freedom matters. Universities matter. Truth matters.

The History of My Case

I was first denied promotion in 1993, ostensibly on the basis of deficient scholarship. That same year, Cecilia Konchar Farr and David Knowlton were denied continuation on the tenure track because of their own supposedly deficient scholarship. In response, George Schoemaker, Sam Rushforth, I, and others formed an Ad-hoc

Committee on Academic Freedom to support our colleagues. We collected publication lists from everyone who had passed a third-year review that year and compared them to Cecilia's and David's publications. When we published the results that showed they ranked among the very best of those with positive outcomes, university administrators corrected themselves and admitted that the deciding issues had been related to citizenship.

My department chair Alan Keele did not immediately give me the letter denying my promotion, but spent over a month engaged in an informal appeal of the decision. I passed Rex Lee one day in the administration building and he gripped my arm and said: "We're trying to do what we can for you." It made no sense to me—I knew nothing about Alan's appeal—but I appreciated the personal attention from Rex. A month later, on his way to Lake Powell, Rex called Alan to report that "We can't take Scott's name to the Board at this time." Alan then gave me the official letter denying promotion on the basis of insufficient scholarship.

The real basis for the denial was a paper I had read at the 1992 *Sunstone* Symposium: "One Lord, One Faith, Two Universities: Tensions between Religion and Thought at BYU." Rex's admission to Alan was a clear indication that someone on the Board of Trustees had taken umbrage at the article and that the scholarship issue was an attempt to appease that person or persons while keeping the real issue cloaked.

During the demonstrations against the Knowlton and Konchar-Farr decisions, my colleague Bill Davis was asked by a TV reporter if he was calling our administrators liars. Yes, he said. The next morning, he joked that he had heard the word "lawyers." Lawyer, liar—how can we respect an administration that scrambles to do someone else's bidding and then lies about the reasons?

This spring, stung, perhaps, by our disclosures of their earlier perfidy, the administration was straightforward about their decision being related to my role as a university citizen. My application for promotion was denied for reasons I will address in turn.

Zeal to Change Policy

A careful look at what I have written since arriving at BYU will show that my concerns have been not to change policy but to oppose changes in policy and practice that threaten the university I chose to be part of in 1988, leaving a newly tenured position at Vanderbilt University. I have been critical of the following changes, some of them official, others unwritten but still enforced.

- Departments of Religion have steadily undermined their previously strong academic base by hiring teachers rather than scholar/teachers. I documented this and noted that it weakened the role of religious studies at a university supposedly committed to religious studies.
- The unwritten and thus unofficial but still threatening ban on participation in symposia like the annual *Sunstone* symposium undermines our academic freedom. Members of the Sociology Department protested this limitation and I discussed its problematic nature as well. Administrators clearly understood the embarrassment of an outright ban and attempted to have it both ways: limiting participation while appearing to support the right to present results of research at conferences.
- The new contract requiring annual ecclesiastical endorsement added a coercive aspect to our employment and to our religious practice. I published an essay arguing against that new policy.
- The new academic freedom document placed institutional prerogatives over academic freedom as traditionally defined. I argued against this in a series of memos for the Faculty Advisory Council, in a public debate, and in several publications.

- New limitations on hiring non-Mormons and increased administrative scrutiny of Mormon candidates have impinged on departmental responsibilities. The fact that administrators give no reasons for their decisions leaves us scrambling in the dark as we go about the difficult work of hiring good colleagues. I argued against this in a series of internal memos and in a publication.

My zeal, then, has been to defend reasonable policies that have been changed in ways that harm our mission as an LDS university.

Lack of Affirmative Contributions

I'll simply note the statement concerning positive contributions of my work as a critic by the College Committee on Advancement in Rank (which unanimously recommended promotion):

> ... that both the possibility and the actuality of thoughtful dissent are, themselves, essential to the flourishing of any truth-seeking community, and especially to a university community, requires no defense. . . . At his trial, Socrates described his gadfly function as a form of divine service and humorously asserted that no greater good had ever befallen his beloved fellow-Athenians than this service to his god. We are similarly disposed to value Scott's gadfly function at BYU. Whatever the merits finally of any of his particular challenges to BYU policy or practice, we find the challenges, themselves, stimulating and provoking of self-examination, and hence, salutary. BYU, like Athens, very much needs some citizens like Scott Abbott.

Of course Socrates didn't fare too well. And of course I am no Socrates. But it feels good to have five of my colleagues see my work in this light, as it does to know that colleagues in my department likewise see my contributions as worthy of promotion.

Appropriate Methods

Jim Gordon writes that we "should not abuse the moral climate of discourse on campus." Earl Woolley summarizes my career at BYU as a series of "personal attacks, contentious criticism, making false statements, and using methods that were uncivil, disruptive, manipulative, and contentious." And Van Gessel, my dean, says that I have held BYU up for ridicule. As troubling as these crimes are on their own, they are exacerbated by being committed in public. "Appropriate methods for expressing disagreement with University policy and decisions exist," Jim Gordon writes, and then lays out a list of where and how I should have appropriately disagreed. His list dovetails beautifully with methods I employed prior to the public statements:

- Emails arguing against new policies and decisions, written to Rex Lee, Clayne Pope, Bruce Hafen, Merrill Bateman, Alan Wilkins, and Jim Gordon, repeated emails to which the answer, if answer was given, was that those are established policies that must not be disputed.
- Service as a member of the Faculty Advisory Committee. Discussions of questions I raised there were routinely tabled before meaningful action was taken. There is essentially no faculty governance at BYU. Contrary to AAUP guidelines accepted and practiced by nearly every university in the United States, the critically important University Faculty Council on Rank and Status is not elected by faculty members, but appointed by the administration and chaired by an administrator. The Council on Rank and Status has overturned departmental and college-committee recommendations in every recent controversial case relating to academic freedom.

- I argued my case against the new academic freedom policy in a debate with a member of the Religion Department before a full house in the Varsity Theater.
- My comments on the ecclesiastical endorsement policy were civilly argued, first in a committee of the FAC (see 1992 report), and then in this letter to Academic Vice President Alan Wilkins, dated 5 February 1997:

    Dear Alan,

    In the place of a positive vision for BYU as a university in the context of faith, it seems to me that our current driving principle, despite President Hinckley's assertion that "trust comes from the top down," is distrust. Convinced by the worst of the arguments made in *First Things* about the secularization of American universities (arguments that have led, most recently, to the editor's advocating that the U.S. government be overthrown because it refuses to rule this as a Christian nation, a position that has led Gertrude Himmelfarb and other Jewish contributors to the journal to resign), we have been running scared. The new ecclesiastical endorsement policy, egregious limits on academic freedom, and current hiring policies excluding non-LDS and many LDS candidates evidence a pervasive lack of trust. In place of trust, we have micromanagement and attempts to control that are, to paraphrase an unfortunate phrase used to describe actions of Gail Houston, "enervating the moral fiber of the university." There is hardly a department on campus that is not disheartened by recent administrative actions undercutting departmental decisions.

    I don't expect you will agree with that assessment. But there are ways, if you wish, to weigh the possibility that I am right.

- Ask Kendall Brown and Tom Alexander how the history department feels about your unexplained refusal to clear Grant Hardy and others for candidacy, about your refusal to allow them to bring Pulitzer Prize winner Laurel Thatcher Ulrich to campus for a lecture, about how you have treated Steven Epperson, and about recent academic freedom limitations on members of the history faculty.
- Ask Jim Kearl and Clayne Pope how the economics department feels about your recent decision not to clear the three candidates for jobs in economics, again without explanation. In fact, ask the chairs of all departments how your hiring decisions (which have drastically undercut traditional departmental prerogatives to determine and work toward their futures) have demoralized faculty.
- Ask Lynn England and Tim Heaton how the sociology department feels about your treatment of Larry Young in his tenure bid and about limitations on academic freedom for Mormon sociologists.
- Ask Bert Wilson, Doug Thayer, Jay Fox, Grant Boswell, Merlin Forster, John Robertson, Tom Plummer, Jamie Lyon, and others in the humanities how it makes them feel to know that President Bateman asked Gene England to leave the English department and the university.
- Ask Bill Hess, Duane Jeffery, Bill Bradshaw, and others in the sciences what it means to them that Rex Lee and Bruce Hafen asked Sam Rushforth to leave the university because he "would not be comfortable with the directions BYU will be taking."
- Ask professors in the fine arts how the administration's efforts to control their art and drama, an absolute aversion to risk of any kind, affects their ability to do what they were hired to do
- Do an anonymous survey to determine whether faculty feel the ecclesiastical endorsement policy has strengthened or weakened their own spirituality and their relationship to the Church.

- Ask yourself why morale is so low at BYU at the moment (note the accreditation report, if you don't sense this yourself). And ask whether the answer, in general, might be that attempts to control that grow out of distrust create an environment analogous (if not equal in scope or violence) to those in countries with totalitarian governments. Rather than doing their best work, rather than risking displeasure in any form, citizens of such countries notoriously resign themselves to lives of quiet desperation, or they flee.

Let me recount a recent incident, with which you may be acquainted, to demonstrate the consequences of distrust. Dave Babbel, who was just offered Ned Hill's chair in the business school, decided to stay at the University of Pennsylvania because the ecclesiastical endorsement policy struck him as pharisaical—he didn't want some bishop determining his continued employment (although he is a bishop himself), and because he felt that current restrictions on academic freedom would inhibit his ability to speak about matters meaningful to him. The representative of the business school suggested that conditions weren't as bad here as he thought. Babbel said he had decided, and that he would write a letter outlining his two basic reasons for refusing the offer. Don't do that, the representative warned him. If you ever change your mind and decide to come here, that could be used against you. QED, said Babbel.

We need people like Dave Babbel here. But we will only attract them (and keep them) if they sense here an atmosphere of mature trust and of shared responsibility. I can imagine that you perceive the actions of myself and the other seventy faculty members who put together the AAUP investigative visit as undermining that positive atmosphere, that if we had said nothing, Babbel and others like him would not have such a negative image of BYU. We may have made mistakes, and we may make mistakes in the future. But isn't it

> possible that our insights are important to BYU? Isn't it possible that what we are saying about the debilitating effects of distrust, of the ecclesiastical endorsement policy, of broad (as opposed to narrow) limitations to academic freedom, and of taking hiring out of the hands of departments, is a diagnosis that could lead to positive change?

Those, then, were some of my attempts to work through appropriate channels. Silence has been the most common response. Reasonable people can disagree. One of the highest compliments a person can make to the author of an argument is to engage with the argument. Perhaps the lowest blow in this same public arena is to ignore the argument and to blame the author for making the argument at all, or in this case, for not making the argument through appropriate channels. What other members of the faculty, I wonder, have offered critique through appropriate channels to the extent of my letter to Alan Wilkins?

Where there is a true place for faculty governance (as opposed to simple affirmation of administrative decrees) there is less need to speak publicly about university issues. And where cooperative governance is taking place, public discussion is welcome. Finally, what does it matter through which channels criticism comes? A healthy organization is grateful for the kinds of questions that lead to better performance.

I'll end this section with a quotation from the "Recommendations from the FAC Subcommittee on Academic Environment, April 9, 1998":

> Our review finds that in some cases where disagreements have not been swiftly resolved incidental errors of discretion have been treated as serious or stubborn ones; respectful disagreement has been treated as deliberate attack; cases of a single offended student have been treated as behaviors adversely affecting the entire university or church. . . . What often results from the communication of administrative concern

or displeasure about such issues is a chilling climate of self-restraint in the face of potential challenge, a self-censorship that serves the interests of administrative convenience rather than that of truth-seeking and integrity of inquiry.

Uncivil and Contentious Criticism

While making my arguments in published essays and public speeches, I have occasionally used strong language. Earl Wooley highlights my use of the word "unctuous" in regard to new hires in religion and bemoans the fact that I called BYU in its current state "sanctimonious." Yes, I said those things and more. Were they contentious and uncivil? Yes, they were. Does the context matter? Yes, it does. BYU administrators fired my dear friend Steven Epperson after he reviewed a book by two members of the Religion faculty, pointing out that their pseudo-biological arguments were racist. BYU administrators fired our colleagues David Knowlton and Cecilia Konchar Farr and lied about the reasons they were fired, admitting the real reasons only after our Ad-hoc Committee on Academic Freedom published the facts. BYU administrators fired our colleague Gail Houston in a case that drew sharp censure in the report published by the AAUP. BYU administrators required colleagues to forego publishing research on Mormon topics. And so on. The administration perpetrates these atrocities and accuses me of contentious criticism and incivility?

Factual Errors

I wrote the speech Jim Gordon calls un-factual for an AAUP conference on Academic Freedom at Religiously Affiliated Institutions. Two statements made in that talk are incorrect, according to Jim Gordon, and he concludes that "Your false assertions and failures to cite references and verify your information are inconsistent with the standards of professionalism expected of a faculty member." We do require of one another certain standards of professionalism. Because Jim Gorden judged my statements false, I was not promoted. What will be the consequences for him if he can be shown to have erred in calling my statements false? And shouldn't the consequences be more severe because he not only erred, but punished me as a result of his errors?

First, Jim faults my claim that "numbers of non-Mormon faculty have declined precipitously." Earl Wooley cites figures Jim Gordon has furnished him. Although I am leery of accepting numbers provided by my prosecutor, it seems that the reduction of non-Mormons at BYU between 1992–93 and 1997 was 17%, or 15 of 89 faculty who left for one reason or another. On a graph, 17% doesn't look especially precipitous. But if you note that we only had 89 non-Mormon members of the faculty and that we lost 15 of them, the loss *feels* precipitous. Add to that projections for the future, given that there is a virtual, if not absolute, freeze on the hiring of non-Mormon faculty and it feels *really* precipitous.

I chose the word precipitous to indicate a qualitative loss as well as a quantitative loss. During the weeks I wrote my talk, I felt personally the effects of the stricter policy concerning hiring and retaining non-Mormons. In my department, non-Mormons Johannes Evelein and Raisa Soloviovna, both gifted teachers, talented writers, and members of our department for several years, were unanimously chosen to fill open tenure-track positions. The administration turned them both down, carefully skirting the fact that they are not Mormon.

In the Math department, Arkady Vaintrob, a Russian Jew with a special genius for math pedagogy, was chosen by his colleagues for an open tenure-track position. The administration refused to allow the hire. He was not Mormon. Arkady said later it didn't bother him that much; he had experienced similar discrimination as a Jew in the Soviet Union. So the Math Department lost Arkady Vaintraub, and Arkady's wife, Julia Nemirovskaya, a tenure-track faculty member in our department (she was hired before the new restrictions went into effect), left with him. Johannes Evelein took a job at Trinity College. And Raisa Soloviovna's future at BYU is uncertain.

While this was happening, and because this was happening, two non-Mormon tenure-track members of the Math faculty, Andreas Stahel and Tom Brady, left after passing their third-year reviews. They were disturbed by the new restrictions and felt they had little future here.

In this context, feeling the loss of friends and colleagues, sensing the decline of departments built up so laboriously over time, I spoke of a precipitous decline. A 17% loss in numbers of non-Mormons, the loss of three colleagues crucial to the success of my department, a Math Department in sudden decline—surely my statement was not wrong. Refuse promotion because I and others brought AAUP investigators to campus if you will. Don't pretend that my use of the word "precipitous" makes me unfit for promotion.

Additionally, Jim Gordon cites my claim that "several dozen members of the faculty have been forced to leave or have left on their own" as factually incorrect. Earl Wooley points out that the word "several" means at least three.

Consider the following list:

- Anthropology: David Knowlton
- Communications: Joseph Straubhaar
- English: Bert Wilson, Gene England, Cecilia Konchar Farr, Gail Houston, Brian Evenson, Daryl Spenser, George Schoemaker
- Germanic and Slavic Languages and Literatures: Bill Davis, Sandy Straubhaar, Johannes Evelein, Julia Nemirovskaya
- History: Steven Epperson, Martha Bradley, Michael Allen
- Mathematics: Andreas Stahel, Tom Brady, Mike Lundquist, Arkady Vaintrob
- Physics: Bill Evenson

- Psychology: Tomi-Ann Roberts, Hal Miller
- Sociology: Bonnie Mitchel, Martha Nibley Beck, Jim Duke Jr., Stan Albrecht
- School of Social Work: Karen Gerdes
- Spanish: Russell Cluff, Tom Matthews

This surely incomplete list comprises only thirty and not the requisite thirty-six names. *Mea culpa.* But isn't the basic argument correct? As a result of a series of administrative decisions, many of them related to academic freedom, morale is generally poor among faculty and we are losing valued colleagues (see the 1996 accreditation report, the 1997 AAUP report, Martha Nussbaum's 1997 book *Cultivating Humanity*, the 1998 FAC report on academic freedom, and the anonymous article in *Sunstone*, all of which I cited in the Chicago talk, for independent iterations of this theme).

What kind of administration would strain to call this "factually incorrect"? Where is the real harm here: in my use of the generalizing "several dozen" or in an administration that punishes me for stating that faculty are discontent and leaving the university?

Finally, let me ask a couple of questions:

Are faculty members here more or less willing to speak out on controversial issues than they were five years ago? Will your decision on my promotion free up discussion or shut people up?

Are faculty members here more or less trusting of the administration than they were five years ago? What effect will your decision have on that trust?

Earl Wooley writes that I'm a bad citizen because I used the word "unctuous" and because I called BYU "sanctimonious," but he doesn't address the question of whether the words are appropriately applied. Van Gessel writes that I'm a bad citizen because I held the university up to ridicule, but he doesn't ask whether the university has become ridiculous. Jim Gordon writes that I should have made more affirmative contributions to the university, but doesn't ask about the long-range contributions that even stinging criticism can bring.

Somehow, and I'm not sure how, we have arrived at a place where we are, in the recent words of Slobodan Milošević regarding the University of Belgrade, "obligated to safeguard the [university] and may not disseminate [ideas] directed against the interests of our [university] or spread fear, panic and defeatism or act contrary to the resolutions of parliament.... Absolute unity is required on issues of vital ... interest" (October 7, 1998).

My arguments over the years have been that academic freedom, for whatever reasons, is being progressively undermined at BYU. Because I made those arguments I have twice been denied promotion. Perhaps that proves my argument.

Shortly after the appeal, Jim Gordon wrote and said he "regretted" that the committee did not find grounds for overturning the original decision.

Fisher Tower

ELEVEN

Lighting the Way with Autos da Fé

Brigham Young University's Record with Respect to Academic Freedom, Women, and Homosexuals

Boston Sunday Globe, *Ideas* Section, October 27, 2002

In late 2002 I received a query from the editor of *The Boston Globe*'s Sunday *Ideas* section, wondering if I would write something about Mitt Romney and his substantial gift to BYU's School of Business. After the piece appeared, the *Globe*'s message board lit up with dozens and dozens of responses. Many agreed with my argument. Others were apalled that I had the gall to undermine Romney's chance to become Governor of Massachussetts. If that had been my intention, which it wasn't, my piece appeared to no effect. Romney was elected and BYU continued to crack down on what Boyd Packer called contemporary enemies of the Church: feminists, gay rights activists, and "so-called scholars and intellectuals."

Brigham Young University, founded in 1875, stands on a foothill overlooking Utah Valley, overshadowed by the sharp peaks of the Wasatch Range. It has approximately 30,000 students, ample funding, and keen desire to "stand as a beacon to the world." The university's mission statement, "Aims of a BYU Education," declares that "The intellectual range of a BYU education is the result of an ambitious commitment to pursue truth. Members of the BYU community rigorously study academic subjects in the light of divine truth." In many remarkable ways, the faculty and students of BYU live up to these ideals. The devil, however—and Mormons believe in him—lies in the details.

Mitt Romney, the Republican candidate for Massachusetts governor and BYU graduate, says he supports gay rights and abortion rights. I can't judge his sincerity, but I do know a few things about positions on these matters held by his alma mater, which in 1998 accepted his gift of a million dollars to establish the George W. Romney Endowment in the Romney Institute of Public Management. Mr. Romney did not establish BYU's positions on gay rights and abortion rights, and he is not responsible for enforcing them. But his support of BYU effectively helps underwrite them, and so they are a legitimate subject of discussion as he seeks elective office.

I was an Associate Professor of German Literature at BYU in 1993, the year leading up to Mr. Romney's unsuccessful bid for Edward Kennedy's senate seat. Although Utah is thousands of miles from Massachusetts (in many respects), a charismatic, wealthy, and politically active Mormon is always big news in Mormon country. Reports that Mr. Romney, an active Church member, was taking a pro-choice position were slightly disconcerting to conservative Mormons, but in this case they could overlook that fact.

Officials at BYU, however, could not overlook a carefully stated pro-choice position of one of my colleagues, Cecilia Konchar Farr. Konchar Farr, an assistant professor of English, was personally opposed to abortion but supported its legal availability—just as Mr. Romney did. She had been hired by the English Department to fill a need for a feminist scholar, but during her third-year review was fired on the grounds that she had spoken at a pro-choice rally at the Utah capitol and, what's more, "politicized the classroom." The Administration said she had violated BYU policy, which explicitly endorses full academic freedom except where "faculty behavior or expression seriously and adversely affects the University mission or the Church." As examples, the policy cites "expression with students or in public that . . . contradicts or opposes, rather than analyzes or discusses, fundamental Church doctrine or policy. . . ." The chair of the English department wrote that Konchar Farr's activist and prochoice positions were "behaviors that move from difference to contention."

Along with the dismissal of Professor Konchar Farr came the denial of tenure to English professor Gail Houston and the dismissals of anthropologist David Knowlton and historian Steven Epperson—all, in part, on the basis of charges of "seriously and adversely affecting the University mission" (Professor Houston on gender roles, Professor Knowlton on why Mormon missionaries were targeted by South-American terrorists, and Professor Epperson on a racist book by two professors of religion). In another incident, sociologists Karen E. Gerdes and Martha N. Beck were ordered not to publish their study of Mormon women whose sexual abuse as children had been ignored by Mormon churchmen.

In response to growing concerns about academic freedom at BYU, I and several other faculty members formed a campus chapter of the AAUP. Like over 95% of the faculty, we were practicing Mormons who had chosen to teach at BYU because we wanted to help educate our co-religionists. Our disagreement was not with BYU's distinctive religious and education mission; we were concerned rather with the university's claim to have only clear and narrow limits on academic expression, when in fact we felt it enforced unwritten policies with disturbingly broad limits. For more details than I can provide here, see philosopher Martha Nussbaum's 1997 chronicle of BYU's failure to live up to its own vision in *Cultivating Humanity*. Nussbaum unflatteringly contrasts BYU with Notre Dame's success at remaining true to its religious values while also encouraging vigorous debate on subjects like abortion and homosexuality.

In 1997, nearly a year before Mr. Romney's gift to BYU, after an intensive investigation of the Konchar Farr and Houston dismissals, the AAUP published its report. One section is especially relevant here:

> Numerous women, some in groups and some alone, spoke to the investigating committee about the hostile climate for women on campus.... Instead of being based on principles of intellectual freedom or doctrinal policies of the Church, academic freedom at BYU strikes the investigating committee as often subject to the political concerns of Church officials.... Faculty members who resist the pressure to alter or stop their research are at risk of losing their positions, as in the case of Professor Knowlton.... Women who defend the civil rights of pro-choice advocates in extramural remarks are subject to nonretention, as in the case of Professor Farr.... Feminist faculty members who question the soundness of gender roles in the Church may be denied continuing status [tenure] ... as in the case of Professor Houston. Much more than an isolated violation of academic freedom, the investigating committee's inquiries into complaints at BYU have revealed a widespread pattern of infringements on academic freedom in a climate of oppression and fear of reprisals.

These findings were widely reported in the press in the fall of 1997 and the spring of 1998. It was in this climate that Mitt Romney made his donation to BYU's Marriott School of Business. Interpreting that gift is complicated. Mr. Romney does not have to answer for everything that happens at BYU, and I imagine he doesn't agree with all of BYU's policies. The program in public management is a worthy enterprise, and it made historical sense to tie the Romney name to such an institute. And of course Mr. Romney has every right to donate his money to whatever institution he wishes.

What concerns me is not Mr. Romney's intent, but the effect of his $1,000,000. That gift just months after the September/October 1997 AAUP report lessened the moral force of the AAUP's censure. BYU's Trustees and administrators surely read Romney's gift as a statement that women's reproductive rights, gay and lesbian issues, and academic freedom are not issues of consequence to donors like Mr. Romney.

BYU has continued to thrive since the AAUP censure. In 1999 I was turned down for promotion to full professor by a Dean who found that my campaign in favor of academic freedom had exposed the University to "national ridicule" and by a Vice President who argued that my AAUP activities to "pressure the University to change policies of the Board of Trustees" violated " the standards of citizenship expected of a full professor at the University." I sought and accepted a job at Utah Valley State College, a public institution where the law protects women and gays from discrimination and academic freedom is more than an empty slogan.

Brigham Young University Replies

Brigham Young University has always been open about its mission to provide an excellent university education in an environment consistent with the ideas and principles of The Church of Jesus Christ of Latter-day

Saints. BYU's Academic Freedom Statement protects the individual academic freedom of faculty and the institution's academic freedom to pursue its religious mission. BYU's major accrediting body, the Northwest Association of Schools and Colleges, has found that BYU's Academic Freedom Statement fully meets its accreditation standards.

During BYU's most recent reaccreditation, the Northwest Association examined some of the allegations made by Professor Abbott. This group of independent scholars from across the country concluded that BYU had not violated academic freedom and renewed the university's accreditation.

———

Readers of the *Boston Globe* responded enthusiastically.

Scott Abbott is attempting to create an issue where none exists, the classic tactic of the amoral left. Abbott is a self-serving, intellectually bankrupt hypocrite. Kevin, Chelmsford

I am disappointed at what seems to be the foregone conclusion that BYU is anti-gay and anti-women's reproductive rights. That simply isn't true. Scott, Boston

I'm a democrat. I am not voting for Mitt Romney. But his donations to BYU mean nothing more than he supports his church's educational institutions. Does one question Shannon O'Brian on her contributions to the Catholic Church or to Catholic colleges? Catholic teaching also forbids abortions and homosexual acts. Does that mean Shannon O'Brien has some sinister motive in her contributions? Donald, Hampden, MA

I find it somewhat ridiculous that he is being criticized for a 1 million dollar donation to his alma mater. Obviously ex-professor Scott Abbott still holds a grudge because he was not accepted as a full professor and is attempting to take this out on Mitt Romney. Scott Abbott

should really return to his hideaway at Utah Valley State College before he makes more a fool out of himself. Peter, Carlisle

I think, to some extent, a politician's personal choices are, indeed, political statements. In this case, it is obvious that Mitt Romney supports his religious academic institution's fascist practices regarding human sexuality, including women's reproductive rights and homosexuality, and limiting the ideas of academic freedom to their brainwashed notions of how the world should be. Jonathan, Becket, MA

The Mormon Church has a long history of excluding and censoring men and women in the church who dare to express views that differ from church doctrine. The church is anti-gay and not exactly enlightened about women either. Women are not allowed to hold high positions in the church even though the church boasts that women are equal. Women are acceptable as long as they remain obedient to the men who run it and do not question. I do believe that the actions and philosophies of Brigham Young University are rooted in bigotry and are dangerous because they promote intolerance and hatred. Mitt Romney is well aware of what the University stands for and what it does. His support of such an institution should sound an alarm to all Massachusetts voters who treasure personal freedom and who find intolerance unacceptable. Pamela, Arlington, Virginia

I feel that Romney's religion should not be an issue. It seems though that people are missing the point. The author was not criticizing him for being a Mormon, he was pointing out that he donated money to an institution that attacks freedom of speech. For the record: I have been both a student and a teacher at Boston College and have participated in and led discussions on sexuality, church corruption, abortion, and the Church in politics (in the 16th and the 21st century!). Several of my professors were openly gay (and have tenure!). In my time as a teacher there, Boston College has never asked me what I do in my spare time or to avoid criticizing Catholicism in my classroom. BC still has issues to work on, but you would be hard pressed to find faculty member who have had their academic freedom impinged upon in the ways this article describes. According to the article, BYU actually tried to block a study on the abuse of Mormon women. No school with such a poor grasp of academic freedom deserves to be called university. Romney should have exercised better judgement. NL, Boston

The Pro-Romney groups who are posting here ignore one major difference between donating to BYU and Boston College. Boston College does not have a policy of expelling students who publicly acknowledge their homosexuality. But the Romney team wants you to ignore that and pretend that donating to Boston College is exactly the same as donating to BYU, when it is clearly not. This means nothing except for the fact that Romney wants to pretend to be a social liberal so he can have a shot at being Governor. Dan S., Weston, MA

What's next, the Celtics should have passed on Danny Ainge? James, Raynham, MA

Lemons

Two Buttes

TWELVE

Reviews of New Work by Brian Evenson

Mormon Civilization and Its Schizophrenic Discontents

The Open Curtain (Coffee House Press, 2006),
Published in *Catalyst Magazine*, September 2006

and

Affliction Fiction

Windeye (Coffee House Press, 2012) and *Immobility* (Tor, 2012),
Published in *Open Letters Monthly*, May 2012

When *The Open Curtain* was published in 2006, Brian Evenson was teaching in Brown University's Literary Arts program, having taught at Oklahoma State University, University of Denver, and Syracuse University after leaving BYU. He was still at Brown when *Immobility* and *Windeye* were published in 2012. He joined the faculty of CalArts in 2015 and in a press release the California University noted that his

> novel *Last Days* won the American Library Association's award for Best Horror Novel of 2009. . . . *The Open Curtain* was a finalist for an Edgar Award and an International Horror Guild Award. Other books include *The Wavering Knife*, which received an International Horror Guild Award for best story collection, *Dark Property* and *Altmann's Tongue*. He is the recipient of three O. Henry Prizes as well as a National Endowment of the Arts fellowship. His writing has been translated into French, Italian, Spanish, Japanese and Slovenian.
>
> Evenson has also authored ten book-length translations of work by Christian Gailly, Jean Frémon, Claro, Jacques Jouet, Eric Chevillard, Antoine Volodine and Manuela Draeger among others.

More recently, Brian Evenson was chosen as the 2019 Shirley Jackson Award winner for Single-Author Collection: *Song for the Unraveling of the World*.

I read and write about Brian's work because of the questions it explores and because of the precise intelligence of those explorations. The *Father of Lies* (1998) tells the story of a violent pedophile who serves as a lay religious leader. *Last Days* (2009) features a "brotherhood of mutilation" whose members rise in the hierarchy as they accumulate amputations. And even when the stories and novels have no direct connection to Brian's Mormon culture, they probe structures and practices familiar to me.

In his afterword to *The Open Curtain*, Brian discusses his changing and enduring relationship with the Mormon Church:

> I was Mormon when I started writing *The Open Curtain*. By the time I finished it, years later, I had left the Mormon Church of my own volition, first by gradually ceasing to participate in the ceremonies of the Mormon temple, then by tapering back my participation in weekly church services, and finally—finding neither of these to give me sufficient distance from

a culture that objected to my first book of fiction on moral grounds—by formally requesting, in 2000, to be excommunicated....

I intend for this to be my last Mormon-themed book, at least as far as fiction is concerned. It is my departure from Mormonism both as a person and as a writer. Mormonism is a culture that nourished me as a person and as a writer growing up; without it I would not be who I am. And yet at the same time I feel remarkably comfortable having left it and am not sorry to be free of it. Or at least as free of it as one can ever be of a culture whose rhythms of speech and ways of thinking one still finds oneself to lapse naturally into years later. I suspect those rhythms are sufficiently burned into my brain that they'll stay with me until I die. But that relation to language, to me, is the best thing about the culture.

Like Brian, I am marked variously by the Mormon culture that nurtured me with its stories and its unique ways of telling them. I remember an encounter with a patron in the BYU bookstore (sadly, a bookstore no longer). Standing in the fiction aisle, he mistook me for a bookstore employee and asked whether fiction meant it was not true. Fiction means it is true, I told him. Brian Evenson's stories are true stories. And that frightens the hell out of me.

Mormon Civilization and Its Schizophrenic Discontents

What if you had suddenly experienced a break between what you took to be true and what you now perceived to be true—letters to and from your dead father, for instance, that revealed, perhaps, an illegitimate half-brother? What if your mother tightened her lips and claimed the opposite: "It's simple truth.... We know the truth. There's no reason to speak of this again"?

What if you started to "have an odd relation to words"?

What if you read a story in the 1903 *New York Times* about William Hooper Young, a grandson of Brigham Young and the author of an article about blood atonement, who was on trial for a ritual murder?

What if you began "to feel isolated, insulated, buried deeper inside" your body?

What if you received a new name in a secret ceremony and then swore never to reveal it except to God at the veil between life and death? And what if your throat were to be cut again if you did reveal it?

What if it were difficult for you to tell the difference between the person who had your original name and the newly named person, or between yourself and Brigham Young's grandson?

What if you lived in Provo, Utah?

What if you were a character in Brian Evenson's novel?

Even worse: What if most of these things were true and you were not a character in *The Open Curtain*—but rather a resident of Happy Valley reading the book and recognizing damning parallels between the landscape of the troubled character's mind and the map you used to navigate your own culture?

Evenson's new book (following *Altmann's Tongue, The Din of Celestial Birds, Father of Lies, Contagion, Dark Property,* and *The Wavering Knife*) is a rigorously realistic novel about a young man who comes to manifest many of the symptoms of schizophrenia. It is harrowing to be inside the mind of Rudd Theurer in the first part of the novel, "Rudd, Parsed," as he develops what must be hallucinations (neither he nor the reader is able definitively to distinguish between what is real and what he perceives as real). It is doubly harrowing in the second part, "Lyndi, Adrift," to witness Rudd from the perspective of the young woman who takes him in, marries him in the LDS temple, and then experiences his ritual-stoked delusions on her own body. And it is triply harrowing in "Hooper Amuck" to be again inside Rudd/Hooper's mind as he tries repeatedly to make sense of his surroundings: "It took him a long moment to understand where he was. . . . It took him a moment to understand where he was. . . . For a moment he was not certain where he was."

The language of the novel is spare, exact, and almost affectless as it portrays characters themselves without affect. Readers of earlier work by Evenson will recognize this language that blankly states horrors that can scarcely be spoken.

The terror evoked by this novel grew exponentially for me as the disturbed young man walked the actual streets of Provo, sat on Sunday-School chairs stenciled "Edgemont 3rd Ward," did research in the BYU library, traversed the Provo-Springville highway, rode his scooter up local canyons, and participated in a sacred temple ritual—the pre-1990 one still replete with Freemasonic tokens and violent penalties. This novel is David Lynch's *Blue Velvet* staged behind Provo's white picket fences. Rudd Theurer is Dennis Hopper grown up in Utah Valley, sucking on his gasmask while pawing through intimate cultural lingerie.

And that's when the novel turned for me, came alive like dormant maggots in a bucket. A reader who indeed "parses Rudd" finds a character (like him or herself) who has taken on a personality based on various texts: his father's letters, his Sunday School lessons, the *New York Times* articles about the trial of Brigham Young's grandson, the section from *Mormon Doctrine* on blood atonement, the symbols and words of the temple ceremony, newspaper accounts of local murders Rudd may or may not have committed. Given his own mental state, these texts work in him corrosively, structure and de-structure his identity, leave him at the end waiting "for someone to tell him who to be next."

Freud argued in *Civilization and Its Discontents* that humans are instinctually aggressive toward one another and that civilization or culture is created to restrict aggression. But restrictions, commands, or prohibitions that are too strong lead to unhappiness and neurosis. This works, he argues, for individual development as well as for civilizations: "If the development of civilization has such a far-reaching similarity to the development of the individual and if it employs the same methods, may we not be justified in reaching the diagnosis that, under the influence of cultural urges, some civilizations . . . have become 'neurotic'?"

In the context of this novel, a Mormon culture that enforces secrecy on penalty of death, a Mormon culture that abandons its history of polygamy, blood atonement, racism, and violent Freemasonic symbolism without admission of error or productive discussion of the changes, a Mormon culture that thus tells its adherents a schizophrenic story and requires that that story alone structure their lives, a Mormon culture that tightens its lips and asserts that "We know the truth. There's no reason to speak of this again"—is neurotic.

"I was Mormon when I started writing *The Open Curtain*," Evenson writes in the Afterword. "By the time I finished it, years later, I had left the Mormon Church of my own volition."

No wonder.

Affliction Fiction

. . . we see through a glass, darkly . . .
First Corinthians 13:12

The characters in Brian Evenson's dark stories don't wake up one morning to find they have metamorphosed into a bug. They do, however, share with Kafka's Gregor Samsa situations that are both inexplicable and implacable. Their stories begin like this: "In retrospect, it was easy for her to see it had been a mistake to have sex with a mime," or like this: "I have been ordered to write an honest accounting of how I became a Midwestern Jesus and the subsequent disastrous events thereby accruing. . . ." They take place in dream states: "Night after night, Kraus dreamt of a woman with a normal leg and a baby leg." Characters ponder the awkward "Intricacies of Post-Shooting Etiquette," or ask themselves "How do you know the moment when you cease to be human?" In one way or another, Evenson's characters all share the dilemma of the professor in "Mudder Tongue" whose words increasingly have no relationship to his thoughts: "There came a certain point, in his speech, in his confrontation with others, in his smattering with the world, that Hecker realized something was wrong."

What is wrong, horribly (or absurdly) wrong in story after story, is that characters either embrace webs of lies (like the grim worshipers of barbed-wire in "Contagion" or the abusive church leaders in *Father of Lies*) or they live violently (or absurdly) outside the seductive constraints of civilizing language. Either course leaves the characters (and in a somewhat different sense, readers) face to face with absurdity.

The stories in Evenson's first book, *Altmann's Tongue*, perfectly exemplify the book's epigraph—Julia Kristeva's insistence on writing that is "more and more incisive, precise, eschewing seduction in favor of cruelty. . . ." Antoinine Artaud wrote in this vein, as did Thomas Bernhard, both of whom Evenson cites as favorites. Echoes of Beckett and Kafka can be heard in Evenson's work as well. Like their European predecessors, Evenson's characters interact along the border between what seems to be legible and coherent and what appears to be neither.

In *Dark Property*, for instance, readers enter a state of incomplete and uncertain apprehension somewhat reminiscent of a young child's. Early in the novel we read that "The boy fremented as he ran. She could not determine any sense in it." The woman's gradual, approximating comprehension of the scene (two men are killing the boy to eat him) is a study in painstaking phenomenology:

> Smiling, he turned his face upward and the sun angled into the crevasion in which was hid his good eye: pale, pellucid. She hitched the pack higher onto her bone-worn shoulders. Her hands brushed the hair away from her own eyes, spread it off squin across her forehead.
>
> The sack at his feet grew rageous, roiled around itself an aura of dust. He coughed. Turned his face away. His boots afflicted the sack until it quivered, fell still. His boots forbore.

Like the woman, readers experience only fragments of a world that must be interpreted and reinterpreted and that yield tentative meaning at best. To create that experience, Evenson employs dozens of neologisms and otherwise obscure words: crevasion, off squin, sprent, runcated, stammel, benimous, flectubile, greave, spartled, corneous, flittern, flench, ribbard, and so on. The words make sense, more or less, in the context of their sentences; some of them, like frement, "to roar," are historical but obsolete. They remind readers that we see through the glass of language darkly, confronting us with a slippery epistemological condition in which the clear, coherent world of habitual thought threatens to collapse.

The physical dark property of the novel is the body of a woman carried in a bounty hunter's sack. Metaphorically, after Nietzsche's "supposing truth to be a woman," the novel's dark property is truth. The bounty hunter claims that "'Truth cannot be imparted . . . It must be inflicted.'" On its title page *Dark Property* is designated "An Affliction" and the novel excoriates readers with the violence perpetrated by absolute truth claims (it was a patriarch who sent the bounty hunter after the woman).

The truth confronting the detective of sorts in *Last Days* who is forced to investigate a murder (or is it a robbery?) inside the Brotherhood of Mutilation must be inflicted as well. He receives information about the hierarchical institution only as he himself loses digits and limbs to ritual amputation in order to rise in status. With the secrets of its mutilated hierarchy (perhaps all hierarchies require self-mutilation) and its hard-boiled investigator, *Last Days* evokes the generic detective novel only to refuse the resolution the genre demands. Who did it? Not only do we not learn the answer to this standard question, we're left not even knowing for sure what "it" was.

The stories in *Windeye*, Evenson's new collection, repeatedly address archeological and teleological questions. "Knowledge," for instance, is a description of "precisely why I have still not written my detective novel." Mysteries work within a set of assumptions that all crimes are scrutable and that clues will lead inevitably to the criminal. Attempts to solve the case presented in this story, however, require the investigator to make assumptions about the nature of reality that "end up derailing the genre." In *Windeye*'s "The Moldau Affair," to cite a second example, a detective finds it impossible to break out of the logical circles imposed by the circumstances: "Yet, how to know if the logic I think I am following is not in itself its own trap, a distortion of reality prone to do me more harm than good—just as Stratton's logic was a trap for him?" The detective assumes his report will do more good than harm. Readers are left to question his optimism.

In the story "Contagion" from the book of that name, characters fatefully construct metaphors from a barbed-wire fence. The fence is a given, simply there, and the men who ride it are just doing their jobs. Their written notes are a straightforward litany of the various types of barbed wire until they encounter a deadly contagion, when the notations begin to stray to more subjective considerations.

> *Half-rotted posts, top and middle strands of coldweather undulate wire.... Bottom strand: single-wire set with spurwheels: large sheet metal, 14 sharpened points, locked in place with sheet metal tabs.*
>
> All the time I am eyeing Grenniger, trying to determine if he is afflicted. But the contagion only latterly gives up its traits and there is no means to forsee it. One has it or one does not, and once one has it, one is already dead.
>
> Are we already dead?

Past the fence's end the riders find a town dominated by a religious sect whose leader locks one rider in a room to write oracular notes about the barbed wire that has become the sect's object of worship. When he runs out of paper he writes on the walls, encircling himself with sentences that resemble a long, enclosing strand of barbed wire.

As a tool in the real world, barbed wire controls, separates, and imposes order. In light of that fact and in response to the incomprehensible and frightening contagion, the town's panicked populace has transformed the wire until the fact of the wire becomes the coercive truth of the new religion: "You shall know the fence and the fence shall make you free." This is precisely the process of truthmaking Nietzsche wrote about so devastatingly: "What is truth? a mobile army of metaphors, metonymies, anthropomorphisms . . . only insofar as man forgets himself as . . . an artistically creative subject does he live with some calm, security, and consistency." Evenson's work insists on this. We are the artistically creative authors of the truths we live by. We must then, if we are honest, live more tentatively in relation to the security and consistency we achieve through language. The effect of this conclusion, at least for me, at least most of the time, is bracing.

It is not bracing for everyone.

Evenson grew up Mormon in Provo, Utah and was an undergraduate at Brigham Young University. After graduate school he returned to teach in BYU's English department, hired in part because his manuscript for *Altmann's Tongue* was scheduled to be published by Knopf. Evenson soon came under attack by religious leaders for the violence that is the subject of the book. At the time, I too was teaching at BYU, having left a tenured position in Vanderbilt's Department of Germanic and Slavic Languages to return to the university that had given me my first taste of the life of the mind. I had become co-president of the BYU Chapter of the American Association of University Professors, concerned by growing limitations on academic freedom at the private Mormon university. The controversy over Evenson's work grew public and I stepped in to explain to BYU President Rex Lee, former Solicitor General of the United States, that the character in the book's title story was Klaus Barbie, the Butcher of Lyon, who took the name Altmann when he fled his Nazi past. *Altmann's Tongue*, I argued, explores language and the violence that attends fascist truth claims. As little moved by my literary arguments as by ones for academic freedom, Lee and others kept up the pressure and Evenson finally decided to leave BYU and the Mormon religion as well. The university's sense of mission and Evenson's sense of mission were "quite divergent," explained BYU's public relations officer. That was more true than he could imagine. By demonstrating religion's patent and sometimes lethal absurdities, Evenson's work consistently calls into question communities that worship metaphors as truths.

Brigham Young University is the setting of Evenson's new novel *Immobility*, post-"Kollaps" BYU, that is, and community is the target announced by an epigraph: "In the true movement of community what is at stake is never humanity, but always *the end of humanity*" (Jean-Luc Nancy). Mormon theology asserts the opposite. The names and dates and family connections assembled by Mormon genealogists and protected in granite vaults are the prime and everlasting proof of the continuation of humanity.

Immobility takes place after the riots and the bright blast, after a few men reportedly "banded together acting 'rationally' instead of 'like animals' . . . attempting to found a new society, attempting to start over. *Not having learned better*, he thought grimly, *the first time*." The "he" has a name, he remembers, awakening to consciousness after having been frozen for decades in a vault underneath what was once a campus: Josef Horkai. And he has a context sketched by a voice he hears while waking up: "'How are we feeling?'" We. How are we feeling? Who are we? Why are we together? The answers to these questions are the substance of novel.

By some freak of the atomic blast, Horkai is not only immune to the radioactive atmosphere but able to regenerate limbs and even life. When the non-immune people need something outside their bunker, they revive him. They ask him to travel to a canyon east of what once was Salt Lake City to bring back a frozen cylinder stored by enemies in a vault cut into the mountain.

Having been drugged and frozen, Horkai struggles with his memory: "The problem, he began to realize, wasn't just trying to assemble the little he thought he knew into a narrative—it came in determining which of the memories were real, which were things he'd dreamed or imagined." What he knows comes largely from assertions made by Rasmus, the leader of the people in the bunker. Rasmus tells Horkai he is suffering from a degenerative disease that will eventually paralyze him. To slow the degeneration, he says, they have kept Horkai frozen and now that he is awake will administer periodic injections into his spine. Horkai feels intense pain when injected and raises a question: "'If I'm really paralyzed from the waist down, why did I feel that in my legs?' Rasmus just held his gaze. 'You didn't,' he claimed at last. 'You just think you did.'"

When Horkai hesitates to undertake the mission, Rasmus points out the alternatives:

"Either you can lend us a hand for a few days or we can put you back in storage. But if you don't help us, the chances are good there won't be anyone left to get you out of storage later on. We're the ones who can keep you alive, and we're the ones trying to find your cure. Do you want to risk losing us?"

Us. That's the problem. It is also the solution to the problem. That's the problem.

Near the end of their mission, Horkai and the two clones who carry him trip a wire that starts a recording: "Welcome, brothers! . . . We are here for you. We are here to protect you. . . . God has chosen us to stand attendant to you and to guide you in once again founding civilization.'" "'So is it a message or a trap?'" Horkai asks. By this time a reader knows enough about community to answer the question: all messages are traps. Language is a trap. Horkai knows this as well. Welcomed into the vault by a man who calls him brother and who explains that God has sent Horkai to aid in the task of preserving "the history of the human race, a record of births and deaths for hundreds and hundreds of years," he has to decide whether to stay with men he considers religious fanatics to "participate in the reinstitution of the human race. Something he wasn't exactly sure was a good idea." His other option is to steal the cylinder and return to the people who say they are trying to cure him.

At this juncture there are several plot surprises waiting for readers of Evenson's fine novel. I'll make just two further points. The first has to do with Horkai's thought that perhaps reinstituting the human race isn't a good idea. He reflects on human history: "We say no to torture, and then we find a reason to torture in the name of democracy.... We say no to eight million dead in camps, and then we do it again, twelve million dead in gulags. Humans are poison. Perhaps it would be better if we did not exist at all." *Immobility* is dedicated to the profoundly pessimistic Norwegian Peter Wessel Zapffe and to Thomas Ligotti, whose *The Conspiracy Against the Human Race* argues that human consciousness is an unmitigated disaster. The Kollaps is proof of that, as are the coercive communities that compete for Horkai's membership. Nonetheless, Horkai keeps moving: "he wanted to know something about who he was, gain some knowledge that he suspected they might have. Was he committed to some sort of cause? No. Was he opposed to Rasmus and his community? No, not really. Did he side with them? No."

The second point is that there is an alternative to community. Horkai collapses and wakes again to the words "'How are we feeling?'" The man who has rescued him means "we" in a less coercive sense and in fact has strategies to combat community. Horkai asks who he is and he answers with a question: "'Do names really matter? . . . I don't mean to be rude,' said the stranger. 'It's just that's where we went wrong. . . . Back in the Garden of Eden when Adam named first his wife and then the animals. When we started thinking about names rather than the things they were supposed to designate.'" Horkai says he'll have to call the man something and he relents and gives him a word, "Rykte," to use. The man explains that it is not a name but that it means name in one language and nothing in the one they are speaking: "'Now you have something to call me, but I still don't have a name.'" That attempt to simply exist rather than to name what inevitably will become good or evil (Rykte claims it is "'better not to let society develop at all, to leave each person on their own, alone, shivering, and afraid in the dark'") finally isn't enough for Horkai. He makes a decision. The novel and his consciousness approach a fateful end.

But isn't the final joke on Brian Evenson himself? Isn't a writer the ultimate creature of language? Doesn't language speak him even more thoroughly than it speaks me and Josef Horkai and Kline and the barbed-wire worshipers and Rudd Theurer and the woman in the bag? It does. Of course it does. We know that because Evenson (after Herder, Nietzsche, Heidegger, Derrida and so many others) has so skillfully pointed it out, spelled it out, plotted it out. Brian Evenson writes profoundly about the prison-house of language precisely because he has made that place his home.

GWT I

Castle Valley III

THIRTEEN

Hermeneutic Adventures in Home Teaching
Mary and Richard Rorty

Dialogue, **Summer 2010**

In the spring of 2010, I received an email from *Dialogue* editor Kristine Haglund. She said she was going to publish an interview with Mary Varney Rorty in which Mary spoke about a home teacher they had had in Princeton, someone studying German literature, she remembered. Are you that former home teacher? Kristin asked. And if so, would you be willing to write something about it? I am and I would, I answered.

When the issue appeared I was surprised and gratified by the warmth of Mary's memory:

> Princeton was the high point in [Rorty's] encounter with my religion. We had some very, very, excellent home teachers there—very devout, intellectually lively, and interesting people. One of our home teachers, Scott Abbott [my name added by Kristine], was writing his dissertation on German intellectual history. He and Richard were both interested in his topic, so the two had an intellectual relationship independent of the home

teacher context in which they explored things of common interest.

I wasn't writing about German intellectual history and wonder now if Mary didn't mean a previous member of the ward who had worked in the history department. Still, as I hope my essay conveys, home teaching Mary was a high point in my history of home teaching.

Lavina Fielding Anderson was the copy editor for the piece. I hadn't published in *Sunstone* or *Dialogue* since 1997 and Lavina said she had missed my voice. I told her that after I left BYU and after I resigned from the Church I felt like I no longer had the standing necessary to be part of the conversation. Nonsense, she said. Thank you, I replied. Kristine's invitation and Lavina's assurance reminded me that there were still ways I could contribute. *Dialogue* subsequently published three sections of what became *Immortal for Quite Some Time*. Although I had become an outsider of sorts, I began to feel I was an insider-outsider still welcome, perhaps, in my own religious culture.

When philosopher Alastair MacIntyre came striding into my Vanderbilt University office brandishing the *New York Times* in October of 1985, I knew something was up. Congratulations, he said, your church has just entered its Renaissance Period. I was used to seeing him walk into Furman Hall on Ash Wednesdays with a streak of ash on his forehead, and we had talked about Mormonism, but I had no clue what he was talking about. He showed me the front page of the paper. It was the Mark Hofmann bombings, murders to cover up Hofmann's forgeries. It only took you 150 years, Alastair noted. It took us a millennium and a half.

I've told this story a dozen times, maybe two dozen. For just the right audience, Mormons who know that Alastair is one of the world's foremost ethicists, it works beautifully. I never hesitate to tell it, although I'm always a little uneasy because I'm name-dropping. But if I can convince myself that there's more to it than that, that stories about intersections between philosophers and the religious tradition I grew up in might be interesting to others (in ways my story about sitting behind Marie Osmond in the Nashville Third Ward while she chewed off her fingernails and deposited them in her husband's coat pocket is not), then perhaps there's a purpose to writing about my role as home teacher to America's most famous pragmatic philosopher after John Dewey. Well, not technically a home teacher to Richard Rorty, but rather to his wife Mary Varney Rorty, a philosopher in her own right.

About thirty years ago, in a middle-school cafeteria in Hightstown, not far from Princeton University where I was studying German literature, I watched a grey-haired man hold his baby in a circle of priesthood holders while the Bishop of the Princeton Ward gave the child a name and blessing. That's Richard Rorty, someone said. The name didn't mean a thing to me at the time. It did soon enough.

Mary had grown up Mormon in Idaho, and had acquired a Ph.D. in ancient philosophy. Richard had grown up the orchid-loving son of Trotskiite parents. True to his pragmatic philosophy (or was he simply deferring to Mary?), Richard figured it might be good for their new son (or was it their daughter?) to grow up within some tradition, and perhaps Mormonism was as good as any other.

When the Bishop of the Princeton Ward asked me to be the Rortys' home teacher, I hesitated. Do they want a home teacher? The Bishop assured me they did. I told him I would ask Mary, and if she agreed, I would do it. She agreed, although I noticed her eyebrows raising when she said yes. I sealed the agreement by promising I wouldn't be intrusive, and that I would report monthly visits on the basis of whatever contact we happened to have. Mary's eyebrows relaxed.

And so I became their home teacher. Over the course of a year or two, I visited them at their home three or four times, usually bringing my son Joseph as my companion. When we rang the doorbell, there was always a scurry inside. We could hear Richard shouting "the home teachers! the home teachers!" while rushing up the stairs to the second floor. When Mary opened the door, she was always laughing at Richard's antics, theater performed for the children.

Our other visits, not exactly *home* teaching but duly reported to the Bishop, were memorable to me. The only one that occasioned tension of any sort was the morning I delivered Joseph to his class at the elementary school and found Mary there too, talking with some other parents. When she saw me, she slid her cup of coffee to one side. I sat down next to her and said I would resign as her home teacher if she ever felt uncomfortable about me again. Could I have a sip of your coffee? I asked.

Sometime in 1979, Mary asked if I would babysit Kevin and Patricia while she and Richard celebrated the publication of his book *Philosophy and the Mirror of Nature*. When I arrived, Richard handed me the first copy of the book, handsome in its green and yellow jacket. The children are asleep, Mary said, take a look at the book if you want.

I wanted.

It was a magical evening. Starting with the Wittgenstein epigraph that pointed out that when we think of the future we suppose it will be a direct extension of the present as opposed to an extension of the present over a curved or changed line, I fell into a reading reverie broken only by the hope that they would make a long evening of it. Richard was arguing that "pictures rather than propositions, metaphors rather than statements . . . determine most of our philosophical traditions," and that the image of the mind as a mirror that correctly or incorrectly represents what we experience has held philosophy captive for millennia. Instead, he thought, we might better be engaged in the kind of hermeneutics developed by Hans-Georg Gadamer, a turn from attempts to find truth to work that focuses on romantic ideas of self creation. Truth isn't something we find, but something we make. Mary and

Richard finally came home, and because it's a long book, I bought my own copy the next day.

Not long after that visit, Gadamer came to town. His lecture drew hundreds of listeners, and although the 80-year-old German didn't use a single English preposition correctly, he charmed us all. After the lecture, Richard found me and invited me to come to their home for a reception. You're working on Rilke and Heidegger, aren't you? Come talk with Hans about it.

Hans!

I arrived at the small reception, mostly Richard's graduate students, and Richard asked what I wanted to drink. When I hesitated, he took me into the kitchen, found an almost empty bottle of 7-UP, and poured it into a wine glass. It's old and flat, he said. Wish we had something else. Come meet Hans. He told Gadamer I was working on Rilke's "Duino Elegies." Gadamer asked what my angle was, and when I told him about the "standing" metaphor I was tracing through the poems, the poet's attempt to counteract physical and cultural entropy through standing figures, stanzas and *Gestalten*, letters and figures, he nodded vigorously. It's all there, he said. I knew it was remarkable when I first read it, just after it was published, and I knew Martin needed to see it.

Martin!

I gave a copy to Heidegger, he said, and he liked it as much as I did.

And I was grateful for the "hermeneutics of home teaching."

On another memorable evening, the Rortys' friend Harold Bloom was in town to lecture. I sat next to Mary in the crowded auditorium and listed to the big man with the photographic memory talk at great length about some fascinating topic. And although I've forgotten what Bloom's lecture was about, I have a clear memory of Mary, next to me, knitting at a steady pace, her knits and purls accompanying Bloom's ideas.

Mary is not just a knitter. She also has a way with words. One late afternoon, with the setting sun slanting through the tall side window of the Princeton Chapel (our sod laying and funnelcake sales had finally resulted our being able to build the beautiful chapel), Mary delivered a carefully written sermon. The warm light played sensuously on the high wall behind her while she spoke about various kinds of love. Had I given the sermon, it would have sounded like C.S. Lewis' *The Four Loves*. But Mary had done more than read Lewis; she knew ancient Greek philosophy through its original texts, and she knitted and purled a complicated and beautiful story. The literary quality of her sermon was unexpected in our ward; we were, for the most part, people with the skills to pull the electrical wire in the building, or to set the open rafters, and even if our skills lay in the academic sphere, we weren't likely to write our sacrament meeting talks with an eye to beauty. Turning to erotic love, Mary described how the curve of a lover's arched foot was as meaningful as anything in the world. I sat there dumbfounded.

Fifteen years later, I spent five afternoons in Provo Canyon with Richard, looking for a lazuli bunting. He was a passionate birder and had accepted a summer speaking engagement at BYU on the off chance that he might spot one of the beautiful little birds. He was also thinking (or was it Mary who was wondering?) about BYU as a possible place for Kevin and Patricia to go to college (BYU quickly fell off the map of possible universities, for reasons Mary would have to elaborate). Near Stewart Falls above Sundance, I saw a flash of blue and pointed at it. Richard raised his big binoculars and found the bird. While focused tightly on the little beauty, he held out his bird book so I could see the lazuli bunting on the cover. Richard looked and looked and looked. Finally he handed me the binoculars. I glanced quickly at the amazing flash of blue on the back of a striking red, white, and black body and quickly handed the glasses back. That night we had dinner in Sundance's Tree Room. I feigned horror when Richard ordered quail. After that initial sighting, I emailed Richard every spring on the day I spotted the first lazuli bunting in Utah Valley. The year he died it was the second of May.

On his last morning at BYU, lecturing about pragmatic philosophy and its connections with postmodernism, Richard recited a "double dactyl" he had composed, a strict form that announces its playfulness with the opening "Higgledy-Piggledy," and requires that a single word comprise the double dactyl of the sixth line. I'll remember Richard with a double dactyl of my own, borrowing the sixth line from his:

>   Higgledy-Piggledy,
>   Rorty the pragmatist,
>   Trotskiite parenting,
>   "Richard McKay";
>   Challenge philosophy's
>   Phallogocentrism,
>   *Mirror of Nature*,
>   And those who prey.

Landscape

FOURTEEN

New LDS Restrictions on Children of Gay Parents Make Perfect Sense

A Post on the Blog *The Goalie's Anxiety*, November 6, 2015

The day after a new policy was announced by the LDS Church that children of cohabiting same-sex parents could not be baptized, I posted a short response on my blog, "The Goalie's Anxiety." These are my brother's people, I thought. These are people I came to know and respect while writing *Immortal for Quite Some Time*. These men and women who have finally achieved marriage equality are my brothers and sisters. This is my homophobic church.

There were almost 3,000 views of the post that November. About 300 views a month had been average for the obscure blog that focuses mostly on books; there have never been so many views since. Satire felt like the only reasonable response to the church's vicious and patently absurd decision.

Since the new LDS restrictions on children of gay parents were made public yesterday, there have been many angry denunciations of a church that punishes children for the sins of their parents. That will change, I think, when people think through the issue more carefully. I'll try to help with that process.

Let's start with the premise that same-sex marriages are unnatural and thus evil and with the fact that what we know to be evil is now legal and increasingly natural in the United States. That new law makes it harder and harder for us to make people understand that gay marriage is evil.

We have a special problem with children being raised by gay parents. A child whose parents love and support it—and feed and care for and challenge and correct and nurse and weep with and celebrate it—will, unfortunately, understand the goodness of those parents. Their family life may even seem natural to those children. They may love their parents. That puts them in a position of inevitable opposition to the principles of the gospel we are trying to teach, namely, that their parents are engaged in evil and unnatural lifestyles. Were we to allow the children of such parents to be blessed and baptized and to enjoy full fellowship with the rest of us, they might attend church and express their admiration for their parents in ways that would undermine our valiant efforts.

Some of the anger being expressed today is aimed at the fact that while these children can't be baptized, children of murderers and rapists can be baptized and welcomed into the church. That's a different question entirely. Our decision is driven by impeccable logic. Children of murders and rapists will easily recognize those acts as illegal and evil and will not be inclined to defend them in church. But children whose gay parents love them are more problematic.

The only way, then, to protect the delicate faith and true belief of the members of the church is to discipline and punish people in same-sex marriages and to keep their sympathetic children away from our meetings and out of our fellowship. The

LDS leaders who have announced the new policy understand the problem well and have taken appropriate action.

They haven't, however, thought this through to the end. In coming months, as the fruits of their restrictive actions are manifest in fully correlated and homogenized congregations, inspired leaders will realize that additional restrictions are called for. Heterosexual parents of gay children often sympathize with their children and are grateful when they find a supportive and loving partner. That can't be good for anyone. The church will be better off once all parents of gay children are disfellowshipped.

Additionally, siblings of gays and lesbians often know from long and intimate experience that their brothers and sisters are good people. Better disfellowship all of them too. And while we are thinking in that direction, friends of gays and lesbians cannot be trusted and must be similarly disciplined.

In short, while the new restrictions on the children of parents in same-sex families are a good start, parents and siblings and friends and acquaintances must be excluded as well. Appropriate signs can be posted at all entrances to our chapels: gays and lesbians, children of gay parents, parents of gay children, siblings of gays are not welcome here. LDS public relations will come up with inoffensive and still effective signs, I'm sure.

As this retrenchment is enacted, new policy will have to be drafted concerning the words "congregation" and "ward" and "fellow citizens" and "fellowship" and "community" and "saints." None of those old words fit what will be the new reality: henceforth Sunday meetings will be attended by a few bitter and fearful white guys, unless, of course, there is a football game on TV.

Sage IV

FIFTEEN

UVU President Matthew Holland Continues His Battle against Marriage Equality

In *The UVU Review*, November 13, 2017

Utah Valley University is a state university located in what has long been referred to as Happy Valley. Largely Mormon and for the most part conservative Republican, Utah County has two major universities, both of which reflect the makeup of the county's population. The building of the LDS Institute of Religion at UVU is designed to blend in with the university's architecture and stands in such close proximity to other buildings that it is an integral part of campus. Many of our students live in BYU-approved housing, often with BYU students. Nonetheless, we are a state university required by policy to foster diversity of various sorts. Most of us welcome that requirement and do our best to celebrate and support diverse members of our university community.

When the Utah Board of Regents announced that the son of a Mormon apostle, a young and inexperienced BYU professor of political science, would be our next president, my first response was "holy shit!" But there we were.

Matt Holland was clearly aware that he needed to assuage doubts about his ability to rise above his religious connections. Early in his presidency, at the dedication of a new campus theater, Mormon actor James Arrington, chair of the theater department, quoted Brigham Young in his speech. Holland quoted Oscar Wilde. So far so good, I thought, and as the years passed Holland's presidency seemed, for the most part, to be productive.

That changed in 2015 and was followed by a second breach of the church/state wall in 2017. I published the following piece in the UVU student newspaper.

When Matt Holland was chosen to be the new president of Utah Valley University in 2009, my partner and I sent him an e-mail at his BYU address. We were concerned, we wrote, that he was a member of the board of the National Organization for Marriage, an organization founded to oppose "same-sex marriage." Given that affiliation, we wondered how he might represent a diverse student body, staff, and faculty, many of whom are gay. We received an email in response thanking us for the welcome, reporting that he had stepped down from the NOM board, and assuring us that although his personal beliefs would not change, he was acutely aware of the need for him as president to represent the full range of people at UVU.

In 2015, however, "Dr. Matthew S. Holland, University President and Professor of Political Science, Utah Valley University," joined a brief against marriage equality for the Supreme Court signed by "100 Scholars of Marriage." In response, more than 100 members of the UVU staff and faculty signed and published a letter in of the *Salt Lake Tribune* (Sunday, May 3, 2015). We wrote that "as the public face of UVU to the larger community, Holland has a special responsibility to avoid public pronouncements that would harm his ability to carry out his duties as president of a state university officially committed to diversity and inclusion. . . ."

President Holland has never publicly addressed our statement or our concerns.

On November 3, 2017, the Sutherland Institute (which discounts climate science and opposes marriage equality) gave Matt Holland its "New Birth of Freedom" award. The introduction of the awardee featured Holland as the President of UVU with an image of him under a UVU flag atop Mt. Timpanogos. Wearing a UVU-green tie, Holland lectured the Sutherland audience about the advancing forces of modern collectivism that in defense of the rights of "so-called consenting adults" infringe on the rights and freedoms of religious institutions. He cited correspondence between James Madison and Thomas Jefferson in 1789 in which Jefferson asked "May one generation of men have a right to bind another?" Both men believed, Holland said, "that . . . the living generation should make sure that their actions not diminish the freedom that future generations are entitled to enjoy."

Holland argued that "such a theory of government of course would stand firm against many forms of modern progressivism and collectivism that cavalierly diminish the scope and conditions of individual liberty in the name of equality or some utopian vision that will never come to be in a fallen world. . . . Undoubtedly, the requirement to perpetuate the freedom of future generations must sometimes pull back on the freewheeling practices of the current generation, even if those practices are simply what so-called consenting adults want to do."

Our president's history of opposition to marriage equality and now his disrespectful speech denigrating "cavalier" arguments made "in the name of equality" by "freewheeling" and "so-called consenting adults" make our collective work devoted to diverse and inclusive education at Utah Valley University more difficult than he can imagine.

—Scott Abbott
Professor of Integrated Studies,
Philosophy and Humanities
UVU

Matt Holland never responded to this letter. When students affiliated with UVU LGBTQ+ Student Services asked to speak with him, he make them wait for weeks for an appointment and sent instructions that the discussion was not to be about his speech at the Sutherland Institute. So they talked, the students reported, about where they were from and what their majors were and where they had served LDS missions.

Baren

Hillside

Final Thoughts

(for the moment)

What motivated me to write these essays? Why didn't I stay tightly focused on German Studies like colleagues from graduate school who forged distinguished careers as Germanists at Columbia, NYU, UNC Chapel Hill, UC Santa Barbara, UC Irvine, and Notre Dame? Why did I leave a department at Vanderbilt that offered a Ph.D. in German Studies for a department at BYU that only offered an M.A. in German Studies and then move to UVSC where there was virtually no German program? As I noted in *Immortal for Quite Some Time*, I was confronted with the trajectory of these choices soon after I moved to UVSC.

> 7 April 2000
>
> PBS's *Religion and Ethics Newsweekly* just aired its program on intellectuals and the Mormon Church. Lucky Severson and his camera crew showed up at UVSC a few months ago to ask me some questions about academic freedom and BYU. While they were setting up the lighting equipment, Lucky made sure he had my credentials right: So, in 1981 you moved from a lectureship at Princeton to a tenure-track job at Vanderbilt.

After being tenured there, you moved to BYU, and after eleven years moved to UVSC. Is that correct?

It is, I said.

I've never seen an academic career in such precipitous decline, he said.

Fair enough, I told him, but you should know that each step was carefully taken.

They filmed me saying something about how disappointing it was to leave a promising university that had lost its nerve. Then they hurried off for their next interview, the important one, with former BYU and San Francisco quarterback Steve Young.

It's true that each step was carefully taken. But why? I missed the scent of sage, of course, a metonymy for the public lands of the Great Basin whose skies and mountains and deserts feed my soul. The pungent scent of sage has a counterpart for me in the savory religious culture that has nourished another part of my soul. After seven stimulating years at Vanderbilt University and after finishing *Fictions of Freemasonry: Freemasonry and the German Novel*, I moved west because I wanted more intimate interactions with the Mormon religion that had so fruitfully contributed to my identity, in part through institutions like the temple and the university. I wanted to think about more than German literature, to bring the wisdom of those great writers into conversations about broader issues.

Inspired by friends whose scholarship reaches beyond disciplinary bounds, motivated by friends who are creative writers, and encouraged by the writers whose novels and plays and poems I love, I began to write personal essays alongside the scholarly work that had been my singular focus. Steven Epperson's and my "House of the Lord, House of the Temple" is an intimate personal exploration of our shared Mormonism. Novelist and translator Žarko Radaković invited me to travel and write with him in Yugoslavia and then, between the wars, in Serbia—travel and introspection that unsettled and enriched my life and resulted in three books: *Repetitions*, followed by *Vampires & A Reasonable Dictionary*, and *We: On Friendship*. Sam Rushforth and I rode stretches of Utah's Great Western Trail daily for a most of a decade and recorded our conversations about mountain biking, botany, philosophy, and friendship in *Wild Rides and Wildflowers: Philosophy and Botany with Bikes*. During the two decades after my brother John died, I wrote the fraternal meditations of *Immortal for Quite Some Time* that fundamentally shifted my place in the world. And recently, I wrote about the meanings of barbed wire with historian Lyn Bennett in a truly interdisciplinary book called *The Perfect Fence: Untangling the Meanings of Barbed Wire*.

At BYU, as I had anticipated, I began to think more intensely about the religion I shared with most of my colleagues and students. The essay on Zion was an early foray into this appealing genre. Unfortunately, the flourishing university I had chosen to be part of began to change. Administrators adopted increasingly restrictive policies and, under false pretenses, fired friends and colleagues. For reasons I don't fully understand, I cannot stand by and watch institutional power exerted unfairly. I joined the American Association of University Professors because of its two-fold mission: to support scholars whose institutions are treating them unjustly and to help institutions develop and adhere to policies that protect due process, academic freedom, and shared governance. I wrote the essays collected here to argue for fairness and honesty and intellectual openness, principles, I hasten to add, that I first learned from the scriptures and practices of my faith.

I've often wondered what role my unbelief played as I challenged policies and administrative decisions at BYU. I have no patience for or deference to the idea that policies and decisions should be accepted simply because they come from supposedly inspired leaders. That left me free to question and suggest and argue and challenge on the basis of my best judgement and to trust that others would welcome such debate in the service of the university. Because that trust was disappointed, I have since asked myself whether my sojourn as a stranger in the promised land has fostered or undermined a culture I love? It is possible that my answers have been self-serving. I don't think so, but readers may judge otherwise.

While raising questions about my answers, I have been re-reading a book by James K. Lyon, a colleague in my department at BYU: *Bertolt Brecht in America*. Brecht's five-year exile in the United States ended in 1947 when, as one of the "Hollywood Nineteen," he was required to testify at a hearing of the House Committee on Un-American Activities. "Brecht's testimony," Jamie writes, "was a polite exercise in cunning and duplicity." Although he could truthfully say he was not a member of the Communist Party, Brecht was certainly a Communist in spirit and, Jamie's account continues, "from the moment he took an oath in the name of a God in whom he did not believe, he followed his carefully planned scenario" which included smoking cigars throughout and the services of an interpreter who spoke English less well than Brecht himself. Brecht said later that he understood the institutional structure because of his experience as a refugee from the Nazi Committee on Un-German Activities. He flew to Europe the day after his hearing, never to return.

Besides reminding me of my own pragmatic duplicities, Brecht's case shifts attention from the person answering questions to the people asking the questions. As Sam Rushforth pointed out in my defense, Brecht's play *Galileo*, performed while he was in the US, tells the story of a man coerced by a tyrannical institution. Why, I ask, do institutions act that way? Why did the Catholic Church force Galileo to recant? Why did HUAC disrupt the lives of so many Communists and supposed Communists? Why did BYU seek to "clip and control" its students and faculty? Isn't the answer that these institutions wanted to protect themselves from ideas they found threatening? Unfortunately, their coercive actions subverted democratic and academic and Christian ideals that were the pride and inspiration of their members and citizens.

Although the historical parallels make sense on one level, we were not dealing with Nazis or Joseph McCarthy during those years at BYU. We could draw inspiration from Joseph Smith's confident openness: "One of the grand fundamental principles of Mormonism is to receive truth, let it come from whence it may." At its best BYU is an inspiring institution of higher learning. At its worst (and there have a series of historical low points—like the time in 1911 when fundamentalist Church leaders fired professors teaching evolution and like the concerted efforts in the 1990s to cleanse BYU of feminists, so-called intellectuals, gay and lesbian advocates, coffee drinkers, speakers at unnamed symposia, etc.), a university and its sponsoring Church have driven away students and professors and professional employees who have dedicated their lives and talents to the pursuit of "truth, let it come from whence it may."

It is unfortunate that events transpired as they did. Our AAUP chapter didn't win a single case we took up (even the AAUP censure of the BYU administration, as important as it was, didn't feel like a victory). Still, I'm proud to have been involved with activist students and members of the faculty in the service of a university worthy of the name.

At Utah Valley University I became a founding member of a new chapter of the AAUP and with colleagues I have continued to support students and members of the faculty harmed by overreaching administrators. And I continue to contribute to conversations about what a good university should look like. Institutions like universities and churches have great power to foster human development. They can also be oppressive. It is our job as we teach biology or music or German literature and as we serve in Relief Society presidencies and bishoprics to make sure our institutions uplift rather than oppress our fellow human beings.

After all this, am I surprised to find myself still saying "we Mormons"? Yes, I am. And no, it doesn't really surprise me at all.

Greg Prince published a piece in *Sunstone* (Oct. 31, 2018) that gets at some of the issues I have tried to address here. He argues that

> People—particularly younger people—want a church that walks the walk, that takes a stand for values, and that tries to make the world better. They don't want empty talk—and neither do I. There are so many areas in our society that are crying out for the voice of moral authority, and yet those cries go unanswered. Who would not yearn for our church to fill the moral vacuum with not just proclamations, but strong actions that address poverty, disease, climate change, social justice—showing us that character counts, that truth is essential, and that a society that disregards these traits does so at the peril of its very existence?

"Even if people don't see the Church embodying moral authority," Prince continues, "they may stay if the community is nurturing." He concludes with questions: "Can the church be a place where community can flourish despite a 'low rate of coherence in believing the same things?' Can it be a place where kinship and loyalty to one another come first?"

While I was at BYU, these questions were answered with an increasingly emphatic "no." There were many losses, one of them Steven Epperson. That loss was another community's gain. After nineteen years as minister of the Unitarian Church of Vancouver, Steven delivered his final sermon in mid-June of 2020, a sermon that might well have been delivered as a final lecture at BYU had administrators had the foresight to respect and honor his gifts as a member of our community. Imagine his voice in a BYU lecture hall or at a devotional. A few excerpts from the farewell sermon reveal a commitment to a nurturing religious community with courage to take on moral issues beyond the personal worthiness of its members. It is a vision I share and and have argued for since arriving at BYU as a new student in 1967.

The Individual and the Community
Remarks by Rev. Steven Epperson
June 14, 2020
UCV

Four months ago, who would have thought, or even dreamed we were about to get a global pandemic, something like the Great Depression and a world-wide civil and human rights movement at the same time? . . .

We don't have a housing crisis, a food crisis, a crisis of indigeneity and race, a mental health crisis, a policing crisis, or a budget crisis—no! We have a crisis of collective and political will. We have more than sufficient wealth, Canada!; and we have uncommon, untapped reservoirs of goodwill and a wild hunger for fairness, justice and decency. We and our leaders must commit resolutely to build this, our beloved half-built nation; and *then*, persist and keep at it until it's more fully achieved. "Even in the darkest of times we have the right to expect some illumination." And I'm dying for some light. . . .

Which brings me to the last thing I want to say about a truth that has been revealed for all to see during these past couple of extraordinary months and weeks: and that is, our well-being is social and relational; it cannot be achieved individually. To be healthy is to be whole, to heal is to make whole; and to experience that is to belong to and with and for others and the world.

From the very beginning, Unitarians have affirmed that we live and move and have our being, minute by minute, by an inter-involvement, an interdependence with other bodies and a world of living creatures, natural orders, forces and cycles. . . . Our lives, and those of all things, are woven into one indwelling, continuous fabric of being that summons us to wholeness and plenitude. And there are consequences to that world view, consequences summed up in the vision statement of our Canadian Unitarian denomination where it states that *"our interdependence calls us to love and justice."*

When and where it has not been co-opted, religion is an affront to the individualistic ethos of our age, because it dares to say it's not all about you, not about the ego and its satisfaction. Instead, if we'd only get this right, it's about envisioning and working for the common good; it's about the priority of the earth summoned always toward wholeness and healing; it's about justice, equity and compassion—a world upheld and transformed by our care and attuned to and living in harmony with the rhythms and systems of nature—all our relations—beyond the self and for the sake of the seven generations times seven yet to come.

A colleague of mine called it "fierce hope." That's what I've been feeling in these plague-ridden months and weeks of sliding economies and powerful affirmations that black lives matter. . . . Our well-being is social, not individual; it's grounded in the priority of the community, not the consuming ego; it's fed by righteous confrontation, not the quiescence of "realism" and distraction; it's nourished by the well-springs of justice and the bread of compassion.

May these times be truly different, with no going back; and may we, the many beloved communities, find strength in our resolve to be generative and fiercely hopeful for the sake of those we love and the kind of world we long to see break forth into the light of day. And may it be so.

Highway 24 II

Hartnet

Woodcuts

Woodcuts by Royden Card (https://roydencardfineart.com/)

Bluff	x	Canyons	52	Lemons	211
Day's Window	xiv	North of Goblin	87	Two Buttes	212
Peaks	xx	Hidden Valley II	88	GWT I	227
Salt Valley	xxv	Sienna Wall	97	Castle Valley III	228
Sky Stone	xxvi	Grey Hill	98	Landscape	236
Highway 24	xxxi	West Zion II	131	Sage IV	240
Castle Valley	xxxii	Sandstone	132	Baren	245
Sage V	11	Castle Valley	150	Hillside	246
Line Pole II	12	Salt Valley Hills	160	Highway 24 II	255
Wasatch	36	Toward Hite	172	Hartnet	256
Hidden Valley I	51	Fisher Tower	202		

Scott Abbott is the author of *Fictions of Freemasonry: Freemasonry and the German Novel*; *The Perfect Fence: Untangling the Meanings of Barbed Wire* (with Lyn Ellen Bennett); *Wild Rides & Wildflowers: Philosophy and Botany with Bikes* (with Sam Rushforth); *Immortal for Quite Some Time*; and three books with Žarko Radaković: *Repetitions*; *Vampires & A Reasonable Dictionary*; and *We: On Friendship*. He has translated works by Peter Handke and Gregor Mendel. He blogs at "The Goalie's Anxiety" (https://the-goaliesanxiety.wordpress.com). Professor of Integrated Studies, Philosophy and Humanities at Utah Valley University, he lives in Woodland Hills, Utah.

Made in the USA
Columbia, SC
19 June 2022